Created and Directed by Hans Höfer

INSIGHT GUIDES

SINGAPORE

Updated by Joseph R. Yogerst
Managing Editor: Audrey Simon

Editorial Director: Geoffrey Eu

HOUGHTON MIFFLIN COMPANY

APA PUBLICATIONS

Singapore

Fourth Edition (Reprint)
© **1995 APA PUBLICATIONS (HK) LTD**
All Rights Reserved
Printed in Singapore by Höfer Press Pte Ltd

Distributed in the United States by:	Distributed in Canada by:	Distributed in the UK & Ireland by:	Worldwide distribution enquiries:
Houghton Mifflin Company	**Thomas Allen & Son**	**GeoCenter International UK Ltd**	**Höfer Communications Pte Ltd**
222 Berkeley Street	390 Steelcase Road East	The Viables Center, Harrow Way	38 Joo Koon Road
Boston, Massachusetts 02116-3764	Markham, Ontario L3R 1G2	Basingstoke, Hampshire RG22 4BJ	Singapore 2262
ISBN: 0-395-73385-5	ISBN: 0-395-73385-5	ISBN: 9-62421-041-1	ISBN: 9-62421-041-1

Dear Reader,

Insight Guide: Singapore is a sentimental favourite of mine. Singapore has been my home for more than 20 years, so I've had firsthand experience in watching Singapore come of age. In a big way. From a fledgling island state in the 1960s, it has enjoyed outstanding success and developed into one of the most dynamic economies in Asia.

I first came to Asia in the 1960s. From my base in Bali, I created *Insight Guide: Bali*, which served as the blueprint for a subsequent series of critically acclaimed guides to Asia. Bali was noted for its sensitive cultural portrayal, thought-provoking text and vivid photography. These editorial characteristics have since become trademark features in every Insight Guide.

The original *Insight Guide: Singapore*, first published in 1971, was just the second in a travel series that now spans some 185 titles and dozens of countries. The book has undergone several updates and revisions, but the edition you now hold is the result of a comprehensive revamp, dedicated to reflecting the Singapore of the 1990s.

It was revised, rewritten and edited by Singapore-based freelance journalist **Joseph R. Yogerst**, who is fast becoming an Apa regular, having edited *Insight Guide: Southeast Asia* and written recent *Insight Pocket Guides* to Hong Kong and Macau. Yogerst, who writes for various international newspapers and magazines on a wide range of subjects, has won several awards for travel writing. He has also published a novel and is hard at work on a second. **Julia Clerk** researched and compiled the extensive Travel Tips section at the back of the book.

Credit must go to members of the original editorial team for laying the groundwork for this new book. American writer-photographer **Star Black** helped me devise the concept for this book. After years of travel in Asia, she now lives in New York City. Other members of the original team include **Sharifah Hamzah**, **Cynthia Wee**, **Ilsa Sharp**, **Eric Oey**, **Ng Swee San**, **David Pickell** and **Colleen Lye**, inveterate traveller and longtime Apa contributor **Marcus Brooke** and Singapore-based writers **Marianne Rankin** and **Henry Yap**.

This book combines rich stores of cultural and historical information, making it a perfect reference for where to go, what to buy, where to eat and how to have a great time in Singapore. I hope you'll make the most of it.

Hans Höfer
Publisher

History

People & Culture

Activities

Places

Maps

Travel Tips

Compiled by Julia Clerk

**For detailed Information
See Page 263**

Minutes after landing in cool, clean Changi Airport, the visitor is whisked down a wide highway lined with glorious tropical palms and bright bougainvillea. Nearby, ships from all over the globe wait their turn in the world's busiest container port. Ahead, the silver highrise towers of the city sparkle in the sunlight.

There's more to Singapore than luxury hotels, enticing shopping centres and high-tech offices. Everywhere, tradition and modern ways co-exist – sometimes in apparent contradiction – such that the appellation "Surprising Singapore" is indeed a fitting one. Thus huddled below smart highrises where futures are traded are a jumble of red-tiled roofs, where ancestors are worshipped in some corner of the house. Computers rule the commercial hub but the abacus and ancient *daching* scales are used to calculate the price and weight of pearls, for use in traditional medicine. Singapore's skyscrapers speak to the world by fax, but its herbalists, medium, and craggy-faced shopkeepers keep the traditional ways alive.

On a world map, the island of Singapore is just a dot at the tip of the Malay Peninsula. Despite well-founded fears for its survival as an independent entity, the tiny 625-sq-km (250-sq-mile) island has blossomed into one of Asia's economic dragons. Its success has gone far beyond what Sir Stamford Raffles, its founder, envisioned when he bought the island from its Malay ruler in 1819 and set up as a trading post. Raffles determined the layout of the town and established a free port which rapidly grew in importance because of its strategic location on the great East-West trading routes. The opening of the Suez Canal and the rubber boom resulted in increasing prosperity during the latter part of the 19th and early 20th centuries. From a sleepy Malay village, Singapore grew rapidly, drawing migrants from China, India and neighbouring Malaya and Indonesia.

Invasion and occupation by the Japanese during World War II spelled the end of British colonial rule, as the local populace never fully regained confidence in their erstwhile masters.

After independence in 1965, the driving force behind Singapore's success was Lee Kuan Yew who, as Prime Minister until 1990, led his people from rural slumber into a high-tech awakening. Grandson of a Hakka coolie from China, and holding a double first degree in law from Cambridge University, he and his People's Action Party have given Singaporeans the second highest standard of living in Asia, next to Japan.

His vision, like that of Raffles about 170 years earlier, was of a prosperous, well-ordered society, with religious and racial tolerance

Preceding pages: Surprising in Singapore: The General Post Office sits in the shadow of modern Singapore high-profile skyline; a vestige of the past – colourful but faded facade in the historical district; tropical foliage abounds in a controlled environment at the Jurong Bird Park; the Orient's cosmic significance is symbolised in this hi-tech video mural at Haw Par Villa. Left, the city's historical heart features a green expanse of land known as The Padang.

and equal opportunity for all. Massive public housing projects and the establishment of educational facilities were the initial priorities. Economic stability achieved through cooperation between unions and employers and an efficient infrastructure made Singapore attractive to multinationals, resulting in phenomenal economic growth.

Now moving into the 21st century under the second generation of leaders, Singapore is setting its sights on becoming an "intelligent" island. High technology will be available to all, with information at the touch of a button and instant communication worldwide possible.

With affluence comes a growing recognition of the importance of history. Conservation is the watchword as efforts to preserve cultural heritage gain momentum. New buildings still spring up, but no longer at the expense of the old.

Careful planning has turned Singapore into a Garden City and everywhere, imaginative landscaping softens the hard edges left by modern concrete complexes. Recent efforts to save endangered species and stringent anti-pollution laws bring Singapore to the vanguard of world environmental consciousness.

Life is changing for Singaporeans, and for the better. More and more leisure parks, golf courses, tennis courts, shopping centres, cinemas and theatres are springing up for families to spend time and relax together.

As the island grows in wealth, so its self-confidence increases. Fresh ideas and different values pose less of a threat. The hitherto strict censorship laws are slowly being relaxed and for the first time, "restricted" films and heavy metal concerts are being allowed.

Asian and Western culture and values meet and mix in this cosmopolitan city. But Confucian precepts still temper ideals of personal freedom. Society is kept on a tight rein, with fines for failing to flush public toilets, littering and other social misdemeanours. The result, however, is an immaculate public mass rapid transport system which puts London's Underground to shame and probably the cleanest streets outside Switzerland.

Singapore's population of 3 million is a melting pot of cultures comprising 77.6 percent Chinese, 14.2 percent Malays, 7.1 percent Indians and 1.1 percent other ethnic groups. Most of the younger generation have been born in Singapore and are proud to call themselves Singaporeans. This national identity is intensively fostered by the government and emphasised with slick media campaigns and elaborate national day celebrations. In deference to the original settlers, Malay is the national language, but the *lingua franca* is English. For Chinese, Mandarin is encouraged as the unifying spoken language. Chinese and Tamil, are official languages.

For visitors, Singapore offers the charms of Asia in unequalled comfort. Services are efficient, English is widely spoken, and there's always the reassuring knowledge that "things work". This book draws together the diverse peoples, the different parts of the island and all the facts, figures and handy tips which give an Insight and a Guide to Singapore.

Young, cultured Singaporeans can look forward to a bright future – with no strings attached.

About 1,700 years ago, there was an island called P'u Luo Chung, which in time became Temasek, Singapura and eventually Singapore. Throughout this period, the island's importance in the history books has been disproportionately large for such a small place.

Poised at the tip of the Malay Peninsula, smack in the middle of one of the world's richest trade routes, Singapore has since the 3rd century, and possibly earlier, been a stopover, tanking up point, and sales floor for the wheeling and dealing of tradesmen.

head and white breast, the king asked his aides what manner of beast it was. One of his advisers suggested it was a lion, and thus the king conceived the name Singapura.

In any case, by the 14th century, the name Singapura had become attached to the little trading community, which by the end of the century, was thriving.

Junks and riches: Even before the birth of Christ, Tamil seamen from southern India were plying their heavy ships through the Straits of Malacca and back. Our words for

Singapore's early history, apart from a brief reference to P'u Luo Chung in ancient Chinese texts, is shrouded in mystery and legend. Even the story of how the place came to be named Singapura – "Lion City" in Sanskrit – reads like a fairy tale.

The *Malay Annals*, or *Sejarah Melayu*, written in 1612, tell of the exploits of Sri Tri Buana, the King of Palembang. He was out searching for a good place to establish a city when his ship was struck by a sudden storm. He was able to save himself and his men by casting his crown into the waves, and they came ashore on an uncharted island.

Seeing a creature with a red body, black

pepper, rice, ginger and cinnamon have their origins in Tamil: *pippali, arici, injiver* and *karppu*. Later the Greeks and then the Romans sought tortoise shell, spices and sandalwood from the archipelago.

By the 5th century, Chinese junks were sailing down into Malayan waters braving "huge turtles, sea-lizards, and such-like monsters of the deep" enroute. The Arabs and Persians hauled goods to and from the Straits region as well.

Thus trade grew, and by the 14th century, Singapore was well established on this East-West trade route. Although the island's various rulers exacted duties from the passing ships, what most worried the traders were the "freelancers": the pirates.

According to the 1350 Chinese text *Description of the Barbarians of the Isles*, the traders were unmolested as they sailed west. But on the way back, loaded with goods, "the junk people get out their armour and padded screens against arrow fire to protect themselves, for a certainty two or three hundred pirate junks will come out to attack them. Sometimes they have the good luck and a favouring wind and they may not catch up

evidenced by the succession of invasions it suffered. The Chola kings of India, the Thais and the Javanese all took turns trying to acquire Singapore by force.

Singapura, often called the "Temasek" in literature of that period, was most likely founded around the middle of the 13th century by the Javanese Sri-Vijayan. The settlement withstood attempted invasions for more than 100 years, but towards the end of the 14th century it fell to the Javanese Majapahit empire.

The *Sejarah Melayu* ascribes this con-

with them; if not, then the crews are all butchered and the merchandise made off with in short order". While the scale of the pirate fleet seems somewhat inflated, there is no doubt the threat was real.

Invasions: Despite such risks, Singapore had become a valuable piece of real estate, as

Preceding pages: Life on the River: A colonial captain takes time to admire the scenery from Fort Canning; the view of Fort Canning from the sea offers a slightly different perspective; the same view about 50 years later. <u>Left</u>, Temenggong's *kampong* at the foot of Mount Faber in 1837. <u>Above</u>, the advantages of Singapore's natural harbour were apparent from the very beginning.

quest to a personal act of revenge against the island's monarch. Apparently the king's wife had been repeatedly accused of infidelity by jealous concubines. When the king had her impaled in public as punishment, the woman's father was distraught. As the invading Javanese were then at hand, the man found a ready outlet for revenge and cast the city doors open to the invaders, giving the Majapahits enough of an advantage to conquer Singapore.

The Majapahits (1292–1398) were the last of the great Javanese Hindu rulers, and the first people who strove to unite all the Malay Archipelago into a single political entity.

Much of regional culture as we know it today derives from Majapahit times, including various architectural and artistic motifs, *gamelan* music, the use of the *Ramayana* and other Hindu epics in classical dance and puppetry, and even traditional fashion.

The empire disintegrated into rival states near the end of the 14th century, and within a hundred years many of the princes and sultans had converted to Islam, essentially changing the archipelago from a Hindu to a Muslim zone.

Singapore essentially vanished from the history books for more than 400 years – give or take a few accounts by European traders – becoming, for all we know, nothing more

"I observed his habit was always to be in deep thought. He was most courteous in his intercourse with all men. He always had a sweet expression toward European as well as native gentlemen. He was extremely affable and liberal, always commanding one's best attention. He spoke in smiles."

Raffles was born in the year 1781, aboard his father's ship, at that time sailing through the Caribbean. Fifteen years later, he became a clerk for the British East India Company, working in the Far East. At the age of 30, he had become the lieutenant-governor of Java. By this time he had learned both the Malay language and the ways of Malay politics; knowledge he was to put to good

than an overgrown jungle home to the *orang laut* ("sea men") whose main occupation was usually piracy.

Sir Stamford Raffles: The abandoned little island on the tip of the Malay Peninsula underwent a dramatic change in the 19th century, thanks to an ambitious young British East India Company official, Sir Thomas Stamford Bingley Raffles.

Raffles was the founder of modern Singapore, some even say its creator. And there is no doubt that he was a capable, clever, and even visionary colonialist. This was how Munshi Abdullah, a Malay clerk, described his boss:

use in time to come.

In 1817, British and Dutch trading interests were competing for control of the lucrative Far East exchange, and the Dutch control of Malacca and Sunda threatened British dominance of the region. Although Britain held Bencoolen and Penang, it was considering trading these to the Dutch in exchange for territory in India. This situation worried Raffles. He pleaded with the governor-general of India, Lord Hastings, to establish a settlement in the region from which the British could secure the Straits of Malacca. Hastings approved the idea in 1818, and on 29 January 1819, Raffles landed in Singapore.

The Singapore deal: The Briton found Singapore thick with swamps and jungle, its only settlement a ramshackle *kampong* (village) of 100 Malay huts by the mouth of the Singapore river. Further up the river lived 30 or so *orang laut* families.

It was, to put it mildly, pretty bleak looking. Raffles' scribe later wrote: "All along the beach there were hundreds of human skulls, some of them old but fresh with the hair still remaining, some with the teeth still sharp, and some without teeth."

The island at the time was controlled by Dato Temenggong, who was the Malay chief of the southern part of the Malay Peninsula. The Temenggong did not, however, own the

land; it was formally held by the Johor empire. The sultan of Johor had died, leaving behind four wives but no clear heir.

The two wives of royal blood had been childless; the two commoners bore the Sultan one son each. When the Sultan died, Tengku Hussein, the oldest son, was away travelling. So the viceroy decided to place the younger son on the throne, and the legitimacy of his rule was immediately recognized by both the British and Dutch. Tengku

A view of Singapore and its harbour from Mount Wallich in 1856. Mount Wallich was long ago leveled to fill in Telok Ayer Bay.

Hussein, hearing of the appointment, went into exile.

Raffles watched these intrigues with interest, and despite the recognition of the younger son by the two European powers, he knew that the new ruler was still under scrutiny, particularly by the Dutch. He further knew that the man would never permit the establishment of a British presence in Singapore.

Raffles concocted his own plan and invited the exiled Tengku Hussein to Singapore. As soon as he arrived, the canny Briton proclaimed him rightful heir to the throne of Johor. On 6 February 1819, Raffles signed a treaty with the Temenggong and the new Sultan giving the British East India Company permission to establish a trading post in Singapore. In return, the company agreed to pay the Temenggong 5,000 Spanish dollars a year and the Sultan, $3,000. Raffles appointed Major William Farquhar as Singapore's first resident.

"(I)t is my intention to make this my principal residence," wrote Raffles, "and to devote the remaining years of my stay in the East to the advancement of a Colony which bids to be one of the most important."

Raffles retained ultimate control of the island for himself, in his position of lieutenant-governor of Bencoolen.

The Dutch, of course, at first protested against Raffles' acquisition, and initially it was unclear whether the British would support their new port. But Singapore's success as a trading outpost came so quickly that the British were soon convinced.

The settlement grows: The island's population surged, and by June 1819 topped 5,000, mostly Chinese immigrants. Resident Farquhar cleared the jungle, constructed buildings, and dealt with Singapore's pests. A bounty was placed on the resident tropical rats, which were so large that no cat would contend with them. The island's rat problem was soon solved. The first settlers in Singapore were mainly traders and other itinerants of all types, the bulk of them Chinese, though there were also those from the Middle East, Europe and Malacca.

Raffles was away for the first three years of the new British trading post, and when he returned in 1822 he found a city that had – under Farquhar's leadership – developed in directions at odds with his instructions. To counteract this, Raffles drew up a detailed plan for the development of the Singapore he envisioned. To avoid conflict in a rapidly-developing multi-racial society, he designated separate areas of the city for immigrants from the various corners of the globe. Chinatown was established, west of the river, where it still is today. Arab Street and "Little India" remind us of Raffles' now nearly-170-year-old plan.

Like most trading outposts, Singapore was a town of little moral compunction; Raffles set about to remedy this situation by abolishing gambling, enforcing his wishes by ordering all owners of gaming houses to be flogged in public. In 1824, the British took formal control of Singapore. They traded off other

It was under Crawfurd, in 1824, that the colony first made money for the British. Crawfurd ran a tight ship, and his strict adherence to the bottom line alienated many Singaporeans. He made no friends among the Europeans either when he resumed licensing gambling houses. Gambling was a natural "disease" of the Asian races, Crawfurd claimed, and he figured his government might as well profit from the situation.

As Singapore's developers hacked their way back into the island's jungles, many of the settlement's members were lost to tigers. In the middle part of the 19th century, records show that as many as 300 citizens a year were being eaten by the creatures.

regions to the Dutch and made increased payments to the Sultan of Johor and the Temenggong in exchange for more control.

Raffles, his health failing, left Singapore in 1823 and returned to England where he died three years later of a brain tumour. The British, meanwhile, put Singapore under the Indian colonial government and, at Raffles' urging, appointed a new resident, John Crawfurd.

Getting down to business: By 1824, the island was home to some 11,000 people, mostly Malays, with a large number of Chinese and Bugis, and fewer Indians, Europeans, Armenians and Arabs.

With the imposition of a government bounty, this problem was soon eradicated. Thanks to the "Tiger Club" and its ilk, the big cats have long ago become extinct on the island. Although many experiments with agriculture were attempted on the island, the sandy coastal soil seemed to support nothing other than the native coconuts. But Singapore was never destined to be a farming community; with its strategic position between the Pacific and Indian oceans, the settlement's future lay in trade.

Among the goods traded in the mid-19th century were Chinese tea and silk, ebony, ivory, antimony and sage from across the archipelago and nutmeg, pepper and rattan from Borneo. From India and Britain came cloth, opium, beer, whisky and haberdashery for the expatriates. By 1860, Singapore's trade reached £10 million a year.

Immigrant entrepreneurs: "The Queen of the further East" was how British writer George W. Earl described Singapore in 1837. It was an apt description of this pretty city with its bustling harbour, lush greenery and fine houses.

By the middle of the century, a sense of permanence had been established in the city; three banks had been set up by the year 1860, and many elaborate houses of worship – mosques, churches, and temples – had been

In these early days, Chinese men outnumbered the women 15 to one, and the social lives of young Chinese bachelors revolved around the activities of secret societies and clans. These societies grew to have tremendous influence, and like Western "syndicates" they used all manner of coercive tactics to run criminal rackets and secure territory. Professional thugs called *samseng* were the societies' operatives.

The situation became so uncontrolled that in 1877 the government eventually decided to step in – with the Chinese protectorate, headed by the savvy W.A. Pickering, the first European in Singapore who could read and speak Chinese.

built. Wealthy Europeans built spacious Palladian-style houses with sprawling courtyards and grounds.

By this time, the Chinese population had swelled to 61 percent of the total and showed no signs of slowing down. Most Chinese immigrants came as indentured labourers, and after their requisite time was served working for their employer, the *sinkehs* – as the new immigrants were called – often struck out on their own.

<u>Left</u>, the genteel life of colonial Singapore (1905) along Queen Elizabeth Walk. <u>Above</u>, Raffles Place, circa 1925.

Babas: By this time, a generation of native Chinese had grown up in Singapore, the Straits Chinese or Peranakans (see chapter on *The Chinese* page 77 for more details on history and life of the Peranakans). While retaining their Chinese physical characteristics, the *Babas* (men) and *Nonyas* (women) incorporated much of the Malay culture into their lifestyles: food, fashion and the distinct Singaporean/Malay patois.

The number of Malays also increased progressively, but not at the same rate as the Chinese. Immigrants from India, chiefly from the south, came as well. Some came as free merchants and labourers; others were brought in as convicts by the British to build Singapore's system of public works.

In 1867, the Straits Settlements were made a Crown Colony under London's direct control, and a governor was appointed. In the early days of the colony, sailing ships were giving way to steam vessels, and Singapore became of extreme importance as a coal station for the many ships travelling to Europe through the Suez Canal, which opened in 1869.

In 1888, botanist H.N. Ridley, first director of the Singapore Botanical Gardens, brought rubber tree seedlings from South America and encouraged their cultivation as an export crop. The trees flourished, and this

even acquired an English taste in sports, playing cricket, tennis, billiards and hockey.

In 1911, Singapore's population stood at 312,000 and included, according to the census takers, 48 races speaking 54 separate languages. Underscoring the truly phenomenal amount of immigration into Singapore is the fact that until 1921, deaths in the colony exceeded births.

During this same period, a large number of Europeans immigrated to Singapore and it marks perhaps the nadir of colonial snobbery on the island. The Europeans distanced themselves from the "locals", eating continental food shipped in at great cost, surrounding themselves with local domestic help, and

new cash crop as well as the increasing quantities of tin being mined in nearby Malaya further contributed to Singapore's good fortunes. By 1903, the little island had become the world's seventh busiest port.

The 20th century: Singapore's future appeared bright at the turn of the century. The *Babas* ushered in a new era in 1900 by forming the Straits Chinese British Association, which provided a forum from which a new generation of leaders emerged. The association's members, chiefly professionals and legislative or municipal counsellors, became British subjects formally and culturally; they sent their children to British schools, and

barring all but those of their own race from their social clubs and, in fact, from prestigious posts in the civil service.

Roland Braddell's *The Lights of Singapore*, describes life on the island in 1934 thus: "When you come into Singapore the whole place seems so new, so very George the Fifth. Up overhead seaplanes circle; opposite the wharves is a brand-new railway station; you roll into town along a road both sides of which implore you not to be vague but to order Haig, or to try somebody's silk stockings or somebody else's cigarettes; the streets are full of motor traffic; most of the big buildings which you pass seem quite new; and, if you are English, you get an impression of a kind of tropical cross between Manchester and Liverpool."

Singapore's airport was built a few years later and the city seemed headed straight along the rails of modernization. Hollywood found Singapore an intriguing subject for celluloid – although the naughty bits were scissored out for the locals – and all seemed well for this bustling little centre of Southeast Asian trade. Then came World War II.

Colonial life: In the more rollicking days of the settlement, epitomized in Joseph Conrad's seadog tales, the social atmosphere of Singapore was relaxed. The races mixed easily and many westerners were said to be

troduced the conventions and petty proprieties of British suburbia to Singapore, separating the whites from the Asians for the first time. However, defenders of the "*mem*" point to her undeniable sterling service as a social worker, particularly during the immediate pre- and post-war periods.

The position of Western women in Singapore remained a problem. Many of them entered Singapore only as dependent wives, unable to work, no matter how experienced or well qualified they might have been.

The problem of colonial life in Singapore for white women was well described by that intrepid if caustic female traveller, Isabella Bird, in her book, *The Golden Chersonese*,

Singapore. Collyer Quay.

"going native". Many a lonely white man had comforted himself with an Asian female companion.

Several observers, perhaps jaundiced, have theorized that we can blame the tangible stiffening of Singapore's social mores in the 1920s and '30s on the arrival of white women in larger numbers after the turn of the century. These women, say their detractors, in-

Left, England's King George V and Queen Mary parade past the Singapore post office during a 1901 visit to the colony. Above, the Collyer Quay impressed visitors with its big buildings and broad roads.

published in 1883: "I think that in most of these tropical colonies, the ladies exist only on the hope of going '*Home!*' It is a dreary, aimless life for them, scarcely life, only existence. The greatest sign of vitality in Singapore Europeans that I can see is the furious hurry in writing for the mail."

There was almost no entertainment, apart from sports or homespun amateur theatricals, in which only a handful of women – those daring enough to go against social mores – took part.

Colonial women hid their pallor behind shuttered windows, leading "half-expiring lives," said Isabella Bird, "sleeping much of the afternoon". They were fanned by the patient "*punkah wallah*", usually an Indian or Malay who would rhythmically tug a string attached to a flap of cloth or woven cane – the "*punkah*" suspended from the ceiling, to create a draught of cooling air. Or else they frittered away time in idle gossip and games of bridge.

They emerged only at twilight for the almost mandatory evening "turn" around the Padang, that welcome green lung which still serves as a cricket pitch. There, bobbing to the governor and waving to friends from their horse-drawn carriages, they would parade themselves and their marriageable daughters until the sun had gone down.

then, now Raffles Place) to trade the latest business intelligence until about 10.30am, when at last, he would get down to his desk work. But only until tiffin, at 1pm, a fairly "light" lunch of curry and rice with beer. Some time would be devoted to reading the newspaper, then he was off to the Exchange at about 2pm.

Bored young European bachelors – "commercial assistants" as these young company clerks were called then – sometimes amused themselves at lunch by pelting local boatmen and coolies with the crimson-staining skins of the mangosteen fruit from the verandahs of their company *godowns* (Anglo-Indian for warehouses), or with eggs "that looked

The Race Course, SINGAPORE

Tiffin, tittle-tattle and sport: Life for colonial men also conformed to a fixed, although much busier, routine. The morning gun went off at 5am every morning on Government Hill. After a walk, the typical colonial would take tea with bread and butter and fruit, after which he would lounge around reading or writing letters until the breakfast gong sounded at 8am.

After bathing Malay-style – dousing with cold water ladled from a tall Shanghai jar – breakfast he had in the shape of curry and rice with egg, washed down by a tumbler of claret. A carriage would then arrive to convey him to "The Square" (Commercial Square

rather too hoary to eat".

Work would cease at about 4.30pm and the men would prepare to head toward the Esplanade and Padang for games, or gossip at the aptly-named "Scandal Point" nearby. Sport had become something of a mystique among the empire-builders, the key to "character" and the hallmark of "a decent fellow." Many a civil servant or company executive was hired more for his proficiency at cricket or rugby than for his academic or his professional prowess.

Roland Braddell wrote in 1924: "I doubt if

Race day at the Farrer Park course, circa 1909.

the English can point to anything that they have done here which has been more to the good of their Asiatic fellow citizens than the teaching of games and good sportsmanship."

Dinner was substantial: soup, fish, beef or poultry with vegetables and potatoes, followed by curry and rice with beer, as well as sherry (they believed alcohol was good for the health in the tropics) and pudding – plus cheese and fruit, with pale ale.

Before he retired, the man of the house took a turn of billiards in his own billiard room at home (the *de rigueur* equivalent of today's swimming pool). He went to bed at about 10pm.

Literary history: For more than a hundred years, Singapore has been kind to the travelling scribe. Many of them stayed at Raffles Hotel, as the hotel became a home away from home for scores of authors, ranging from erotic existentialist Hermann Hesse to mainstream master James Michener. But more than any other genre, Singapore played host to the literery lions of the British Empire – Conrad, Kipling, Coward and Maugham – for whom the island was a source of both inspiration and succour.

Joseph Conrad spent 16 years (1878–94) as a seaman in the Far East, with Singapore as his most frequent port of call. He was partial to bunking down at the Sailors' Home, where he could enjoy the company of his fellow seafarers.

Like many other authors, Conrad drew material from news events of the day. For instance, *Lord Jim* (1902) was inspired by a real-life incident in which a ship called the *Jeddah* – with 950 Muslim pilgrims aboard – was abandoned by her British crew when the vessel began taking on water after leaving Singapore.

Another rich source of material was Conrad's own life. He was first mate on the *Vidar*, a schooner making a circuit between Singapore and Borneo. "In terms of Conrad's reaching out toward writing… this was the most important berth he was to take," says one biographer. A number of works can be traced to the *Vidar* journeys including Conrad's first novel *Almayer's Folly*, as well as *An Outcast of the Islands*, *The Rescue* and *Victory*.

Rudyard Kipling came to Singapore at a most interesting time in his career. It was 1889, he was 24, and he had just left his

beloved India on a journey that would forever change his life. Kipling had spent the previous seven years in India writing for several English-language newspapers including the *Pioneer* in Allahabad. Clever and often biting dispatches earned Kipling a reputation as a rising star of British journalism. At the same time he began to churn out quite brilliant short stories like *The Man who would be King*.

The *Pioneer* offered to pay his passage to America, if Kipling would send dispatches back from his ports of call. He was utterly surprised by the pervasive Asian atmosphere of Singapore. "England is by the uninformed supposed to own the island," he quipped.

Kipling kept his kit aboard ship in Singapore's harbour, but he was fond of strolling up and down the waterfront. He seemed to have stumbled upon Raffles Hotel almost by chance. "Providence conducted me along a beach in full view of five miles of shipping – five solid miles of masts and funnels – to a place called Raffles Hotel, where the food is as excellent as the rooms are bad," Kipling wrote in his dispatch to the *Pioneer*. "Let the traveller take note. Feed at Raffles and sleep at the Hotel de l'Europe."

The Sarkies brothers incorporated the "Feed at Raffles" bit into subsequent advertisements for their food and beverage outlets – displaying both dramatic license and shrewd marketing in their elimination of the offensive portion.

When **Hermann Hesse** reached Singapore in 1911, he was already well known in Germany for works such as *Peter Camenzind* (1904) and *Gertrude* (1910). His descriptions of Raffles are highly intriguing, not the least because he was a German observing the English at play. In one passage, he anticipates the era of the modern football lout: "When we returned at one o'clock, a few tipsy Englishmen played around in the hall with the brutality of football players, shattered the show window of the poor postcard dealer to smithereens and shouted, fooled wildly around and fought with each other half the night like pigs."

More than any other writer, **Somerset Maugham** is indelibly linked with Singapore. Already one of the world's most respected and successful bards, Maugham made the first of several visits to the island in 1921. He spent mornings writing in the cool shade of the Palm Court at Raffles, his afternoons in Room 78 correcting galley proofs of *The Trembling of the Leaf*, his first collection of short stories.

It was during the 1921 visit to Singapore, and a similar sojourn in 1925, that Maugham collected material for magazine articles that would later go into his most famous collection of short stories, *The Casuarina Tree*. Among these sordid tales of British colonial life were *The Letter*, *The Outstation* and *Yellow Streak*.

The Letter provoked outrage from Singapore society. Based on a true incident, this is the story of Leslie Crosbie, a rubber planter's wife, who murders her lover while the husband is away on business.

In the course of these stories, Maugham devised some quite brilliant descriptions of Singapore. "The Malays, though natives of the soil, dwell uneasily in the towns, and are few," he wrote in *The Casuarina Tree*. "It is the Chinese, supple, alert, and industrious, who throng the streets; the dark-skinned Tamils walk on their silent, naked feet, as thought they were but brief sojourners in a strange land… and the English in their topees and white ducks, speeding past in motorcars or at leisure in their rickshaws, wear a nonchalant and careless air." And we learn from *A Gentleman in the Parlour* (1930) that Maugham tried opium for the first time in Singapore.

Noel Coward was another of the great British wits who visited Singapore. He came in 1929 in the company of Lord Amherst, on the outbound leg of a journey to China. Although he was barely 30 years of age, Coward was already the darling of the London stage.

Among the other illustrious bards have bedded down in Singapore over the years are German avant-garde writer Gunter Grass, American novelists Arthur Hailey, Englishman Noel Barber – who penned a classic tale of Singapore called *Tanamera* (which was later made into a mini-series for television) – Maxine Hong Kingston, Gavin Young, James Clavell and Paul Theroux.

The South Pacific heats up: Although allied with the Japanese in World War I, Britain, at the Americans' suggestion, severed her treaty with Japan in 1921. As war tensions increased, Britain developed the "Singapore strategy," grooming the island as a base for British warships in the event of an outbreak of hostilities in the Pacific.

In 1927, Japan invaded China, occupying Manchuria by 1931 and withdrew from the League of Nations. Six years later, the Japanese formally declared war on the Chinese. Airfields and dry dock facilities for the British fleet were completed in Singapore in 1938. The defences looked so substantial that the *Sydney Morning Herald* dubbed the island "the Gibraltar of the East".

The Japanese, in a manoeuvre that has become legendary in the war annals, simply chose to invade the island from the north, via Malaya. Tomoyuki Yamashita, head of the Japanese 25th Army, a stern veteran officer, led the invasion. Yamashita's regimental discipline was known to be "as rigorous as the autumn frost".

On the same day that Japanese aircraft were devastating US ships and airfields in Pearl Harbour, 8 December 1941 (Singapore time), Japanese aircraft raided Singapore. When he was roused and given the news, Governor Shenton Thomas seemed to have been more nonplussed at having been woken up than by news of the invasion. He said to commander A.E. Percival, "Well, I suppose you'll shove the little men off."

The governor's nonchalance proved misplaced, however, as the Japanese soon established land and air supremacy in the fight for the region. The Royal Navy had arrived a few days before, and quickly lost two battleships. The Japanese pushed south through Malaya, marching and riding bicycles through the jungle paths. Percival, realising that his northern border was unprotected, grouped the last of his troops along the northeast coast of the island. However, this proved to be futile as the Japanese, using collapsible boats and other makeshift vessels, cut around the northwest flank and invaded the island on 8 February 1942.

Prime Minister Winston Churchill cabled that Singapore must hold and that "there must at this stage be no thought of saving the troops or sparing the population. The battle must be fought to the bitter end…" However, after days of shelling by the Japanese, Percival finally surrendered.

Percival met Yamashita – by then "The Tiger of Malaya" – at the old Ford Motor factory in Bukit Timah village (now a Bridgestone tyre outlet) and the British commander agreed to an unconditional surrender; Churchill called it "the worst disaster and the largest capitulation in British history." Yamashita wrote later that his success was based on nothing more than "a bluff that worked." The Japanese troops were outnumbered more than three to one by the island's defenders and a more protracted defence would probably have repelled the aggressors.

The Syonan years: The Japanese renamed Singapore "Syonan" – Light of the South – and began a reign of terror soon after. The Europeans were classified as military prisoners or civilian detainees. The Malays and Indians were urged to transfer their allegiance to Japan or be killed. The Chinese

and the word "examined" stamped on their clothes and tattooed on their bodies. Those that failed – i.e. signed their names in English, dressed in a Western way, etc. – were imprisoned or executed.

The Japanese Kempeitai were as feared in Singapore as the Gestapo in Germany or France. People were killed, imprisoned, or tortured for the flimsiest of reasons. Meanwhile, children were being taught in the Japanese language, the clocks were reset to synchronize with Tokyo time, and students began their day by facing Japan and reciting the Japanese anthem.

The prison camps were tropical hell-holes of rats, disease and malnutrition. Prisoners

A Japanese painting of the British surrender.

were singled out for the most brutal treatment by the Japanese invaders. The Imperial government was more willing to assimilate the Malays and Indians and many served in the institutions of Syonan.

Japanese fascism was preached through the "Great East Asia New Order" which consisted of purifying the Asian races of Western influences. Three days after occupation, all Chinese males were ordered to report to detention centres where they were imprisoned and "cleansed". Those that passed were released with the appropriate papers

were sent off to work camps in the jungles of Southeast Asia where many succumbed to heat and starvation.

Syonan's economy deteriorated. Their currency was nicknamed "banana money" for its design, and also its value. Inflation skyrocketed, food was scarce and corpses were a common sight on the city's streets.

The Japanese surrendered to the Allies on 21 August 1945, and the British returned to the island in September. But the resistance to the Japanese, organized by the communists in Singapore, had changed the political climate. The people had plans for their own destiny, and the British were not invited.

World War II radically altered the face of global politics and the experience of Syonan drove home the point to Singaporeans that survival was neither something that could be taken for granted, nor something that could be left in the hands of the British. Although the British were welcomed upon their return to the island, there was a palpable feeling that the Crown was no longer going to be considered the benign and judicious paterfamilias of Singapore.

"Neither the Japanese nor the British had

military rule of the Straits Settlements and set up separate Crown Colonies in Singapore and Malaya. On the island, the new governor instituted a measure of self-government by allowing for the popular election of six members to a new 22-member Legislative Council. Elections were set for 1948.

The only party to participate in the first election was the conservative nationalist Progressive Party, and three of its members – in addition to three independents – were elected. Turnout was slim; only 13,000 votes were

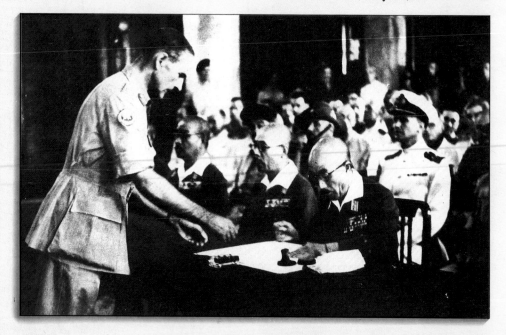

the right to push and kick us around," said former Prime Minister Lee Kuan Yew in 1961. "We determined that we could govern ourselves and bring up our children in a country where we can be a self-respecting people."

Towards *merdeka*: Even before the war ended, political activity began in Singapore; in 1945 the Malaysian Democratic Union was formed with the express goal of ending colonial rule and further, of merging Singapore with Malaya. "*Merdeka*" – Malay for independence – became the rallying cry.

This nationalistic itch among Singapore's population was not ignored by the British. One year after their return, they ended their

cast. Both independents and Progressives engaged in a dialogue only with the English-speaking minority. The Chinese majority did not identify with the candidates and even the local press showed little interest in the election. Following another poorly-attended election, Sir George Rendel was appointed by the British in 1953 to review the colony's constitutional statute. He recommended that all citizens be automatically registered to vote and that a Legislative Assembly with 32 members – 25 of them elected – be established with broadened powers.

The constitution was enacted in early 1955 and later in the same year, Labour Front member David Marshall was elected Singapore's first chief minister. Very soon, Marshall, a flamboyant criminal lawyer, grew impatient with the slow implementation of the new constitution and early the following year, led an all-party delegation to London to negotiate complete independence from the Crown. It quickly became apparent that the British had no intention of allowing Singapore to manage its own defence and security arrangements, so Marshall returned to the island and resigned for failing to keep his

member and young Cambridge-educated lawyer named Lee Kuan Yew – eventually accepted roughly the same terms Marshall had been offered: a fully-elected Assembly of 51 members, no power over external affairs, and representation on – but not control of – an internal security council.

Back home, the Legislative Assembly ratified the terms and in 1959, the British Parliament passed an act which approved the new Singapore constitution. The general election was set for May. The PAP contested every

merdeka promise.

Lim Yew Hock of the Singapore Labour Party, who shared Marshall's views, took over as chief minister and in March 1957 led a second delegation to London.

A new constitution: The second delegation – which included a People's Action Party (PAP)

seat and won an overwhelming majority – 43 out of 51 – with 53 percent of the popular vote. In June 1959, PAP Secretary-General Lee Kuan Yew became Singapore's first prime minister, a position he held until 1990.

PAP struggles for control: The years following the election were not quiet. The People's Action Party, from its inception in 1954, had both left-leaning and moderate factions. And from 1955 to 1961, the political climate in Singapore had grown increasingly to favour the election of left-wing candidates.

In 1960, Ong Eng Guan, the PAP Minister of National Development, impatient with the party leadership's slow progress towards full independence, issued "Sixteen Resolutions" criticizing Prime Minister Lee and his colleagues for being soft on the *merdeka* question. Ong suggested new talks be opened with the British at which the government should push aggressively for full independence.

Lee, who had come to represent the PAP moderates, responded by firing Ong and expelling him from the party. Ong formed his own party and was re-elected to the Assembly in 1961. In another by-election, David Marshall of the Workers' Party was elected. Like Ong, Marshall campaigned vigorously for the removal of the British military presence and full and rapid independence.

On the eve of the 1961 election, eight PAP

more particularly its industrial expansion, is the basic problem which the PAP must solve or else risk disappearing as a political force."

The context of this statement was an offer by Tunku Abdul Rahman, the Malayan Prime Minister, to accept a merger with Singapore.

Joining Malaya: Merger with Singapore's northern neighbour had been on the political agenda of nearly every party since World War II. Lee sought to join Malaya for a number of reasons, but primarily because it offered both raw materials and a market for Singapore goods.

An independent Singapore, Lee said at the time, with no domestic source of raw materials and no appreciable internal market, was "a

assemblymen, representing the more radical faction of the party, joined pro-communist trade union leaders in condemning the ruling faction's failure to bring about full self-government. That same year, Lee Siew Choh and Lim Chin Siong – leading members of PAP's radical wing – formed a separate party that was to become Lee's chief opposition in the coming years: the Barisan Socialis.

The Prime Minister was banking on overcoming this "threat" from the left by providing increased employment and affluence through economic expansion. In 1963, Lee said: "Our expanding population stares us in the face – Singapore's economic expansion,

political, economic and geographic absurdity". A further advantage, from his point of view, was that the Malayan government was right-wing and would support the moderate Lee in his struggle with the Barisan Socialis.

Malaya – which had rejected earlier merger offers – did not relish the thought of extending citizenship to Singapore's one million Chinese. Nevertheless, the perceived threat of an "Asian Cuba" in Singapore persuaded the strongly anti-communist Tunku to offering unification.

Singapore, F.M.S.: The PAP and the Barisan Socialis disagreed on the terms for merger although they both supported the move. On

1 September 1962, a referendum was put to the voters and the PAP proposal won – against a backdrop of blank protest votes.

The merger took place just over a year later, and on 22 September 1963, just five days after the announcement, the PAP held a general election. The opposition was caught by surprise and the PAP, benefiting from its recent success in bringing Singapore into the newly-formed Federation of Malaysia, won 37 seats against 13 for the Barisan Socialis.

Crackdown: Immediately following the election, the PAP arrested and detained 15 prominent leaders of the opposition. The moves, which decimated the Barisan Socialis, were explained by the PAP as necessary in order ful union. With the "Asian Cuba" threat crushed, the merger no longer seemed like such a good idea to the Malaysian government. On 9 August 1965, the two countries parted ways and Singapore became an independent country.

Survival: When Singapore gained its independence, the prospects for the tiny nation looked grim. One-tenth of the country's citizens were out of work. The government was cash poor. The then Foreign Minister S. Rajaratnam said Singapore had a "near-zero chance of survival politically, economically, or militarily".

However, the government had already mapped out its economic development plan

to wipe out the "communist plot to create tension and unrest in the state".

Once the moderates had consolidated their power in Singapore, progress towards a permanent federation ended. The PAP had aggressively entered the Malaysian political scene, but differences between Singapore and its federation partners caused tensions to rise. One reason was the PAP's insistence on an immediate common market between the two states, a move which met Malaysian resistance and soured chances of a success- in 1961, centred around growth and employment based on foreign investment. Starting in 1965, the country began a massive industrialization drive.

Economic textbooks say that to attract foreign investment, a developing country must offer political stability, cheap labour, a good location and few or no restrictions on currency movement. Taking this to heart, Lee Kuan Yew's government provided all of the above and succeeded (from 1968–1972) in achieving one of the highest rates of growth the world had seen – Singapore's industrial sector grew an average of 23 percent a year during that period.

Left, Lee Kuan Yew leads the PAP victory march in 1959. **Above**, the PAP at a party conference.

Unemployment fell to 5 percent by 1972 and full employment came soon after. This growth, however, did not come without a price. In 1968, the government, in order to assure cheap labour, passed laws limiting the rights of organized workers and effectively put a ceiling on their earnings through wage and overtime restrictions.

In a way, industrialization was a curious step for an established entrepot like Singapore. Most developing countries move to an industrial economy from an agrarian, raw materials-based economy. Trade and financial services normally follow industrialization. But Lee Kuan Yew took Singapore a step "backward" and in the process created phenomenal

95 percent had telephones, 80 percent had washing machines and 75 percent had video cassette recorders. At the same time, Singaporeans became the world's third best savers (after Japan and Switzerland) with a per capita average of S$31,037 in the bank.

Public housing: In 1960, the government established the Housing and Development Board (HDB) with the express purpose of providing decent living quarters for Singapore's citizens. The performance of the HDB has been one of the greatest public housing success stories.

From 1960 to 1980, the HDB built almost 400,000 apartments at an ever increasing rate; by the early '80s, one apartment went

growth, employment and prosperity.

The Singapore economy, despite recessions prompted by the oil glut in the '70s and by a changing world economy in the middle '80s, has proved a boon to the island's inhabitants. The overall growth rate averaged almost 13 percent a year until the oil glut, and 9.3 percent a year from 1976–1984.

The 1990 census revealed just how successful Singapore had become – and the extent to which that success has trickled down to ordinary citizens. The average household income more than doubled in the 1980s, to S$3,076 per month. More than 97 percent of homes had refrigerators and televisions,

up in Singapore every 15 minutes. Today, more than 87 percent of the population live in government-built housing.

By Western standards, life in one of these "boxes in the sky" does not particularly appeal. But set within self-sufficient "new towns" with their own commercial, shopping and recreational facilities, HDB living has become very much a Singaporean way of life. Improvements in design and upgrading programmes in older neighbourhoods ensure a pleasant environment. Estates are kept clean and, increasingly, green.

Visitors to the island often comment on the HDB apartments which they compare – unjustly – to government "projects" in the United States or Britain. In fact, Singapore's public housing bears no resemblance to the slums to which people in the West are accustomed, and the Singapore's housing programme is studied by public planners around the world who consider it a model of success.

A spinoff of the public housing programme is the fact that Singapore has the world's highest rate of home ownership. By 1990, more than 90 percent of Singaporeans were living in their own homes. People are encouraged to purchase HDB flats, using funds from a compulsory savings programme called the Central Provident Fund (CPF) to finance most of the mortgage.

Malay, and Tamil schools have become Chinese-, Malay- and Tamil-stream schools, with English as the other language.

In fact, as English has become the *lingua franca* of business in Singapore, and English fluency has grown to have economic benefits, most Singaporeans now choose to send their children to English-stream schools.

The language and cultural barriers that threatened to divide Singapore's population 20 years ago have been largely erased. The sense of national identity among today's Singaporean is very acute; as much as 90 percent of the population prefers to be called "Singaporean" rather than Chinese, Malay or Indian.

Multi-racial society: Although instances of racial confrontation in Singapore's history are relatively rare, the government has, at every turn, sought to inculcate a national identity among the members of its 77 percent Chinese, 14 percent Malay, and 7 percent Indian society.

Perhaps the most important step the government has taken in building a Singaporean identity has been its policy of bilingualism in the schools. What were formerly Chinese,

Left, government housing can be a colourful affair. **Above**, modern youths in a relaxed moment.

Armed Forces: Three years after independence, in line with the "Nixon Doctrine" in Asia, the British announced the accelerated withdrawal of British forces from Singapore by 1971. This posed a problem for the then-struggling nation not only in the perception of vulnerability, but also because the British bases provided a major source of employment. But a high rate of industrial growth, as well as the accelerated development of a domestic armed forces, blunted the effect of the British withdrawal.

Mandatory 2½-year national service for all 18-year-old males was established in 1967. This, coupled with today's arsenal of sophisticated weaponry, provides for a Singapore Armed Forces that serves as an estimable deterrent.

Single-party democracy: Singapore has evolved into a what is basically called a one-party state, with a government that is cautious, paternalistic and free of corruption. Elections are held every five years. Voting is compulsory for all citizens over 21 years of age. Since independence in 1959, the PAP has been in power, with at most four opposition members in an 81-seat Parliament.

The constitutional head of state is the president, which is now an elected office after decades as a purely ceremonial job. Ong Teng Cheong – former deputy prime minister

The one-party system gave Lee and the PAP remarkable autonomy in shaping the nation. And it is not only economic growth that has been carefully planned and executed.

The Singapore government keeps a careful lid on many aspects of Singapore life. The number of children a couple has, how to behave at work, on the road, and at home are all officially encouraged through legislation and splashy government media campaigns.

In the early days of the Republic, Singapore's population increased at a rate the government found alarming. Abortion and sterilization legislation, and later, tax and schooling advantages to those families of two or fewer children, have brought the

and secretary-general of the National Trades Union Congress – became the first elected president in August 1993. Ong received 58.7 percent of the vote against 41.3 percent for opponent Chua Kim Yeow. The president has veto power over the prime minister and parliament as part of a broad mandate to carry out "judicious checks and balances" on the nation's political system and guarantee a high standard of government.

In Singapore, unlike most democracies, policy-making is not the business of the legislative branch. Instead, the prime minister and his cabinet introduce policy, and Parliament then debates means of implementation.

population down to a growth level of just over 1 percent a year.

But with labour shortage, the government, in 1987, began encouraging couples who could afford it to have a third child. The population has now reached 3 million and an increase of up to 4 million is envisaged.

Communist threat: The Singapore government has retained the privilege of detention without trial since colonial days, and since the arrests of the Barisan Socialis members in the early '60s, the government has periodically invoked the Internal Security Act to round up "communists and communalists."

In a famous sweep in 1976, more than 50

Singaporeans were rounded up and detained for allegedly trying "to undermine Singapore's stability by rekindling the flames of subversion and terror". And speaking in 1987 of the government's arrest of 22 people that year in an alleged Marxist plot to overthrow the Singapore government, the then Senior Minister S. Rajaratnam spoke of an "unholy trinity" of communism, racialism, and religious fanaticism: "This unholy trinity is not a bogey. It is real. It is real because this hybrid beast, red in tooth and claw, is today laying waste to many lands."

Despite Western complaints about Singapore's detentions without trial, restrictions on assembly and lack of press freedom –

for individual dissent and questioning, but stop short of allowing interest groups to organize and participate in policy-making.

However, acceptance of this began to change as the '80s began. In a by-election in 1981, for the first time in 15 years, an opposition member, lawyer and Workers' Party candidate, JB Jeyaretnam was elected to Parliament. And in the 1984 general election, voters returned Jeyaretnam and added another opposition member, Chiam See Tong.

After the last elections in August 1991, opposition members now total four, three from the Singapore Democratic Party (SDP) founded by Chiam and one from the Workers' Party, while at the same time voters

luxuries, local officials have repeatedly stated, a vulnerable country like Singapore cannot afford – Singaporeans have repeatedly demonstrated confidence in the PAP government. The PAP government has provided its citizens with the essentials, housing and employment, and produced a strong measure of affluence.

Recent setbacks: The political structures of Singapore's single-party democracy allow

Left, conscripts on parade during National Day. **Above**, the Boy Scouts, one of the many uniform groups which help the nation mould responsible, civic-minded citizens.

returned the ruling PAP with its lowest percentage of the popular vote.

The new generation: The political changes wrought by a younger population and a shifting economy have not been ignored by the PAP. True to its method of political evolution rather than competition, it began, in the early '80s, a programme of "self-renewal".

Younger "Second Generation" candidates were fielded by the PAP in the 1984 election, and faces in the Cabinet changed. On 28 November 1990, after 31 years in power, Lee Kuan Yew handed over the reins of power to his chosen successor, Goh Chok Tong, and his team of second generation leaders. Although remaining as Senior Minister in the cabinet, Lee had thus smoothly guided the leadership of Singapore through the transition from the old guard who achieved independence, to the new generation.

Under Goh's leadership, the new generation of PAP ministers has shown itself to be flexible and accommodating. Opportunities were created for community participation in government – particularly at "town council" level where HDB residents were given a say in the running of their estates. Goh also gave the economy something of a push with a $100 million venture capital fund and a cut in the employer contribution to the mandatory CPF scheme.

69 percent of the youngest group of voters wanted an active opposition party.

This desire encouraged the opposition to field more candidates for the 1988 election than ever before. The opposition challenge failed to win any more seats but some of the PAP wins were considerably narrower than in past elections.

Into the Nineties: More than 20 years of affluence has created a society that is beginning to desire things less tangible than housing or a decent income.

By the early '80s, the government had begun to realize that its tight-reined style had created a society that was culturally and artistically wan. A retro trend towards recog-

A political science professor at the National University of Singapore, Chan Heng Chee, wrote in 1986: "If over the years the population in Singapore had come to understand the essence of democracy to reside, firstly, in efficient and non-corrupt government, secondly, in the increase in the welfare of the citizens, and thirdly, in a benevolent paternalistic government, it now rediscovered a fourth element, that is, checks on absolute power."

Two polls taken in 1984 found that most Singaporeans hoped to see an active opposition party in Parliament. The second poll, taken by *The Straits Times*, also found that

nition of racial heritage and language, and a number of programmes to stimulate cultural growth started. In 1987, even the normally sedate *Straits Times* commented: "(The censorship board) must take note that there are voices at other forums which are equally legitimate expressions of public values even if they do not carry the weight of authority."

The subject was the censorship of the Academy Award-winning war film *Platoon*. But the sentiment could be applied more broadly, and would accurately reflect the feeling of Singapore's growing well-educated elite.

In response to this feeling, the Ministry of

Information and the Arts was created in 1990 and under the dynamic leadership of Brigadier-General George Yeo eased censorship laws in 1991, paving the way for greater freedom and encouragement of the arts in Singapore. Many artistic films are now shown without censorship – even full-frontal nudity. Even films that were once banned are now released on home videos. Movies such as *Mad Max I* and *II* are now available for rental. The first Western heavy metal music acts have been allowed to perform in public. Acts such as Metallica, Deep Purple and Scorpions were well-received with sold-out concerts in Singapore.

A nation of campaigns: Since independence

in this "war" against disagreeable behaviour. In marked contrast to most other cities, Singapore is clean and green, and its people are for the most part honest, polite and healthy.

The tendency towards uncouth behaviour is countered with posters, slogans, exhibits and TV exhortations against either specific vulgarities – "No Spitting!" – or more generalized bad manners – "Courtesy Month!" In fact, the annual courtesy campaign of 1993 took on "overseas element in an effort to quell the image of the "Ugly Singaporean" barging his way through foreign countries.

The tab for all this public interest promotion is picked up by both the government and local businesses. One of the most recent

in 1965 the Singapore government has often relied on broad public education campaigns to put across its goals and aspirations to the man (and woman) in the street.

Campaigns on the subjects of spitting, littering, flushing public toilets, courtesy, keeping fit, teenage smoking, chewing gum and speaking Mandarin instead of dialects, have sought to create a more hygienic and well-behaved population.

Singapore has been remarkably successful

Left, Goh Chok Tong has been at the country's helm since November 1990. Above, art competitions encourage creativity among the young.

anthems – "We are Sing-a-pore, hear the lion roar!" – for example, was backed by the Cold Storage Supermarket chain.

In 1987, Singapore launched its "National Ideals and Identity Programme" which includes a whole slew of slogans, programmes and symbolism, including a stunning computer-generated TV spot: "Courage, Strength and Excellence."

One of the corporate sponsors of the drive, whose company contributed some $40,000, told *The Straits Times* the following when asked why his company supported the campaign: "People outside view Singapore in two ways – if they see Singapore as a clean country, they will view companies here as clean. If they see companies here as clean, they will also view Singapore as clean."

In its methods, the government seems to have picked up a few tips from the Madison Avenue taste-makers, and its current efforts are much more polished and probably more effective than its earlier campaigns.

"MALES WITH LONG HAIR WILL BE ATTENDED TO LAST" shouted a poster from the early '70s. The drawings illustrating the government's definition of "long hair" were crude and roughly sketched. The whole effect was as that of a wanted poster or something out of an immigration handbook.

Some of the more important campaigns

At least once, however, Singaporeans signalled that the government went too far. In the early '80s, having noticed that – statistically – children of graduate mothers were more successful in school and in the economy, the government suggested that women graduates have more children, and proposed some legislation to "encourage" them to do so. The public decided that while spitting was one thing, "sociobiology" – as critics called the proposal – was another. In the face of such strong objections, the proposed legislation was withdrawn.

Campaigns serve a purpose wider than mere behaviour control or policy enforcement. They promote national solidarity and

are backed by legislation. For example, "Please Stop at Two" smaller family drive was reinforced with tax and schooling benefits for those less fecund couples.

By the early '80s, the birthrate having shrunk somewhat too drastically, a new "Have three or more if you can afford to" campaign began, with primary school registration benefits for those children of larger families. While visitors are often bemused at the volume and breadth of advice the Singapore government gives to its citizens, for their own part most Singaporeans have been willing to go along – resulting in Singapore becoming a better place to live.

even provide entertainment. The 1987 "Courtesy Month" celebration, headquartered in the Raffles City shopping complex, took on the dimensions of a small theme park.

For adults, there were videotape morality plays depicting the horror and chagrin of, for example, returning to an HDB apartment drunk. In addition – for the kids – a plywood maze with signs that warned "Throwing Litter from Apartments can Kill!" and other such admonitions.

If you think that Singaporeans don't have a sense of humour when it comes to social behaviour, consider the fact that a shop in Lucky Plaza specializes in T-shirts emblazoned with "SINGAPORE: A FINE CITY" and other satirical phrases based on some of the famous campaigns.

The 1990s and beyond: In typical Singapore fashion, the second generation is looking ahead and planning the future. Their aims are set out in a colourful, well produced book, reasonably priced to be available to all.

In "The Next Lap", Goh Chok Tong and his team pointed the way forward for Singapore. The island state is viewed in an international context, and is set to become an international hub, economically, due to its excellent infrastructure and products and services, as well as culturally. With the nurturing of the arts, more emphasis will be placed on

strives to push those figures even higher. The Edusave scheme involves the government opening and contributing to an account for every child between the ages of 6 and 16. Parents are encouraged to contribute and the money is to be used for education-related expenses. Between 4 and 5 percent of the GDP is spent on education today.

The National University of Singapore (NUS) was established in 1980 by the merger of the University of Singapore and the smaller Nanyang University in 1989. In July 1991 the Nanyang Technological Institute became the Nanyang Technological University (NTU) giving Singapore its second fully-fledged university. The Open University is

improving the quality of life in Singapore.

The educational and welfare needs of Singaporeans are to be better taken care of by the "Edusave" and "Medisave" schemes respectively, and facilities in both fields are to be improved.

Education: By 1990, more than 90 percent of Singaporeans could read and write, and roughly 40 percent of adults had secondary or university education. But the government

Anti-social behaviour is discouraged via a series of on-going campaigns, frequently directed at the country's youth (**left**), and the imposition of prohibition fines (**above**).

to become a reality for mature students in the year 1994.

Health: Medisave ensures that people are able to meet medical bills by compulsory saving by employees. The public and private systems offer a wide choice, with six government hospitals providing 8,000 beds and the 11 private hospitals a total of 1,800 beds.

Preventive medicine, in the form of a clean environment and encouragement of sports and prevention of smoking is promoted by the Training and Health Education Department of the Ministry of Health. Physical education is encouraged in schools as are regular medical checkups.

The compulsory savings of all employees in the CPF, which are increased by contributions from their employers, are designed to take care of expenses in retirement. Savings may also be invested in housing and to make certain approved investments.

Economics: Singapore is now reaching across international boundaries as the hub of a huge business and industrial area that encompasses Johor State in Malaysia and the Indonesian province of Riau. Dubbed the "growth triangle" by Prime Minister Goh, the project is expected to increase the economic attractiveness of all three areas and maximize local resources. The concept is simple: Singapore has limited space, not

constructed by Singapore companies in Suzhou, west of Shanghai. Meanwhile, the Singapore Broadcast Corporation (SBC) has found a lucrative market selling its Mandarin-language soap operas in China, and Singapore publishers are selling close to two million books a year in the "Middle Kingdom".

Singapore itself will continue on its high-tech road to become "an intelligent island." Already known for its efficient communications systems, Singapore is planning to add satellite links, submarine cables and high capacity optic fibres and is also working towards its own communications satellite. A highly sophisticated data transmission utility called Integrated Services Digital Net-

enough labour and scant natural resources, but plenty of expertise and investment capital. Johor and Riau have abundant land, inexpensive workers and ample resources. The growth triangle is already reshaping the face of Johor and Riau, as factories, transportation facilities and resort complexes rise on what was previously unused land. (More on Johore and Riau on page 245).

Further afield, Singapore entrepreneurs are forging new business links in a number of countries including Thailand, Vietnam and China. One of the largest China projects is a 70-sq-km (27-sq-mile) "Singapore style" industrial township that will be designed and

work (ISDN) – which can transmit simultaneous voice, data and image – and other microchip and fibre optic innovations are expected to greatly improve telephone communications by the turn of the century. Computer networks like Tradenet for trade documents, Globalink for global information, Portnet for port business and Teleview for the home will continue the high-tech development of the island. Meanwhile, Singapore's workers – voted the best in the world by the Washington DC-based Business Environment Risk Information service (BERI) for 12 straight years through 1992 – are constantly urged to strive for further excellence.

Singapore International: Singapore is now ready to take its place on the international scene, not just in the commercial world, but politically, in the United Nations, GATT, the Commonwealth, the Non-Aligned Movement and the Association of Southeast Asian Nations (ASEAN), the six-nation cultural and economic bloc comprising Brunei, Indonesia, Malaysia, Singapore, the Philippines and Thailand.

An armed forces medical team was sent to the Middle East during the 1991 Gulf War and Singapore diplomats worked through ASEAN to broker a peaceful solution to the Cambodian crisis. Meanwhile, Singapore troops were dispatched in 1993 to help su-

set up Singapore International Foundation which will provide a link between Singapore and its expatriate sons as well as encouraging talent to come to the Republic. Given past precedent, these future goals seem well within the capabilities of Singaporeans.

Historic conservation: Boat Quay is the latest triumph in a series of building conservation efforts that stretch back more than a decade. Local authorities spent much of the 1960s and 70s tearing down old buildings. It wasn't progress for the sake of progress. Many of the old buildings were little more than slums, perilous fire traps with outdoor toilets and open sewers. In parts of Chinatown, population density had reached

pervise the Cambodian elections and help survivors of the Mount Pinatubo volcanic disaster in the Philippines.

Plans are afoot to create a peace corps to enable young Singaporeans to assist less developed countries. Technical aid is already given in the fields of housing, communications, the environment, health and education. Coordinating these efforts is the newly

Left, the well-equipped container port at Tanjong Pagar. **Above,** just beyond the container terminal is a conservation area, featuring terraced shophouses that have been converted into offices, restaurants, bars and hotels.

2,400 people per hectare. (Details on the development of Boat Quay is found in chapter on *Chinatown and Financial District*, page 206).

But almost overnight, Singapore changed tack, from a position of disdain for old buildings to a course on which almost anything older than 50 years was deemed historically important. Great swaths of the central city like Chinatown, Little India, Kampong Glam and Boat Quay have been spared the wrecking ball and are now in various stages of renovation.

The first large-scale conservation effort was Emerald Hill in 1981, a project which showed that old buildings could be refitted for modern use and that there was money to be made from historic renovation – not just money for architects, contractors and antique dealers, but big bucks for anyone who speculated on such properties.

By 1986 the Singapore government had approved a five-year development plan and pledged S$1 billion towards conservation. But before a single brick was mended or a floor board restored, a delegation was dispatched to study heritage sites in America and France.

At about this same time, the Singaore Tourist Promotion Board (STPB) came to a rather alarming conclusion that Singapore's

of renovation, including the restoration of Raffles Hotel and the National Museum.

The Urban Redevelopment Authority (URA) has now marked 3,300 buildings for preservation. Once gazetted, experts "diagnose" the structure and provide computer drawings to aid renovation. URA strives to preserve the original fabric of the building, while adding modern amenities like indoor toilets and kitchens. Meanwhile, authorities have moved rapidly from the preservation of single structures to the renovation of entire neighbourhoods like Chinatown and Boat Quay.

High Tech: Singapore wouldn't be what it is today without the blood, sweat and tears of

historical, cultural and architectural heritage was in danger of being destroyed. Preservation was suddenly seen as an important initiative in enhancing Singapore's tourism appeal. STPB quickly jumped on the conservation bandwagon as the driving force behind the restoration of Empress Place, one of the island's finest examples of British colonial design.

It was necessary to call in restoration experts from Europe and America who could reteach old skills like woodcarving and plasterwork. And through diligent detective work, a 19th-century formula for paint was rediscovered. Empress Place inspired a flurry

human labour. However, at present the islanders march to the beat of a different drummer – the buzz, grind and whirl of computers and automation.

Everywhere you go in Singapore, you can see the results of this love affair with machines. Robots are starting to replace workmen on construction sites. Longshoremen have turned over their toughest tasks to huge cranes and computers. In other countries, kids play football or watch cartoons on Saturday mornings. But in Singapore they flock to computer software shops or information technology tutors.

Singapore invests roughly 38 percent of its

Gross Domestic Product on machinery – more than Japan, Germany or Switzerland.

There is now a computer for every 12 people in Singapore – the world's seventh highest figure. And 70 percent of business firms use information technology. Government, finance, transport and industry are linked by a complex system of computer networks such as TradeNet, BizNet and EcomNet. MediNet gives doctors and hospitals instant access to patient medical files, while School Link unites the academic records of more than 400 schools. In addition to these networks, the government aims to put a computer in every home through the revolutionary Teleview system.

statistics on the number of passengers and their commuting habits so that train movements can be adjusted daily for more efficient use.

Hawker centres are starting to install computerized dish-washing systems and toilets that flush themselves with the aid of an infrared sensor. Singapore can boast the globe's first post office system linked by a single integrated computer network. And local banks aim to eliminate queues all together by establishing computer systems that allow customers to do everything from withdrawing cash to negotiating a million-dollar business loan through ATM machines.

With a population of just three million,

Just over the horizon is the Land Data Hub, a massive computer data base that will literally detail every inch of the island by compiling every property map, survey and deed issued since 1823. No other nation has anything like this.

The Mass Rapid Transit (MRT) system is a model of high-tech efficiency with computers that keep constant tabs on everything from the air conditioning and lighting, to

Left, the Empress Place Building at the mouth of the Singapore River is used as a venue for arts and crafts exhibitions. **Above**, the MRT will eventually link up the whole island.

Singapore needs to rely on machines and micro chips to make up for the lack of manpower. Automation is also great for the bank account. Robots make less mistakes than human workers which means the overall quality of products is vastly improved. Automation also frees workers to move over to the "brain" sector – research, development, service and managerial professions that in turn create more profit potential.

What lies ahead? A group of companies recently pooled their engineering expertise to create a "robo-waiter" that can make a cup of coffee from start to finish, hand the cup to a customer and then wash the utensils.

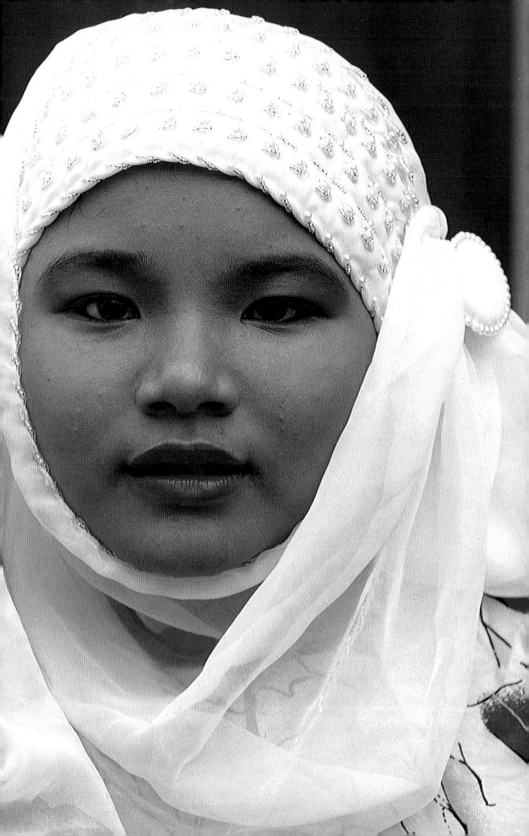

A Singaporean executive, in his designer shirt and well-cut trousers steps out of his Mercedes, clutching his hand phone. He's heading for his favourite lunch spot. He stops at a tiny hawker stall and laps up noodles at S$3.

A luxurious hotel is built just off Orchard Road, and when things don't go as well as they should. The *feng shui* man (geomancer) is called in. The main doors are re-angled, and profits soar. Why? Because the cashier's desk had been directly opposite the main door, so of course money and luck was flowing straight out.

A Singaporean may be sophisticated, prosperous and often completely at home with western ideas, but he is not above hedging his bets with dismissing the gods of fortune, just in case.

The Chinese Singaporean can happily set fire to a paper mansion, complete with swimming pool – a paper effigy to send on to a deceased relative. Once a year, the Muslim will fast for a month and once in his life make the *haj* (pilgrimage) to Mecca. An Indian can walk on glowing coals and pierce his body with metal skewers to carry a *kavadi* at Thaipusam. Many gods are worshipped in temples, shrines, mosques, churches, temples, shrines or in highrise banks where Bible study groups gather during lunchtime.

A Singaporean may be Chinese, Malay or Indian, Eurasian or even European, but really he's not quite any of these. Although Malays were the first settlers, it was the British who realised the potential of the island and the Chinese who came to fulfil dreams of prosperity by sheer hard work. Indians joined the throng and the island's population has been expanding ever since.

As the island developed, so did its people, making them different from those who lived in Malaya, China or India. Racial differences within Singapore remain under a veneer of modernism, but tolerance is the watchword. Most people, if asked, would say their nationality was Singaporean.

Although apparently westernised in so many ways, Singaporeans remain essentially Asian. One agrees with elders and superiors so that they do not "lose face". Authoritarian rule is, therefore, not as resented as might be expected. In general, Singaporeans are happy to maintain the status quo which has done them proud.

Locals tend to be reserved in conversation, but they will immediately ask "How much you pay, ah?" when you've bought anything from a new Volvo to a bunch of flowers. When their response to your reply is "Too much, lah" it isn't easy for visitors to understand that this is not meant as criticism.

Is there anything which unites Singaporeans, old and young, Chinese, Malay? Yes, and it's not football but food. Talk to a Singaporean, not about the weather, but about food and you're on the right track. Neatly dressed Singaporeans put in long hours at the

Preceding pages: The Multi-cultural Face of Singapore: Kids at play; Muslim school girls; Hindu festival dress. Left, thoroughly modern in many ways, many Singaporean Chinese still retain traditional Confucian values.

office, but they'll never just grab a sandwich at the desk, however hard-pressed. It has to be a decent cooked meal, even if it is served on polystyrene plates.

This brings us back to the smart executive. He, like any Singaporean worth his salt, knows just where the noodles are exactly as he likes, and just how much he should pay, whether eating stylishly in top-class restaurants, or down at the hawker centres.

The Singaporean has become urban and urbane. Having long since left their *kampongs*, picturesque villages of yesteryear, they are now used to city life. During a recent spate of unusually hot weather, the local press complained that locals couldn't even take the heat as they used to, having become too accustomed to cool air-conditioning. They live in high-rises and are just as horrified at the thought of cockroaches and snakes as any tourist.

Constantly urged to strive for excellence, Singaporeans are only happy with straight "A"s. They have become afraid to lose out to the next fellow. This trait is now humorously termed the "*kiasu* syndrome" and is the subject of jokes and ironic comment. For example, parents, anxious not to lose out in their children's education, queue up overnight just to get their kids into a nursery school of their choice. Getting a bargain is more than mere monetary satisfaction for the *kiasu* Singaporean, it is almost a moral victory.

That they can laugh about all this is a refreshing thing. Singaporeans are more relaxed, opening up and beginning to enjoy life more. Satirical and even critical books are beginning to appear and censorship is being eased. Things are changing slowly, paving the way for more original thought, less censorship and a more open society.

Right now, there are just over 3 million Singaporeans, but if the efforts of a government match-making service called the Social Development Unit (dubbed Single, Desperate and Ugly) are successful, there will be a million more taking their place on an "intelligent" international island and ensuring a continuation of the good life.

As Singapore moves towards the 21st century, racial differences are fading with shared common experiences and Western influence. Young singles want their own pads, and married couples prefer not to live with their in-laws. Marriage and starting a family have taken a back seat as getting ahead in one's career takes priority. Yet family ties remain fairly strong and the sight of a bent old grandmother being helped along by a young trendily dressed granddaughter is not unusual.

Singaporeans have left their days of immigrant and post-colonial struggles behind and are now finding their place in the international community, a niche between east and west, and they are attempting to combine the best of both worlds.

Ready to party during National Day, August 9th.

DONATIO
BOX
廣種福田

A middle-aged Chinese stands behind the counter in a department store, his fingers deftly punching an electronic calculator. Then, before counting out his customer's change, he moves to a centuries-old abacus and, in practically the same time he spent on the adding machine, he checks the figures. A Singapore Chinese is a Singaporean, but he's still a Chinese.

The visitor will see it long before he spots the abacus. Singapore's skyline is a splash of Chinese characters. Gigantic posters advertise Chinese films in which heroines with powder-white faces and long black hair dispatch legions of villains with mighty whacks of a balsawood sword. High-pitched string music and cascading voice tones hover in the humid night. Boiling garlic and frying pork season the air. If Singapore is mainly anything, it's mainly Chinese, making up 77.6 percent of the total population.

And that is no recent phenomenon. For centuries, Chinese junks have roamed the neighbouring seas. A Buddhist pilgrim named Fa-Hsien passed through the Straits of Malacca from Ceylon in AD 414. A trader called Wang Ta-Yuan visited in 1349 when Singapore was a swampy outpost named Temasek and he reported finding Chinese in residence even then.

When Sir Stamford Raffles hoisted a Union Jack ashore and founded modern Singapore in 1819, Chinese planters, pirates, fishermen and traders were already installed. Five years after the colony was established, Singapore had 3,000 Chinese and more were arriving weekly. In fact, Raffles had already complained about the noise from firecrackers and had pushed through a law stipulating "80 blows with a cudgel on the breech" for anyone caught gambling.

Straits Chinese: Singapore's Chinese population can be broken down into nearly a dozen ethno-linguistic groups, but broadly speaking the nation has two distinct Chinese categories:

the descendants of more recent immigrants who were born in China and the descendants of long-established "Straits Chinese."

The Straits Chinese began settling in the Malay Peninsula and Riau islands more than 400 years ago in order to take advantage of the rich trade along the Straits of Malacca. They often intermarried with the local Malay Muslim population, adopting customs different from those in their homeland. After centuries of melding, a hybrid Straits Chinese culture developed with its own distinct

language, architecture, cuisine, and clothing. Their *lingua franca* is Malay, but an idiosyncratic version of Malay. Peranakan food is unique in its lavish use of spices and shrimp paste for cooking. The Straits Chinese women still wear the traditional Malay *sarong kebaya*. This is a society that is neither Chinese nor Malay, but something entirely different.

Due of the fact that they could speak Chinese as well as Malay – and sometimes English – the Straits Chinese in Singapore enjoyed a clear commercial and political advantage over immigrants from mainland China. In fact, many of the colony's most successful businessmen in Victorian days were Straits Chinese.

Today thousands of Straits Chinese can be found living in Malacca, Penang and Riau, as well as Singapore. Straits Chinese culture is often called by a different name: Peranakan. And the people themselves are sometimes called *Babas* and *Nonyas*. They no longer dress in a distinctive manner except as weddings and other special occasions, but Straits Chinese influence is still readily apparent in the shophouse architecture of places like Chinatown and Geylang; in local restaurants that specialise in Nonya food and in the many "Singlish" phrases that pepper local language.

fifths of the Chinese in Singapore. They are still mainly merchants and office workers.

Other Chinese came in numbers, speaking distinct dialects, cooking different foods and engaged in doing other work. The Chinese had fled from mainland China and away from the despotic Manchus. They took on back-breaking jobs that no one else wanted like building roads and working as dock labourers. Today just over a fifth of Singapore Chinese are Teochews from the Swatow region in Kwangtung province, not far from the Hokkien homeland. Teochews dominate port and maritime work forces.

There are slightly fewer Cantonese – perhaps 19 percent of Singapore's Chinese –

Two of the best places to learn about this unique local culture are the small museum at Peranakan Place on Orchard Road, and the Straits Chinese Gallery in the National Museum, where Peranakan clothing, furniture and *objects d'art* are on display.

New immigrants: Shortly after Singapore was founded, junks started bringing waves of immigrants from coastal areas of southern and eastern China. Some of the largest waves comprised Hokkien Chinese from southern Fukien province.

These hardy Chinese were usually traders and businessmen, largely the roots of today's Hokkien population which account for two-

who are also from Kwangtung province but with a well-defined identity. Cantonese, largely craftsmen and artisans in Singapore, make up most of the huge army of "overseas Chinese" in Hong Kong, San Francisco and just about everywhere else.

The Hainanese came from Hainan Island off Kwangtung and are largely to be found in hotel and domestic service.

Others came from Kwangsi province and other southern areas. In later years, northern Chinese joined the flow of immigration in smaller numbers.

Their common link is Mandarin, or *Hua-Yi*, the language of the Beijing (Peking) area, which is taught in schools and spoken increasingly by Singaporeans, under a concerted government effort to promote the language. "Speak Mandarin" campaigns are held annually in Singapore.

However, unity has a long way to go. Almost from the moment immigrants first arrived, secret societies were formed with emphasis on clan lines. Violence staggered belief. In 1854, for example, Chinese set upon Chinese with axes, knives and sharpened sticks. Six hundred were killed and 300 homes were destroyed. No one guessed the total injuries but details of mutilation and maiming made grim reading. It is unclear how it was all started but one prevalent

The gangs controlled crime, dividing up areas of the colony like Mafia lords. They offered protection for a price. Aside from their money-making ventures, the societies offered immigrant Chinese security in a rough frontier atmosphere. If a newcomer off the boat from Canton found a Cantonese society, he could feel fairly safe that anyone stealing his clothes and rice pot could be found and properly chastised.

Opium, gambling and prostitution ran rampant in early Singapore as Chinese, without women from home and with growing cash reserves, sought diversion from work. Controls were established, with drug laws formulated after heated debate, but enforce-

account is that a Hokkien and a Cantonese argued over 2.7kg (6lbs) of rice.

Secret societies: Secret societies grew so strong that law and order in Singapore at times was at the mercy of their leaders. One early government official, fluent in several Chinese dialects, kept things under control by getting secret society chiefs to rule for him. Otherwise, he found policing and protecting the teeming, winding lanes of Chinatown, where a wrong gesture could be fatal, too much to handle.

<u>Left</u>, Chinatown street scene. <u>Above</u>, posing for posterity on their Special Day.

ment was difficult.

Power was in the hands of men like Tan Che Sang, a rich man in the style of his time. He was the *towkay* in charge of the fish market, so much in control that when Raffles ordered it torn down and moved in 1822, Tan offered to build a new one at his own expense if he could just hold it tax-free for a period of time.

Tan, addicted to gambling, vowed one night after a heavy loss that he would give up the habit. He lopped off his little finger at the first joint just to back up the promise. It didn't work. He died at 78, still a regular fixture at Singapore's gaming tables.

Tan was known for his boast that if he

simply gave the word in Chinatown, Singapore would be emptied of Europeans in one gory fell swoop. He never tried it, but many people had little doubt he was right. And he wasn't the only one who could have given the word.

Manchus: Singapore was psychologically vital to the Chinese who sought an end to the Manchu emperors in Peking. In Singapore, Chinese could cut off their queue – the pigtail which the northern Manchus obliged all Chinese to wear to certify subservience. Accounts from the late 1890s until Sun Yat-Sen's movement overthrew the Manchus described how students enroute from China to Europe would snip off their queue in

By the late 1950s, when Singapore developed self-government, the leaders were almost all Chinese but of a different world from that of the robed and whiskered men of Singapore's past. Men like Lee Kuan Yew, Goh Keng Swee and Toh Chin Chye were educated in Britain and reared in an atmosphere in which the East and West blended.

Today's Singapore has a curious mixture of the new and old Chinese, broadly called "English-educated" and "Chinese-educated". The latter tend more toward Chinese chauvinism and strong links to their heritage, responding more slowly to the new national identity. They sometimes look upon English-educated Chinese with shades of the old

Singapore, buying a false pigtail of black silk for their return home. Plotting and preparing for the resistance was done partly in Singapore's Chinatown.

As time passed, Singapore mellowed somewhat with age, tamed partly with a continuing influx of women and a greater effort toward government by the British. Reformers fought against the smoking of opium, the pulling of heavy double rickshaws and the growing squalor of urban areas. The degrading term "John Chinaman" was heard less often and prominent Chinese, decorated and honoured, took over key civic and government positions.

contempt that their great ancestors held for barbarians not of the Middle Kingdom. The English-educated frequently look on them, in return, as being more conservative (stick-in-the-mud) and unprogressive.

Festivals: Singapore's holiday schedule is spearheaded by Chinese New Year, customarily a period of 15 days of merrymaking during which the whole city is splashed in the luck-bringing colour of red. Part-time chauffeurs are snapped up months in advance and special dining rooms in restaurants and hotels are booked solid.

A Chingay parade is held a week or so after the Lunar New Year and the streets of Chinatown are brightly lit and thronged with people buying and selling traditional decorations and delicacies.

Another important day is the festival of the Hungry Ghosts. It falls in the seventh lunar month when, Chinese believe, the souls of the dead are released from purgatory. The dead are honoured with wild profusions of day-glo colour in puppet shows, pageants and plays. In marketplaces, the devout spread huge tables with every manner of delicacy, carefully prepared in abundance to nourish ghosts out for their first lunch hour in 12 months. Then, when it is certain the ghosts have had time to enjoy the feast, those around eat what is left over. Paper "money" and

are sought carefully. Geomancers are consulted on the layout of brand new offices and their advice meticulously followed to bring good luck and prosperity. Faithful to old remedies, the Chinese patronise, herbalists in Chinatown, wise Chinese proprietors from behind scratched glass counters who prescribe grisly-looking roots from giant apothecary jars to cure everything from warts to aching wisdom teeth. Deer horn helps to prevent "heatiness" and ground pearls work wonders for the skin. Acupuncture specialists continue to practise centuries-old science that is only now becoming recognised by the West.

Food: As in festivals, and in everything else

other symbolic paper objects are burned to ensure that the ghosts have all they need.

The Mooncake Festival soon follows and this is usually celebrated by eating moon-shaped pastries with fillings of lotus paste, red bean paste, nuts or preserved duck eggs. Colourful lanterns are on display at the Chinese Garden.

The Chinese have always been regarded as being superstitious. And where business is concerned, auspicious moments and actions

Chinese, food is a superstar. A Cabinet Minister recently quipped: "If a Chinese sees a snake in the grass, he'll think of a way to eat it." He was only half joking. Restaurants, stalls and private kitchens offer every sort of Chinese dish from Peking duck to Cantonese casseroles. Street vendors sell salted prunes and candied ginger.

As soon as any Singapore Chinese begins talking about Singapore, the "true Singapore" that each visitor should experience, it generally takes him about 30 seconds to arrive at his country's most vital enticement: food. And less than a minute later he is inviting you to join him for a meal.

Left, lavish celebrations are usually held during the month-long Hungry Ghosts Festival. **Above**, when it comes to durians, the smell's the thing.

THE MALAYS

A Malay taxi driver taking a young American couple house-hunting pulled up to a likely looking bungalow, switched off the ignition and lounged back in his seat. When they emerged two hours later, he hadn't moved. He was studying the holy *Koran* propped up against his steering wheel and hadn't noticed the meter running.

Malays, caught in the middle of a society driven by profit, are still Malays. And they are still at the heart of the island they sold to the British.

For all its Chinese-ness, Singapore sings its national anthem in Malay. *Satay,* skewered pieces of grilled meat, is as much a symbol of Singapore as *Hokkien Mee* (noodles). Cultural shows never fail to produce black-clad youths in sashes thrusting their hands in *Bersilat*, the Malay's graceful art of self-defence, or girls in trim *sarong kebayas* dancing the *joget*.

Malays were here first, and they still make up 14 percent of the population. However, generations of aggressive British traders, Chinese businessmen and others have pushed the gentle, genteel life of the Malays to Singapore's far corners.

In earlier centuries, everyday Malay life centred around *kampong* settlements where food was grown to feed the community and life was simple. Fishing sloops and canoe-like war *prahus* explored the neighbouring seas, but little impact was made by outsiders to the Muslim way of life of the 19th century.

A changing role: Today, many Malays have simply adopted the prevalent philosophy and melted into the economy. Typically familiar as clerks, communication and transport workers, policemen and messengers, Malays also confound the statistics as successful lawyers and influential politicians.

Others have succeeded in combining the modern hard-driving ambitious approach with the easy style of their parents. Many have held to their old patterns, spending long hours studying Islamic teachings or lounging on the front porch in a *sarong* to watch the sun go down.

To the traditional Malay, a growing stack of assets is far less important than family life and religion. For many, home was an old-

style wooden slat house on stilts in a *kampong* (village) where banana trees and utility bills were shared among relatives and friends.

Children wander from one house to the next and everyone is a baby-sitter for all. There is little crime. When someone has a problem, he rarely has to look past his neighbour for help.

Kampongs once lined most of urban Singapore but are now increasingly rare. Today, they are tucked away in clumps of trees on the way to Changi, Punggol and at the edges of the island. More and more people have moved to government apartments where they must adapt the old ways as best they can to high-rise living.

Islam, followed closely by Malays, calls for hours of prayer and study of the *Koran*. The gentle drone of the *muezzin* echoes above traffic junctions from the lofty minarets of the Sultan Mosque – centre of Islam in Singapore. The *surau*, or village mosque, lies at the heart of every Malay neighbourhood.

Like Muslims everywhere, orthodox Malays save hard for the time when they make a holy pilgrimage to Mecca. Today, the trip no longer spells danger at sea, or calls for a hike across the sands, but only the price of the airfare and the patience to put up with the rigours of the *haj*.

Some of the old meaning is gone, but Malay status still increases greatly with the title "*Haji*" and the white *songkok* cap earned from pilgrimage.

For a month every year, Muslims eat and drink nothing from dawn to dusk, praying five times a day and thinking of their faith. They end the *Ramadan* fast on Hari Raya Puasa – a day of great joy and importance to

all Muslims. Many homes will prepare a feast and have an open-house for their friends and relatives

The young: But modern Singapore is changing the Malays as it is changing every other race in this nation state. Youngsters grow up, not to the Hindu-influenced shadow figures flitting behind the screen of the *Wayang Kulit* shadow puppet play, but to the egalitarian diet of modern television (mainly

American) programmes. Malay children now cure their stomach aches with Pepto-bismol, seldom bothering to enlist the help of enchanted mumbling, chants and folk medicine of the *bomoh*.

These magicians who hobnob with the spirits and once enjoyed an awesome prominence in village life, still exorcise haunted homes and cast love spells today, but their faithful followers are fast dwindling. Youths are adapting or discarding ancient practices as they find little practical use for the old ways.

Stigma: Malay education has had a reputation of lagging behind that of the Chinese and English school systems. In recent years the government, aware of the problems of the Malay community, has set up Yayasan Mendaki, a special organisation to promote Malay studies among talented students. Malays are encouraged to compete with the other races in Singapore, and many succeed. Gone is the often undeserved stigma attached to the Malays.

Gone too are the days where education is not necessary for a Malay girl. She is required to get married and keep house for her man. In 1990 alone 597 Malay girls graduated at tertiary level, 182 more than the number of Malay boys. Adding to the number of Malay graduates, both male and female, has been the aim of the Malay community for the last decade.

With this educational inequality comes a whole new set of social problems. The single graduate Malay woman is finding it increasingly difficult to find a partner of equal educational background. There is just not enough educated Malay man to go around.

In neighbouring Indonesia, where they are an unquestioned majority, the Malays have no identity problem. In Malaysia, an even closer neighbour, Malays are a relatively small majority and, though they hold political control, their efforts to improve their economic position make racial issues extremely sensitive.

In Singapore though, with historic nervousness, Malays must seek their own position and identity – not so much as Malays but as Singaporeans, and not in a group but more so as individuals.

Lord Budha

You can reach India three ways from Singapore: by air, by sea and by walking down Serangoon Road. The aroma of incense and freshly pounded curry floats over several square miles of Little India, as it is often called. In tiny doorways, ageing men in soiled white *dhotis* and rough pointed sandals carry on never-ending commerce. Restaurants and food stalls dot the street corners with dark-skinned Tamils ladling rich and spicy curries onto banana leaves for customers to eat with their fingers.

Women, fingers stained yellow by tumeric spice and teeth smeared red by betel nut, sell garlands of sweet-smelling flowers used by Indians for welcoming guests and honouring the gods. Young housewives glide gracefully along in bright saris, braided hair shining and jewellery sparkling in the sunlight.

Shop after shop is jammed to the ceiling with silks, muslins, batiks and cottons from India, Indonesia, Thailand and Malaysia. Sprawling markets deal in every exotic fruit and vegetable.

Traces of Hinduism are everywhere, from brightly coloured and elaborate temples to wall calendars with pictures of the elephant-headed god, Ganesh.

That's on Serangoon Road alone. There are also the Nattukkoai Chettiars along Market Street who sit on straw mats in crude shops and handle millions of dollars a year over tiny teak boxes that serve as desk and safe.

The Chettiars, a caste of Tamil money-lenders from Madras, have a hand in everything from hawker stalls to rubber estates. Then there are the Sindhis, Sikhs and Gujaratis along High Street, the North Indian neighbourhood. Sikhs are the easiest to spot with their whiskers and uncut tresses tied together under a turban.

Sixty percent of Singapore's Indians are Tamils, from the eastern part of Southern India, and approximately 20 percent Malayalis Hindus from the Kerala state on the other side of the subcontinent. The rest are Bengalis, Punjabis, Tamils and others – among whom one finds a colourful mixture of Hindus, Buddhists, Christians, Sikhs and the Parsis, a small yet close-knit community.

A 6½ percent minority, Indians pervade every aspect of life on the island. In downtown shops, Tamils make the deals. At glinting hotels, turbaned Sikhs open car doors, yet others (though rarely seen now) sleep on *charpoys* (hemp-strung beds) guarding office blocks.

Indians can be found in food centres deftly

twirling *prata* (leavened bread) in the air and frying it on the iron grill. Then again, many work as journalists and as politicians. Professor or restaurant owner, Indians are known for their eloquence and oratory skills.

History: Since early settlers borrowed the Sanskrit words "Singha Pura" (Lion City) in the naming of the island, Singapore has drawn heavily from the Indian subcontinent. Seven centuries before Christ, Indian craft were crisscrossing the Bay of Bengal to Malaya, known then as Suvarna Dvipa, "the golden peninsula". Ancient traders returned home laden with legendary cargoes: gold dust, tin, emeralds and coral.

Preceding pages: long-lashed lady in contemplative mood; poster display in Little India. **Left**, the distinctive Sri Mariamman Temple on South Bridge Road. **Above**, Sikh and ye shall find.

Many merchants stayed on, founding coastal settlements along the peninsula where they gained high status, wealth and power among native villagers. A thousand-year-old Hindu temple survives in the northern part of Malaysia. Sanskrit is the origin of hundreds of words in the native tongue. Hindu ceremonial graces the courts of Malay rulers to this day.

Prisoners: Many others who came had no choice. Officials of the British East India Company in Calcutta decided that Singapore would be a handy place to send prisoners. So Indian prisoners under guard built much of the colony. St Andrew's Cathedral, steepled and oaken in white elegance, looks as if it

Most prisoners were pardoned and given the choice of returning home or remaining in Singapore as free men. Many stayed. With a stream of voluntary immigrants and indentured labourers brought over to tap rubber and pick coffee, the Indians grew to a community.

World War II: During World War II, strong support grew for the Indian National Army (INA) under Netaji Subhas Chandra Bose, showing clearly the general Indian links toward the homeland. Singapore and Malaya were considered, for the most part, temporary homes which promised opportunities to make money for sending home to families in India. The Japanese Occupation offered a

was transported brick by brick from an English countryside – an amazing feat, observers noted at the time, because the Indian architects and foremen had never seen a church before. They cleared acres of forest and put up an enormous residence for the governor. Today, the residence is called the Istana and is where Singapore's president lives and where its prime minister works and practices golf. Convicts also built hospitals, canals and major roads.

Indian convicts numbered about 1,200. During the 1860s a penal colony was built on the Andaman Islands and Singapore-based prisoners were transferred there.

chance to work toward freeing the homeland of colonial status.

When the war ended, the British punished INA stalwarts, but there was little doubt Singapore Indians' efforts helped bring about Indian independence. But there were ill feelings by the Chinese against the Indians in Singapore because so many had collaborated with the Japanese.

In the years afterward, Indians who stayed in Singapore and Malaya began to look at the area as their new home. The new Indian government discouraged Indians from flooding home. Conditions in India changed. Governments in Singapore and Malaya worked toward creating societies that included Indians as a basic component.

Even the Chettiars, noted as expatriates, brought over their families. Today, Indians still travel to Madras from Singapore, but they usually hold return tickets. Ageing Tamils frugally save their hard-earned dollars for a trip to what they still consider home; but young Indians, whose roots in Singapore date back generations, no longer consider themselves so much as an Indian but rather as a Singaporean.

Nevertheless, Indian communities still stick closely together, carefully maintaining a rich range of religious, social, dietary and professional customs. Tamil newspapers

cages of steel spears weighing up to 32kg (70lbs), sticking into their flesh.

Deepavali is a calmer and most important Hindu family festival, celebrated by lighting homes with oil lamps, eating delicacies and calling on relatives and friends. *Deepavali* means "Way of Light" and commemorates how Lord Krishna wiped out the mythical despot, King Narakasura. A visit to Serangoon Road on this occasion is a must for anyone who wants to experience this Hindu New Year. Little India is a riot of lights, lamps and garlands.

The Hindu gods are honoured by at least 20 major temples, not counting the profusion of smaller shrines and statues. The oldest and

carry every scrap of South Indian news they can find and the passing on of old Indian statesmen still manages to cause sorrow in many of the local Indians.

Rituals: Some Tamil rituals are observed with greater fervour than in India. On Thaipusam, an awesome two-day ritual in late January or early February, Hindu devotees keeping vows, asking forgiveness and offering thanks to Lord Subramaniam, dance and spin barefoot for miles under *kavadis,*

Left, shopping in Serangoon Road (Little India). Above, Hindu wedding ceremony in the Sri Veeramakaliamman Temple.

most important is the Sri Mariamman temple on South Bridge Road in Chinatown. Convicts built the original structure in 1862, expanding a wood and thatch temple put up by one of Singapore's first successful Indians, businessman Narayana Pillai. An ethereal gallery of shrines and paintings honours the mother-goddess Devi and Mariamman, goddess of rain.

Much of the classical Indian culture has survived in Singapore, from old-style recipes to dance, art and literature. The casual traveller wanting a three-day taste of India might well find the taxi fare to Little India a better investment than a plane ticket to India.

Eurasians: The largest of the "minorities", the Eurasians are a mixture from two continents. Some are half English, others part Dutch, many part Portuguese. The Eurasians carry family names such as D' Souza, Pereira, Theseira (Portuguese), Westerhout (Dutch), Scully (Irish) and Young (British). Many of them are also partly Filipino, Chinese, Malay, Indian, Sri Lankan or Thai. About 0.5 percent of Singaporeans are Eurasians. Most of these are the offspring of mixed marriages, which were common in Singapore's 170

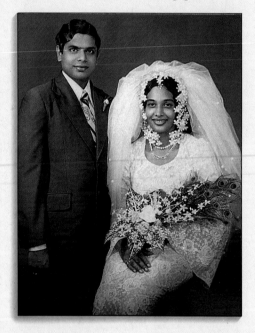

years of modern history. Others are immigrant Eurasians who came from Indonesia, Malaya, Thailand and other distant lands.

A handsome Eurasian Club went up on the colony's Padang in 1884. It's still there, but is now known as the Singapore Recreation Club, facing the lofty terraces of the Singapore Cricket Club across an expanse of green. The Club's charter membership was then only 37. A publication pointedly calling itself *Our Own Magazine* appeared in 1921, put out by the Eurasian literary association. By then, even a "Eurasian Company" was formed from Singapore's population to fight in World War I.

Eurasian organizations still look after the group's interests, but these interests are not that different from those of other Singaporeans. Eurasians fit into the society just as well as any other Singaporean. But on closer look, you will see that the Eurasians are a close-knit community with their own langauge. Patios Portuguese (or *Cristao*) is still spoken among the older generation.

Singapore's census figures list, after Chinese, Malays and Indians, a mysterious category of 60,000 "others". If broken down, the list would run far off the page. Apart from Europeans and Eurasians, minority groups are measured in hundreds.

Sri Lankans: Making up one of the biggest little groups are the Sri Lankans, formerly Ceylonese. They often get confused with Indian Singaporeans, but if in doubt ask. A Sri Lankan is a Sri Lankan, and he'll tell you about it. Most Sri Lankans in Singapore are Tamils, who began migrating to Singapore last century with the Tamils from Madras, brought in to tap rubber and pick coffee.

Boatloads of Sinhalese also came from Sri Lanka, from the lush middle and southern parts of the island. They speak Sinhalese, Sri Lanka's national language, and follow the gentle life of Hinayana Buddhism. Sinhalese in Singapore, as in Sri Lanka, generally prefer the finer trades to manual labour and are found largely in jewellery and gem shops. They have less in common with Indians of the subcontinent's mainland, but they followed the same routes of migration. With them came small numbers of Sri Lankan Burghers – Eurasians – who went to work mainly on the railroad.

A prosperous Muslim community moved in from farther up the subcontinent. When they left they were Northern Indian Sindhis, Punjabis, among others. But now they're ethnic Pakistanis and many would prefer not to be categorized any other way.

Armenians: The western sea-lanes brought huge colonies of Armenians and Jews in Singapore's early years, but new patterns of migration have depleted their ranks.

There are not many Armenian families in Singapore. In the generations after 19th century when Russian and Turkish rivalry sent

Armenians on migrations across the world, Singapore had a colony of about 5,000. The Armenian Apostolic Church of St Gregory the Illuminator stands on Hill Street where it was built in 1835, but the tiny congregation has no spiritual leader and they can't afford to get one. Most of Singapore's Armenians decided to move on to Australia after World War II and probably half of those remaining are now over 50 years old.

Jews: The Jews, too, were once a thriving community. Urban renewal has spread over many of the old buildings on Sophia Road, Queen Street and Wilkie Road, but Hebrew lettering is still engraved in cement on some of the ageing shophouses that remain. Jews in Singapore were largely Sephardic, migrating from Persia and India where their ancestors settled during the Diaspora. Ashkenazi Jews moved to Israel or Australia, or they have scattered around Singapore from the old neighbourhood they once dominated. Until a few years ago, ageing Jewish women wearing flowing loose gowns with high waist-lines, were a common sight on Queen Street. They're still around, listening to Sabbath Torah readings with visiting reform Jews from New York.

Bugis and Boyanese: A number of settlers came from the other direction. Bugis from the Celebes in the Indonesian Archipelago and Boyanese from Madura, a few islands up the line, have moved ashore after centuries of trading. Bugis pirates were on the island before Raffles arrived, operating a prosperous buccaneering industry on the marshy edge of the strategically-placed island. Bugis quickly went straight, amassing fortunes in land and property which their heirs today still hold. The Boyanese live in tight communities called *pondoks,* each with a headman looking after the general welfare of his flock. Both groups are Muslim and are closely related to the Malays.

Other Asians: Small communities of Filipinos, Japanese and other Asians have woven themselves into Singapore's social fabric. In a dozen ritzy restaurants and discos, young Filipino musicians entertain diners and teenyboppers. They come on contract to sing, swing and entertain for a year, then move on to the next big city in their musical tour through Asia. On Sundays, gaggles of giggling Filipino maids gather at the Botanic Gardens and shopping complexes, enjoying their day off.

Orang Laut: Some of Singapore's most colourful communities are the smallest. A few

pure *Orang Laut* ("Sea People") remain. They are descendants of the sea gypsies, original aborigines in Johor, who lived in waterborne villages of boats in the creeks around Kallang, Seletar and Jurong. They gradually came ashore and until just after World War II there were still *Orang Laut* ("Sea People") settlements by the rivers. Today most have intermarried and have disappeared into the Malay culture.

A Singaporean can be an Eurasian singing Portuguese folk songs, or a Sinhalese worrying over a wicket, or a Chinese roasting pork. The only way to know Singaporeans is to take a close look at whoever you meet.

Preceding pages: there's a significant pool of expatriates in Singapore. **Left**, wedding portrait for this Sri Lankan couple. **Above**, Eurasian beauty.

Chinese New Year: This major festival usually falls in January or February. Chinese custom has it that the previous year's debts are to be paid off before the new year, houses cleaned, and celebrants ready for feasting and the exchanging of *hong bao*, traditional red packets of "lucky money." For many, it is also an excuse to splash lavishly on new clothes, new hairstyles and new things for the home.

A notable place to catch the festival spirit is Chinatown, which is ablaze with lights, alive with people and overflowing with pink which takes place the weekend after Chinese New Year, on a Sunday. Mini-dramas illustrating the classic Chinese myths, stilt-walkers, and lavish, electrified floats are some of the parade's best-loved features. This annual parade starts at the junction of Orchard and Scotts Road and it winds it way along the stretch of Orchard Road and ends at the Istana, the official resident of the President of Singapore.

Thaipusam: This Hindu festival is observed in the Tamil month of *Thai*, which falls

pussy willow, kumquat plants and plum blossoms for weeks preceding the big day. Dragon and lion dancers throng the streets making plenty of noise to keep the errant mythical monsters traditionally associated with Chinese New Year at bay.

Still, with the government's ban on firecrackers, Chinese New Year has become a more domestic event, with families gathering for celebratory meals, enjoying festival delicacies and titbits, but especially each other's company.

The holiday season ends with the Chingay parade – a procession of floats, acrobats, martial artists, and performers of all stripes between January and February. Devotees honour Lord Muruga, god of bravery, power, beauty and virtue, by performing various feats of mind over pain.

The festival begins at dawn in the Sri Perumal Temple in Serangoon Road where devotees, who have entered a trance, pierce their bodies with skewers and shoulder the *kavadi*, a huge steel cage-like contraption supported by hundreds of steel spikes driven into the celebrant's skin. The procession of yellow-garbed devotees make their way to the Chettiar Temple in Tank Road, accompanied by the chanting and singing of the festival crowd.

Vesak Day: Usually falling in mid-May, this is one of the most important days for Buddhists as it honours the birth, enlightenment, and death of Sakyamuni Buddha on the same day. Celebrations begin at dawn with a candlelight procession in the temple courtyards witnessed by hundreds of devotees. Worshippers offer prayers and later partake in a vegetarian meal. Saffron-robed monks chant, free meals are offered to the poor, and caged animals are released. Some temples also hold vegetarian feasts.

Muslim month – the date varies from year to year. A month prior to Hari Raya Puasa is called *Ramadan*, it is during this month that all Muslims observe a strict fast from sunrise to sunset. The purpose of this is for all Muslims to experience what it feels like to be hungry and thus be more compassionate to the less fortunate.

As soon as the new moon comes, Hari Raya Puasa festivities start with celebrants asking for forgiveness from family, relatives and friends, make new vows and resolutions,

At the Phor Kark See Temple at Bright Hill Drive, devotees go through a three-step-one-bow ritual led by monks round the brightly-lit temple grounds on the eve of Vesak. The ritual is believed to purify negative actions of the past, and is an act of homage to Lord Buddha. Some temples even hold special exhibitions on this day.

Hari Raya Puasa: This is the Muslim celebration, and falls on the first day of the 10th

Preceding pages, Chinese opera is alive and well. **Left**, lion dancing in the Chingay parade. **Above**, hundreds of Hindu devotees carry the *kavadi* to mark Thaipusam.

wear new clothes and feast on special cakes and traditional food such as *ketupat* (compressed rice cooked in coconut leaves) and *rendang* (spicy meat dish).

Dragon Boat Festival: Every June, colourful longboats with prows carved to represent dragons and fantastic birds race under the steam of dozens of pairs of strong arms.

Since 1990, this popular annual meet has been upgraded into an international event, attracting teams from countries like Hong Kong, Australia, Europe and the US to contest the World Invitational Dragon Boat Race with attractive prize-money to be won. The festival honours an ancient Chinese poet Qu

Yuan, a loyal and honest minister of state who drowned himself in the Mi Lo river to protest the corruption and injustices in the court. Fishermen raced to the scene to save his body from the ravages of sharks but they were too late.

Small packages of food (usually rice) were then thrown into the water so that fishes would not eat the body of the beloved man. Drums and gongs were sounded to frighten away predators, and villagers decorated their boats with dragon heads and tails with the same purpose in mind.

Today, the making and eating of rice dumplings and the dragon boat races serve to honour Qu Yuan's memory.

the anniversary of the island gaining independence in 1965.

Hungry Ghosts Festival: Chinese believe that during the seventh lunar month, usually around September, spirits wander the earth. To appease the mischievous and especially wayward spirits, joss sticks and paper money are burned, and feasts are whipped up as offerings. At the markets, lavish celebrations are held including *wayang* – Chinese opera – climaxing in a lively auction. After the ghosts have their fill, the food is eaten by the celebrants.

Mooncake Festival: On the 15th day of the eighth month, the Chinese celebrate the overthrow of the Mongol Dynasty. On this day,

National Day: At least a month before August 9, one can hear school children practise singing various anthems of nationhood, and military bands, acrobats, schoolgirl choirs and dragon dancers working to perfect the National Day Parade which takes place at the Padang, or the National Stadium.

At the Parade, performers with torch lights, flags and flashcards form intricate patterns for thousands of spectators. This colourful celebration of independence usually culminates with singing and fireworks. Each year the parade becomes more and more spectacular. Certainly an event not to be missed. This spectacular display of nationhood marks

which falls in September or October, children parade with brightly coloured and ornate lanterns traditional to the occasion. Mooncakes – rich, delicious pastries filled with lotus seed or red bean paste and the yolks of salted eggs – are eaten. The cakes, as the legend goes, were used by rebel forces to smuggle messages to the populace.

Birthday of Monkey God: During this festival, Chinese penitents pierce tongues and cheeks with spears, and acrobats put on displays of leaping and tumbling in temple courtyards. For the squeamish, *wayang* and puppet shows are also performed. The date of this festival varies. The Monkey God is a famous character from the Chinese classic *Journey to the West*, renowned for his bravery in protecting his master, a pilgrim monk of the Tang Dynasty was sent to India to collect the Buddhist *Sutras*.

Navarathi: In homage to the consorts of the Hindu gods, nine days of traditional Indian music and dancing precedes a procession on the tenth, when a silver horse is carried through the streets. Falls around October. This is a rare opportunity to experience traditional Indian music and dance.

Hari Raya Haji: This is a special holiday for Muslims who have completed the *haj*, or pilgrimage to Mecca. This day falls on the 10th day of the month of *Zulhijah*, the 12th

in order to save two shipwrecked sailors, a Malay and a Chinese. Kusu Island boasts two beautiful swimming lagoons, shady trees, and is a popular spot for swimmers and picnickers.

Deepavali: Also known as the Festival of Lights or the celebration of good over evil, Deepavali is the most important Hindu festival to the local Indian community. Usually falling in October or November, the festival is reflected in the lighting of oil lamps at homes and in the Serangoon area of Little India. Prayers are recited in brightly lit temples and statues of deities are carried round the grounds. Serangoon Road is the place to be on this night.

month of the Muslim calendar. Muslims in Singapore celebrate the day by praying and sacrificing cows and goats.

Pilgrimage to Kusu Island: Kusu's significance is both religious and legendary. During a month-long festival, falling between the 1st and the 15th of the Chinese ninth lunar month, Taoist Chinese take the ferry to Kusu Island to make offerings at the temple and at a Malay shrine.

The legend behind the pilgrimage tells of a turtle (*kusu*) that turned itself into an island

<u>Left</u> and <u>above</u>, city streets are bedecked to bedazzle at festival time.

Christmas: At first glance, Singapore may seem like a strange place to celebrate Christmas. But remember that a large percentage of the population is Christian, and even non-Christians get into the spirit and exchange gifts at the end of December.

Orchard Road is a riot of yuletide lights, displays and decorations, as department stores and shopping malls try to outdo each other for the biggest and brightest displays.

Nevertheless as in all things Singaporean, the visitor should not be surprised to find Christmas here celebrated with a difference – just tuck into the *tandoori* turkey and you will see!

A visit to Singapore embraces a wide variety of encounters and activities. But unlike other cities where sightseeing is of paramount importance, we believe that most visitors flock to Singapore for action – shopping, eating, recreation and nightlife. With that in mind, we start the practical portion of this book with an activities section – a rundown of the island's best places to shop, eat and play. Following is a places section, with prominent landmarks, buildings, museums and parks described as part of suggested itineraries that follow "user friendly" geographical patterns.

Shopping is the number one activity in Singapore for locals and visitors alike. To say that shopping is the national pastime is to put it mildly. Shopping is a national *obsession*, a capitalistic frenzy that reflects how the isalnd has pushed and pulled itself from third to first world in less than 30 years. The 3 million Singaporeans are now the third most prosperous people in Asia after the Japanese and the oil-rich Brunieans, and after years of self-imposed scrimping and saving, they want to show their success off to the rest of the world.

Hong Kong may be king of the hill when it comes to Rolls Royces, but Singapore has the world's highest per capita consumption of another luxury car called the Mercedes Benz. More than 97 percent of the homes in Singapore have refrigerators and television sets; more than 75 percent have washing machines and video recorders. Million dollar condos are considered *cheap* these days, an era when ordinary citizens are willing to line up around the block to buy blue-chip stocks like the Singapore Telecom issue.

When people aren't shopping they are usually eating. Singapore is famous for its food, an eclectic blend of Chinese, Malay, Indian and other Asian cuisines, as well as a range of Western-style restaurants. Hawker stalls, those ubiquitous outdoor food centres, have become a Singapore trademark over the years. They have always been the great social equalizer, the place where tycoons and taxi drivers rub elbows in a wide-ranging search to see who makes the best chicken rice and chili crab in town. Rule of thumb: You can usually tell how good a hawker stall is by the number of taxis and police cars parked outside.

But the rapidly escalating affluence of Singaporeans is creating a new breed of cosmopolitan dining places that offer both upscale atmosphere and upmarket food. Many of the new restaurants cluster in conservation areas like Tanjong Pagar, Boat Quay and Clarke Quay.

The local nightlife scene is also changing. Most hotels feature house discos, but independent dance and live music clubs are sweeping the island like wild fire, bringing eclectic international

Preceding pages: City of Contrasts: Skyscrapers loom incongrously over colonial-era shophouses, reflecting Singapore's spectacular rise to prominence and prosperity; Sultan Mosque dominates the Arab Street area. **Left,** view to the mainland from the Sentosa Ferry.

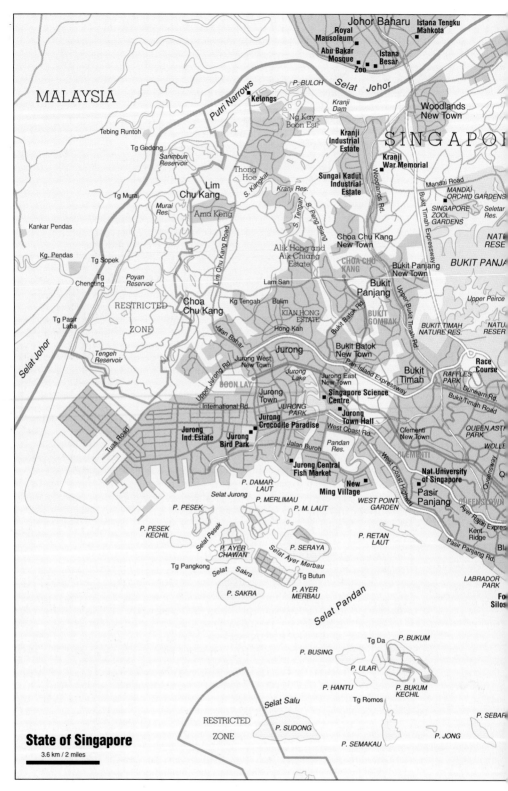

MALAYSIA

SINGAPO...

Johor Baharu
Istana Tengku
Mahkota
Royal
Mausoleum
Abu Bakar
Mosque
Istana
Besar
Zoo

P. BULOH
Selat Johor
Kranji
Dam

Kelongs

Putri Narrows

Woodlands
New Town

Tebing Runtoh

Ng Kay
Boon Est.

Kranji
Industrial
Estate

Kranji
War Memorial

Tg Gedong

Sanmbun
Reservoir

Thong
Hoe

S. Kangkar

Sungai Kadut
Industrial
Estate

Mandai Road

MANDAI
ORCHID GARDENS

Lim
Chu Kang

Kranji Res.

Woodlands Rd.

Bukit Timah Expressway

SINGAPORE
ZOOL.
GARDENS

Seletar
Res.

Tg Murai

Murai
Res

Ama Keng

S. Tengah

S. Peng Siang

Choa Chu Kang
New Town

NATU
RESE

Kankar Pendas

Alik Hong and
Aik Chiang
Estate

CHOA CHU
KANG

Bukit Panjang
New Town

BUKIT PANJA

Kg. Pendas

Tg Sopek

Lim Chu Kang Road

Lam San

Bukit
Panjang

Upper Peirce

Tg
Chengting

Poyan
Reservoir

RESTRICTED

Choa
Chu Kang

Kg Tengah

Bulim

BUKIT
GOMBAK

Tg Pasir
Laba

ZONE

Jalan Bahar

KIAN HONG
ESTATE

Hong Kah

Bukit Batok Rd.

Upper Bukit Timah Rd.

BUKIT TIMAH
NATURE RES.

NATU
RESER

Tengeh
Reservoir

Jurong

Bukit Batok
New Town

Pan-Island Expressway

Bukit
Timah

Race
Course

RAFFLES
PARK

Dunearn Rd.

Upper Jurong Rd.

Jurong West
New Town

Jurong
Lake

Jurong East
New Town

BOON LAY

Singapore Science
Centre

Bukit Timah Road

Jurong
Town

International Rd.

JURONG
PARK

Jurong
Town Hall

West Coast Rd.

QUEEN AST...
PARK

Tuas Road

Jurong
Ind.Estate

Jurong
Crocodile Paradise

Jurong
Bird Park

Clementi
New Town

WOLLE

Jalan Buroh

Pandan
Res.

Nat.University
of Singapore

CLEMENTI

QUEENSTOWN

Jurong Central
Fish Market

New
Ming Village

West Coast Highway

Pasir
Panjang

Ayer Rajah Expres...

P. DAMAR
LAUT

WEST POINT
GARDEN

Selat Jurong

P. MERLIMAU

Queensway

Q...

P. PESEK

P. M. LAUT

Kent
Ridge

Bl...

P. PESEK
KECHIL

Selat Pesek

P. RETAN
LAUT

Pasir Panjang Rd.

LABRADOR
PARK

P. AYER
CHAWAN

P. SERAYA

Selat Ayer Merbau

Fo...
Silos

Tg Pangkong

Selat Sakra

Tg Butun

P. SAKRA

P. AYER
MERBAU

Selat Pandan

Tg Da

P. BUKUM

P. BUSING

P. ULAR

P. HANTU

P. BUKUM
KECHIL

Selat Salu

Tg Romos

P. SEBAR...

RESTRICTED

ZONE

P. SUDONG

P. JONG

P. SEMAKAU

State of Singapore

3.6 km / 2 miles

Selat Johor

Tg Pasir
Laba

Kankar Pendas

Kg. Pendas

111

sounds and top forty hits. Big name acts are also coming to town, ranging from opera impresario Luciano Pavarotti to pop legends like Simon & Garfunkel, Michael Jackson, Elton John and Eric Clapton. And the island has become something of a fulcrum for celebrated stage plays including *Cats, Les Miserables* and *Evita.*

Another change in recent years has been a dramatic shift towards sports and recreation, as Singaporeans take to the beaches and parks in ever greater numbers. The island is said to have more golf courses per capita than any other nation on earth, and despite it's highrise image, Singapore has more green space than any other major city in Southeast Asia. The "great outdoors" ranges from the manicured confines of the Botanic Gardens to great swaths of jungle like Bukit Timah Nature Reserve and the Catchment Area.

If you're not worn out by all that activity, take time to explore the myriad historic, ethnic and organic aspects of Singapore that are outlined in the places section.

Still much in evidence are Raffles' plans for the layout of the city, implemented in June 1819. Clearly recognizable to this day are Chinatown and the Financial District around Raffles Place, the Muslim area of Kampong Glam and the colonial heart of the city, exactly as decreed by the founder. Little India sprang up around the kilns and cattle pens near Serangoon Road. Much later, Orchard Road and the "shopping belt" developed on the main thoroughfare between Singapore and Johor.

As Singapore grew, people began moving out and away from the business centre. The East Coast has been a prime choice for many years and is now dominatd by highrise flats of Marine Parade, Eunos, Tampines and Bedok which extend northwards into huge "new towns" like Toa Payoh, Hougang and Ang Mo Kio, and northeast to Pasir Ris. The terminals, hangers and runways of Changi Airport monopolise the eastern tip of the island.

The western precincts, consisting mainly of Jurong and Clementi, have proved to be a big draw as well. In 1961, development began on the landmark Jurong Industrial Estate on 4,000 acres of swampy land. The project changed the West Coast forever, but it also allowed Singapore to move into the league of industrialised nations.

Since independence in 1965, the southern coastline has moved further south, as Marina Bay was formed through reclamation. Sentosa island is now linked to the mainland by a causeway, and there are plans to develop Pulau Ubin island into a commercial and residential centre if Singapore's population ever reaches 4 million.

But Singapore is also expanding in a different way, linked to Johor state in Malaysia and the Riau islands in Indonesia by an innovative "growth triangle" plan that has induced rapid economic growth in all three areas through an interchange of investment, expertise, workers and resources.

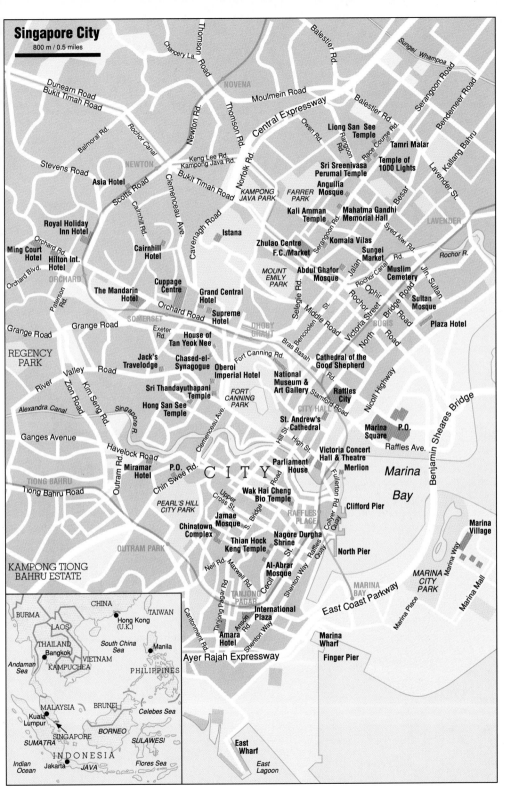

Singapore City

800 m / 0.5 miles

Chancery La.
Thomson Road
Dunearn Road
Bukit Timah Road
NOVENA
Moulmein Road
Balestier Rd.
Sungei Whampoa
Serangoon Road
Bendemeer Road
Balmoral Rd.
Rochor Canal
Newton Rd.
Thomson Rd.
Central Expressway
Owen Rd.
Liong San See Temple
Rangoon Rd.
Race Course Rd.
Tamri Malar
Kallang Bahru
Stevens Road
NEWTON
Keng Lee Rd.
Kampong Java Rd.
Norfolk Rd.
Sri Sreenivasa Perumal Temple
Temple of 1000 Lights
Lavender St.
Asia Hotel
Scotts Road
Cairnhill Rd.
Bukit Timah Road
KAMPONG JAVA PARK
Anguilia Mosque
FARRER PARK
Besar
LAVENDER
Royal Holiday Inn Hotel
Clemenceau Ave.
Cavenagh Road
Kali Amman Temple
Mahatma Gandhi Memorial Hall
Syed Alwi Rd.
Orchard Rd.
Istana
Serangoon Rd.
Komala Vilas
Rochor R.
Ming Court Hotel
Hilton Int. Hotel
Cairnhill Hotel
Zhulao Centre F.C./Market
Sungei Market
Jln. Sultan
Orchard Blvd.
ORCHARD
MOUNT EMILY PARK
Selegie Rd.
Abdul Ghafor Mosque
Rochor Canal
Ophir Rd.
Muslim Cemetery
Paterson Rd.
The Mandarin Hotel
Cuppage Centre
Grand Central Hotel
Middle Road
Jalan Besar
Rochor Rd.
Bridge Rd.
Sultan Mosque
SOMERSET
Orchard Road
Supreme Hotel
DHOBY GHAUT
Bras Basah
Victoria Street
North Bridge Road
Plaza Hotel
Grange Road
Grange Road
Exeter Rd.
House of Tan Yeok Nee
Fort Canning Rd.
Cathedral of the Good Shepherd
BUGIS
REGENCY PARK
Valley Road
Jack's Travelodge
Chased-el-Synagogue
Oberoi Imperial Hotel
National Museum & Art Gallery
Stamford Road
Nicoll Highway
River
Zion Road
Kim Seng Rd.
Sri Thandayuthapani Temple
FORT CANNING PARK
Raffles City
Benjamin Sheares Bridge
Alexandra Canal
Singapore R.
Hong San See Temple
Clemenceau Ave.
CITY HALL
Ganges Avenue
Hill St.
High St.
St. Andrew's Cathedral
Marina Square
P.O.
Havelock Road
Miramar Hotel
P.O.
Chin Swee Rd.
CITY
Victoria Concert Hall & Theatre
Raffles Ave.
TIONG BAHRU
Outram Rd.
Parliament House
Merlion
Marina Bay
Tiong Bahru Road
Upper Cross St.
Wak Hai Cheng Bio Temple
Fullerton Rd.
Clifford Pier
PEARL'S HILL CITY PARK
New Bridge Rd.
RAFFLES PLACE
Marina Village
Chinatown Complex
Jamae Mosque
Nagore Durgha Shrine
North Pier
OUTRAM PARK
Thian Hock Keng Temple
Raffles Quay
KAMPONG TIONG BAHRU ESTATE
Neil Rd.
Maxwell Rd.
Al-Abrar Mosque
Cecil St.
Shenton Way
MARINA BAY
MARINA CITY PARK
Marina Way
Marina Mall
Tanjong Pagar Rd.
TANJONG PAGAR
International Plaza
Anson Rd.
East Coast Parkway
Marina Place
Cantonment Rd.
Amara Hotel
Shenton Way
Marina Wharf
Ayer Rajah Expressway
Finger Pier
East Wharf
East Lagoon

CHINA
BURMA
LAOS
TAIWAN
Hong Kong (U.K.)
THAILAND
Bangkok
South China Sea
VIETNAM
Manila
Andaman Sea
KAMPUCHEA
PHILIPPINES
MALAYSIA
BRUNEI
Celebes Sea
Kuala Lumpur
BORNEO
SINGAPORE
SULAWESI
SUMATRA
INDONESIA
Indian Ocean
Jakarta
JAVA
Flores Sea

SHOPPING

East is east and west is west, so the old saying goes, but the twain met here for business as long ago as 1511. Then the Portuguese scribe Barros wrote, "Singapore was an emporium where all ships went as to… a world fair; for some it was the end of the eastern sea, for others the western." So it has remained ever since.

An exotic port in a faraway place, Singapore was the crossroads from where travellers would return with chests full of oriental antiques and curios. Today Singapore is a place where you can buy absolutely anything, either locally made or imported from all over the world. It is a city of duty-free imports, top-of-the-line technology and a centre of high fashion as well as remaining a centre for Asian exotica.

Buying and selling is the lifeblood of the place. A more recent saying is that in Singapore you can "shop 'til you drop". Whether you prefer slick service in spanking new air-conditioned shopping centres or browsing in the musty, old shophouses of Chinatown, whether you prefer clearly marked, fixed prices or like to try your bargaining skills, Singapore is an enormous bazaar.

In smaller shops, prices are almost always negotiable and shopping is a dramatic performance. The first customer is said to bring luck, so an early start can save money. Find out the seller's "best price", try a little below, plead and joke, perhaps even begin to move towards the exit.

No vendor really has starving children, nor will he really sell below cost as he claims, so don't worry and just enjoy the fun. Buy what you like at a price you are happy with. Comparing prices at different places for the same item is definitely worth your while, especially for cameras and computers.

There are unspoken rules, though, in the bargaining game. Let the vendor know if you intend to pay by credit card, as he will have to allow for the surcharge and if you have bargained for a

Preceding pages: Singapore's reputation as a haven for shoppers is well-earned – there's always something for everyone. Below, traditional provision shop.

while and agreed on a price, you are under a moral obligation to buy!

Shopping hours: Most shops open at about 10am, and stay that way until about 9pm daily.

Complaints: The Consumers Association of Singapore (CASE, Tel: 2705433) is the body to which any complaints should be addressed. Visitors may also take it a step further if they feel that they have been the victim of unethical practices by unscrupulous vendors. A Small Claims Tribunal (Tel: 5309895) has a fast track system for tourists by which cases will be heard within two or three days. A S$10 fee is payable and no legal representation is necessary.

The Singapore Tourist Promotion Board (STPB) aims to ensure that complaints are unnecessary by authorising certain shops to display a red Merlion sticker as an indication of trustworthiness and reliability.

Cameras and audio equipment: Prices for photographic equipment are good, and the selection enormous, from idiot-proof automatics to underwater and video cameras as well as every conceivable lens for the professional. There's even a throwaway camera for those who only want holiday snaps.

The range of hi-fi equipment, video recorders and CD players is vast, and the prices enticing. Cassettes and CDs are often cheaper here than elsewhere.

Either get an international guarantee, or take directly imported goods intended just for the local market, and save on the price. If you don't see what you want in the shop, ask, because it will be fetched for you in no time. A wide range of photographic equipment can be found in **Albert Photo** and **Cost Plus Electronics**, both are located in Orchard Road (see Travel Tips page 287).

Watches: Watches are sold tax-free, with an enormous selection, from a lifetime's investment in a Rolex to a cheap plastic fun watch. Japanese watches compete with Swiss hand-made models that allows you to design your own. There are of course the famous fakes or copy-watches, which keep good time but are nowhere as water-resistant as

Centrepoint is a popular Orchard Road shopping stop.

the originals. Some of the shops that display a wide variety of styles are **City Chain Stores**, which have branches in most shopping centres, **Dickson** in Centrepoint and **The Hour Glass** in Lucky Plaza (see Travel Tips page 290).

Computer equipment: Computer buffs have the choice of local or imported, PCs, laptops or even palmtops and a wide range of software. All kinds of accessories and peripherals are available and good advice for the less knowledgeable is always given. Don't forget to check the voltage. **Funan Centre** and **Sim Lim Square** (see Travel Tips page 287) – two shopping centres packed with numerous computer stores – are a must for all computer enthusiasts.

Gold: It's all gold that glitters in Singapore, pure 22-24 K yellow Chinese gold, which is also an investment, as it can be traded in for cash at the current gold price. Choose from the traditional designs or have something custom-made. Imported gold in glorious designs is also sold at leading jewellers, and top names such as Cartier and Bulgari are all found here.

Jade: Much prized by the Chinese, jade comes in many colours, from the paler nephrite to bright green jadite, made into pendants, rings and earrings or statuettes.

In ancient China, jade was more highly valued than gold. Considered to have magical powers, and a link between man and the gods, jade played an auspicious role in many religious ceremonies. Only emperors were permitted to use jade sacrificial symbols in religious rites.

Jade was also claimed to be the elixir of immortality hence the jade burial suits discovered in the 2,000-year-old tombs of the Han Dynasty.

Ivory: Although the ivory trade is now banned worldwide, there is still quite a lot of the whalebone look-alike, about, some exquisitely carved.

Pearls: Mikimoto pearls are laid out row upon row, in different sizes and hues thus offering the choice of strand length, clasp and knotting. Freshwater pearls of all shapes, colours and sizes are cheap enough to buy several strands for twisting into a collar.

From 'new' antiques to the genuine article, there's something to suit all budgets.

Gems: Diamonds, rubies, emeralds, amethysts and sapphires of different sizes and qualities may be worked into pieces of any design.

Risis has found a way of preserving orchid blooms by dipping them in pure 22K gold to preserve their beauty for ever. They are worn as rings, earrings, pendants or bracelets. Leaves and ferns too are similarly treated to make delicate, unique pieces of jewellery.

S*Pore – created by the finest local craftsmen in Singapore – is an exclusive brand of jewellery that is well received in Japan. Take a look at some of the exquisite jewellery designed with Singapore's multi-faceted culture in mind. It is now available at up-market jewellers along **Orchard Road** and at **Terminal 2**, Sinapore Changi Airport.

Gold and jewllery dealers are centred in **South Bridge Road**, **Chinatown**, **Pidemco Centre**, **Little India** and **Arab Street**. At the shops in these areas nothing is priced as gold items are sold according to the day's gold rate. However, you can haggle over the charge for

workmanship put into the item. For more details see Travel Tips page 289.

Costume jewellery: Brightly coloured bangles, rings and earrings from China, anklets and sparkling gem-studded designs from India, traditional Malaysian and Indonesian pieces make for an enormous choice of inexpensive jewellery. These are available in major department stores such as **Robinson's**, **Isetan** in Orchard Road and **Daimaru** in River Valley Road (see Travel Tips page 291).

Fashion: Whether it's designer labels, local batik or whether you simply want that special dress copied, or a suit made to measure, Singapore offers it all. Chanel, Louis Feraud, Issey Miyake, Gucci, Lacroix and many other top designers have boutiques here. These can be found in **Delfi Orchard** and **Scotts Shopping Centre**.

Local designers like Benny Ong, Celia Loe, Thomas Wee and Bobby Chng offer a combination of eastern fabrics and western chic, good enough even for the Princess of Wales. A list of

Colourful batik dresses and shirts are typical of local fashion.

shops can be found in the Travel Tips section on pages 287–289.

Batiks from Malaysia and Indonesia or locally printed with orchid motifs on soft cotton and silks from China, Thailand, India and Malaysia are just some of the variety of fabrics available.

Many tailors can run up suits in 24 hours, copy clothes or work from patterns. The more time you allow, the better the end result will be, and it's a good idea to be specific and to insist on a fitting. These shops are usually located in shopping centres along the Orchard Road belt.

Silk: The object of the first known incident of industrial espionage, silk was prized as long ago as 2,500 BC. The Romans almost became bankrupt through their love of silk, which had to be transported along the hazardous Silk Road from China. So the Roman Emperor Justinian sent two monks to discover the silk secret. They managed to smuggle silkworm eggs back to Rome in their canes, and thus laid the foundation for the European silk industry.

China, with its plentiful and cheap labour, however, remains the world's largest silk producer. Its climate is also particularly favourable for the mulberry bushes on which the silkworms feed. It takes about 500 silkworms and 15kg (33lbs) of mulberry leaves to produce a kilo of cocoons. About 100 cocoons are needed just to make a silk tie. A blouse requires more than 600 cocoons.

Chinese silk comes in soft *crepe de chine*, satin silks, shantung and raw silk as well as the latest stonewashed silk.

Thai silk is still woven on traditional looms, and is produced mainly in the northern town of San Kamphaeng. Unmatched for glamorous evening wear, this fabric is also made into boxes, photo-frames and jewellery and cosmetic bags.

Japan and Korea produce exotic silks, some extremely valuable. Malay *kain songket* has silver and gold threads woven into the silk. Indian *sari* silks are soft and delicately patterned, some also with gold weaving.

Shops catering for silk lovers are **China Silk House**, **Jim Thompson Silk**

Elaborate oriental carvings are favoured by collectors and souvenir hunters alike.

Shop, both are located in Orchard Road and **Melati Moda** in Joo Chiat (see Travel Tips page 289).

Accessories: Shoes, from the top-of-the-range Charles Jourdan or Bruno Magli to locally-made less expensive and cheerful models tempt visitors to emulate Imelda Marcos. There are handbags and belts of all shapes, sizes, colours and prices to match. Leather goods from India and Indonesia make for more unusual buys.

Singapore is in fact one of the best places in Asia to buy quality luggage at bargain prices. Suitcases in Singapore are rarely pirated (though imitation designer briefcases are common) and at many outlets you can knock up to 25 percent off the list price. A concentration of luggage shops are found in **Far East Plaza** in Scotts Road and **Lucky Plaza** in Orchard Road.

Antiques and Asian exotica: Treasures from all over the region can be found here. Antique desks, chairs, tables, wardrobes, mirrors and opium beds from various regions of China can be restored. A certificate of antiquity can be given. However, reproductions too make attractive buys. A visit to **Ming-Ching Antique House** in Tank Road, **Ming Village** in Pandan Road or **Da-Ching Fine Arts** in Orchard Road is necessary for all antique lovers. See Travel Tips page 286 for the listing of antique shops.

Prints, old maps as well as valuable editions of books on the region can be found, as well as figurines and coins. **Tanglin Shopping Centre** (Tanglin Road), in particular, is well known for its wide range of antique shops.

From China: All things Chinese find their way to Singapore at very reasonable prices. Cloisonne vases, plates, ashtrays and lamps in bright colours make wonderful gifts and souvenirs. Intricately hand-made lace table cloths or mats can be found as well as embroidered Mandarin sleeves, old and new, which look wonderful when framed, or set under the glass of a coffee table. Pretty porcelain of all standards and prices is on sale, from collectors' items

Porcelain ware to brighten up any household.

to pretty reproductions of antique pieces which make wonderful souvenirs.

From other Asian countries: From the Philippines come baskets and shell dishes, place mats and lamps. From Japan come miniature masterpieces of design, tiny sewing or writing compacts the size of a credit card, as well as lacquer ware and exquisite porcelain. From India comes brass ware, as well as rugs, papier mache, sandalwood carvings and silks. There are gems from Sri Lanka and Buddhas from Myanmar (Burma) and Thailand. Sturdy and attractive Royal Selangor Pewter from Malaysia and batik from there and Indonesia, which also produces all kinds of fascinating artefacts.

Oriental carpets: The selection of beautiful Oriental carpets extends from tribal rugs to exquisite silk on silk carpets with glorious colours and intricate designs. The carpets may come from China, India, Pakistan, Iran or Turkey, each with its distinctive style.

Buying at one of the regularly held auctions in a hotel is an exhilarating experience, and not usually totally irrevocable. Uncertain buyers are advised to take their time in shops, however.

As antiques, old carpets often look well worn, but their value increases with age. **Amir & Sons**, in Lucky Plaza, and **Eastern Carpets** in Raffles Shopping Centre (see Travel Tips page 287) may have just what a visitor is looking for.

Rattan: The furniture is one lightweight way to be comfortable without being rich. Singapore is the birthplace of the rattan trade, a skill brought by settlers from Canton. Artisans are capable of turning out just about anything in cane, from sofas, tables and chairs to rocking horses and lamps.

Furniture: Reproduction or old pieces which have been restored are good buys in Singapore. Lovely old marble-topped coffee shop tables and old planter's chairs make for interesting interiors. There are wonderful old brass beds, chests, chairs and carved opium beds. Furniture from all over China as well as antiques and the not-so-old

Baskets of every shape, size and colour are available in Arab Street.

from Malacca and all over the region can be bought and shipped from Singapore. Certificates of antiquity are given with the genuine antiques, however there are plenty of lower priced merely old pieces which are attractive, as are the reproductions.

Where to buy it: Orchard Road is to Singapore what Fifth Avenue is to New York and the Champs Elysees is to Paris – one long line of shops, shopping centres and hotels with shopping arcades stretching from Tanglin Road at one end till **Plaza Singapura** at Dhoby Ghaut.

Starting from the Tanglin end is the lovely **Tudor Court**, with Aussie **Ken Done's** boutique. A little further down is **Tanglin Shopping Centre**, which is a great centre to explore for those who are interested in antiques, arts and crafts and other Asian fare. On the first foor is **CT Hoo**, a store with the widest selection of pearls in Singapore. Do not miss the sumptuous carpets and delightful smaller pieces at **Caravan International**. Just along the corridor is **Renee Hoy Fine Arts**, open from 9.30am to 6.30pm. Exquisite Asian treasures fill the shop, and any questions asked will be patiently answered. A remarkable range of antique prints, old maps and rare books can be found in **Antiques of the Orient** on level 2, and an excellent choice of modern books on the region in **Select Books** on the next floor. Browse around the shopping centre, fascinating artefacts from all over Asia can be found here. Check out **Albert Photo** at the far end for low-priced watches, cameras and jewellery.

Then go straight on to Bangkok's famous **Jim Thompson's** at Orchard Parade Hotel, which sells the world-famous silks and a fascinating biography of the American who started one of the most successful businesses in Asia and then mysteriously disappeared.

Across the road is **Delfi Orchard**, home to a large **Waterford Wedgewood** store and **Scruples**, which has stylish rattan furniture from the Philippines.

Walking down, **Orchard Towers** beckons, with shops selling jewellery, silk, antiques and shoes. Don't miss one

Strolling down an Orchard Road sidewalk.

of the cheapest and best selections of electronic equipment, cameras, watches and binoculars down in the basement at **Electronics Tower**. **Palais Renaissance**, with top designers' labels like **Krizia**, **Karl Lagerfeld** and **Missoni**, is just next door.

Across the road, **Forum The Shopping Mall** is home to **Toys R Us**, the world's largest toy store chain, as well as boutiques and other shops. The exclusive **Hilton Shopping Gallery** is another designers' label haven and the French chain store, **Galleries Lafayette**, in **Liat Towers** is also worth checking out. Next door is the new **Lane Crawford Plaza**, (to be opened 1994) named after the upmarket Hong Kong department store.

Over on Scotts Road, **Shaw Centre** is home to a new super branch of the Japanese department store **Isetan**. There, escalators whisk shoppers to different levels from cosmetics, bags and shoes below, to clothes of all price ranges above and right on up to children's department, complete with nursery and play area.

There are plenty of places to eat in this new shopping complex. On the other side of the street is **Far East Plaza** with many souvenir shops and **Scotts** with **Liz Claiborne**, **Tyan** and **Espirit**.

At the junction of Scotts and Orchard roads, below the high-rise pagoda of the Dynasty Hotel is **Tang's Superstore**, founded by CK Tang, one of the first entrepreneurs to realise the importance of Orchard Road. The business outgrew its original building and is now a spacious department store selling oriental treasures and everything for the household as well as clothes, jewellery, watches and electronics.

If you visit **Lucky Plaza,** be wary, there are some scrupulous traders, but for the most part its just a tourist trap. A little further down the road is The **Promenade**, with **Charles Jourdan** and **Jean Paul Gaultier** and also **Abraxas**, an interesting modern furniture store. Next door is the **Paragon** with **Gucci**, **Lanvin** as well as **Metro** and **Sogo** department stores.

Across the road from Lucky Plaza is

New malls such as Shaw Centre (<u>left</u>) and the mammoth Ngee Ann City (<u>right</u>) have given shoppers more to choose from than ever before.

the big blue building **Wisma Atria**, which houses another **Isetan** as well as hundreds of shops selling fashionwear, electronic and leather goods and restaurants and fast-food outlets. Beside it is the new and impressive **Ngee Ann City**, Southeat Asia's largest shopping mall, with **Takashimaya** department store as its anchor tenant and numerous shops selling designer labels as well as **Tangs Studio** and **Harrods** from London.

Not far off is **Centrepoint**, home to Singapore's original department store **Robinson's** and home to Britain's Marks and Spencer, called **St Michael's**. There is also a wide range of other shops including **The Body Shop**, **Mondi**, **Mothercare** and just about the best concentration of bookstores in Singapore – there's a **Times** and an **MPH** on the same floor.

Next to Centrepoint, explore the newly renovated **Orchard Point** with boutiques such as **Jessica**, **Escape** and **Excursion**, three famous Hong Kong-based fashion houses.

Yaohan, yet another Japanese department store is at **Plaza Singapura**, where there are also shops selling clothes, books and everything for the music lover. **DFS** at **Meridien Hotel Shopping Centre** is a big attraction for tourists because of its duty-free goods and there are some great clothes boutiques on the third floor, including **Anne Klein** and **Man and His Woman**.

Just outside the main Orchard Road area is **Park Mall**. Visit **SA.GA** and **Style Singapore** if you are interested to see what local fashion designers get up to. Park Mall also has a good selection of clothes by other Asian designers from Thailand, Malaysia and Indonesia.

In the narrow streets of **Chinatown** are old shophouses with traditional fare like ginseng and medicinal teas in **Sago Street**, antique jewellery in **Pagoda Street** and porcelain and all kinds of souvenirs in **Smith** and **Temple Streets**. In **People's Park Complex** and **Centre**, shops selling everything from fabrics of every weight and width to watches, CDs and clothes all compete for business from locals and tourists

alike. The new **Chinatown Point** is a haven of Chinese arts and crafts as well as electronics, cameras and watches. **Pidemco Centre** not far away is the place for local gold and jewellery.

In pastel shaded **Tanjong Pagar**, renovated shophouses stock traditional arts and crafts, and fashion items.

Funan Centre in Hill Street and **Sim Lim Square** in Rochor Canal Road are full of electronic appliances and computer hard and software.

Marina Square down at the seaside has **Metro**, and a not-to-be-missed bookshop **Page One** which specialises in art and design, as well as many smaller boutiques and shops. Nearby, **Raffles City** has the **Chinese Embroidery House** and the **Chinese Cloisonne-ware Centre**. Across the road, **Raffles Hotel** shopping arcade has dozens of designer shops plus a gift shop with unusual souvenirs. In Princep Street, **Chan Yew** makes wallets and bags to order in leather of all colours.

Art lovers can browse among books, paints, scrolls, bamboo brushes and all the traditional paraphernalia for Chinese brush painting in **Bras Basah Complex**.

In **Arab Street**, off Beach Road, a Muslim atmosphere lingers from the early years of Singapore when Malays, Bugis and Javanese settled here, sharing a common religion. Prayer mats, holy beads, copies of the *Koran* and *songkoks* (black caps) and lace caps for those who have made the pilgrimage to Mecca are all sold here. It is also the place for batik, especially at **Aljunied Brothers'** and all along the whole street, with fabrics of all colours, patterns and weights spilling out onto the pavement from vivid bales. Baskets of every shape, colour and size are stacked on the floor and suspended from walls, ceilings and pillars. Shops are piled high with leather bags, purses and shoes and bright trinkets glisten invitingly.

Continue browsing along Arab Street to Rochor Canal Road, across the canal is **Sungei Road** and the lively jumble of **Thieves' Market**, where vendors spread their wares all over the street from any-

The posh Raffles Hotel and Raffles City behind it are more than adequately equipped to handle all shopping needs.

thing such as wellingtons to watches (the cheapest fakes in town).

Singapore's **Little India**, **Serangoon Road** and the neighbouring side-streets is the place for anything from spices to Indian silk from the Subcontinent. **Handlooms** is sponsored by the Indian government and has a wonderful selection of rugs, paintings and clothes.

Holland Shopping Centre in **Holland Village**, a little farther out of town, is the expatriate haven. There is a large supermarket on ground level and a host of shops selling bags, shoes, jewellery and clothes from batik to comfortable casuals. There is everything in the souvenir line at **Lim's Arts & Crafts**, a real oriental treasure trove on level two. **The Great Blue Dive Shop** sells everything for divers, as well as arrange diving trips and courses. For casual silks, batiks and other clothing just carry on round the corner. **Jessica Art N' Craft** has lovely Korean furniture and porcelain from Japan. A Chinese emporium, fabrics and furniture, stationery, music, pets and pictures, this shopping centre has it all.

Go down Lorong Liput and explore **Lorong Mambong** behind the shopping centre, a lively little street with a traditional wet market on one side, and baskets spilling out of shops on the other. Rummage through for porcelain, baskets and curios as well as marble-top tables, desks and cupboards at **Wing Mee Furniture** and more antiques further along. There are superb carpets at **Hedges**, exquisite flowers and gifts in Swiss Art and clothes at rock bottom prices at the **Factory Outlet**.

Just along Holland at Jalan Jelita is **Jelita Cold Storage**. There, is a collection of pre- and post-colonial furniture and fascinating artefacts in **Ji-reen Home Boutique**. For furniture, antiques and cane, a visit to the shops in **Watten Estate** along Bukit Timah is a must.

This chapter is just the tip of the monumental iceberg of shopping possibilities in Singapore. The hotel arcades are enticing and shopping centres spring like mushrooms, so do explore and if looking for something in particular, use the *Singapore Buying Guide* directory.

Shopping for food containers in Arab Street.

FOOD

Perhaps nowhere in the world does life revolve around food quite as much as it does in Singapore. Singaporeans talk about food just like the English talk of the weather – all the time! People from all walks of life display remarkable critical abilities in all matters culinary. They can discuss where to get the freshest seafood, the hottest chilli sauce, the best chicken rice, the best chilli crab, best satay or the best fried rice for hours on end, preferably over a meal.

The wide racial mix of Chinese, Malays and Indians as well as an expatriate population from all over the world, has led to an enormous variety of food, available in venues ranging from tumbledown hawker stalls to sophisticated restaurants.

Whether served on polystyrene in a local food centre or on bone china in a world-class hotel, food is the focus. Eating is the national pastime. Wherever you are, whatever the time of day, you'll see people eating. Boxes of cooked food are delivered to offices, shop girls eat fried rice from brown paper wrappings, tea is carried around in little plastic bags so that those who can't get out don't miss out.

Coffee shops, food centres and restaurants are everywhere, packed with elegant couples, jolly families, locals and tourists, all absorbed in the pleasures of the board.

Nouvelle cuisine from France, teppanyaki and sushi from Japan, enchiladas and burritos from Mexico, it's all here, as well as variety of Indian, Chinese, Malay, Indonesian and Nonya specialities, and Singapore's very own home-grown favourite dishes – fish head curry and chilli crab.

Singapore Specialities

As in so many aspects of life, Singapore has gained from the rich variety of its people. Add the spices of India and the

Preceding pages: Thai-style *satay*, *ang ku kueh*, *nonya* cakes; *nasi lemak* is a delicious breakfast dish. **Below**, the new-look Bugis Street.

138

finesse of Chinese cuisine to mild Malay curries and Indonesian ways of cooking and fresh seafood, and you have the much-loved local food. Check out **Telok Ayer Market (Lau Pa Sat)** which serve a variety of Singaporean fare that promises to delight the palate (see page 276 for more details).

Nonya: The combination which really has its own identity however, is the *Nonya* cuisine. This is the product of romance between immigrant Chinese and Malay women from Melaka, Penang and Singapore, who intermarried to give us the Peranakan culture.

The women or *Bibis* fed their *Babas* on a delightful mixture of Chinese and Malay flavours. Young girls of marriageable age learned the complicated recipes with many freshly pounded ingredients, happily putting in long hours in the kitchen in order to become proficient in the art of finding the way to a man's heart through his stomach.

A stone pestle and mortar is used to grind *rempah*, which is a mixture of spices such as chillies, spring onions, lemon grass, candlenuts, turmeric and *belacan* (prawn paste). It is this mixture which gives *Nonya* food its distinctive flavour.

Although best eaten in a Peranakan home, *Nonya* food can be enjoyed at various restaurants here, a favourite being the **Nonya and Baba Restaurant** in River Valley Road. **Oleh Sayang Food** in Holland Village is recommended for some unpretentious *Nonya* food (see Travel Tips page 276).

Seafood: Surrounded by tropical waters, Singapore is assured of a plentiful supply of fresh fish and seafood. You can still see the Malay *kelongs* or little wooden huts on stilts out in the Straits off the coast, where fishermen occasionally still lower their nets to bring in the catch.

However, nowadays most of the fish, fresh and deep frozen, is bought and sold in the pre-dawn hours at Jurong Fish Market out on the West Coast.

Succulent prawns, crayfish, lobster, crabs, pomfret, *ikan merah*, *tenggiri* are featured in many local dishes. Local spices and Chinese cooking methods

Ingredients for a classic indigenous dish – *laksa lemak*.

make for delectable concoctions, favourites such as chilli and pepper crab, steamed prawns and crispy fried *sotong* (baby squid). Fish head curry, sometimes said to be Singapore's national dish, has spicy Indian, Malay and *Nonya* variations.

Another contender for the national dish, chilli crabs are freshly stir-fried in their shells with garlic, sugar, soy sauce, tomato sauce, eggs and of course with lots of chilli. The result is a pile of bright red crustaceans to be attacked with a hammer and fingers, an utterly delicious experience, but a messy one! Pepper crabs too are spicy and some say even better, as larger crabs are used for this dish.

Singaporeans adore seafood and happily make the pilgrimage to the coast to find the best seafood restaurants. Out there, away from the city noise and bustle and the highrise estates, the atmosphere is relaxed, families get together and great food is enjoyed by young and old.

At the **UDMC Seafood Centre** at the East Coast Parkway, choose from a number of restaurants – Red House, Bedok Sea View, Kheng Luck, Jumbo Seafood, and more – displaying an array of lobster, prawn and fish-filled tanks. Not far away are other noted seafood restaurants such as **Singa Inn** and **Seafood International**. **Long Beach** out on Bedok Road is a favourite local evening haunt as well.

Hawker stalls: There was a colourful time when eating out meant eating out – at a rickety wooden table next to a mobile restaurant under a canopy of frangipanis and stars.

Known as hawkers, wizened and wiry entrepreneurs would set up shop at selected spots along the roadside equipped with table, stools, cutlery, kitchen, food and all. Or they would travel through the city announcing their offerings with a high-pitched chant, concocting meals for passers-by and neighbourhood residents.

All were, in a sense, mysteriously ephemeral – vanishing and reappearing from day to night so as to arouse the suspicion that, much like the bakery

Feasting on *rojak* and succulent cuttlefish under the stars.

shop in Mary Poppins, they did not really exist. But in June 1987, street hawkers entered the annals of history, when the last 70 were moved into food centres in the final stage of an 11-year government effort to get them off the street. Improvements in order, cleanliness and convenience have somewhat offset the loss of a part of the old Singapore ambience.

Even with restaurants and all, hawker food continues to be Singapore's favourite (and cheapest) cuisine. A hawker centre is one glorious pan-Asiastic taste tour. Indian, Malay and Chinese stalls are found in close proximity, allowing you to sample half the world's cooking at a single sitting and nominal cost. Far from disdaining them, the true local gourmet when given a choice, will head for his favourite stall, leaving restaurants to foppish millionaires.

Some recommended hawker and food centres are The Derby, Newton Circus, Cuppage Centre, Botanic Gardens (just across from the main gate in Cluny Road), Picnic Food Court, People's Park,

Lagoon Food Centre, Forum Galleria Food Centre, Dunman Food Centre, Odeon Food Centre (for the best *popiah*) and Chinatown Complex Food Centre (where the best claypot rice can be found). See Travel Tips page 276 for more details on food centres.

Chinese

The Chinese have a way with food. Whether it's plain fresh fish or exotic abalone or bird's nest, from so much less, they create so much more. They have given the west a new approach to food. Long ago Marco Polo introduced noodles from China, to what is now the land of pasta.

Now, as westerners take to more healthy ways of eating, out go great lumps of red meat, and in come a range of different fresh vegetables no longer boiled into soggy masses but crisply stir-fried, Cantonese-style to preserve the flavour and goodness, and served with slivers of meat or fresh fish and seafood.

Succulent seafood – a Singapore specialty.

That the Chinese can adapt their cooking to prevailing local tastes is borne out by the popularity of "chow mein" (fried noodles) and bland "sweet and sour" dishes in the west.

Nevertheless, the large Chinese population in Singapore ensures the authenticity of the cuisine, and the meal is best eaten in traditional style, helping oneself with chopsticks from a selection of dishes shared by all, giving new meaning to the saying, "the more the merrier."

The adaptation to regional and climatic demands as well as the absorption of foreign influence has led to a fascinating variety of tastes from the different regions of China. Here in Singapore you don't just say you'll eat "Chinese" – you say, Szechuan, Cantonese, Teochew or any of a dozen distinct types of food from China.

The North and West: The rough-and-ready cooking methods of the invading Mongols and Manchus were absorbed and refined by the Chinese. It was they who introduced cooking with lamb and barbecue techniques. Their influence resulted in the use of wheat flour to make bread the staple.

Beijing: The three courses of Peking Duck are among the most delicious dishes in the world. First the crisp skin is savoured, then the waiter skillfully chops the meat. This is rolled in a wheat pancake with sweet soya bean paste and spring onions. As you eat, the soup is boiling ready for the finale to this superb meal.

Other dishes feature mutton or lamb and are usually served with noodles.

The **Prima Tower Revolving Restaurant** in Keppel Road and the luxurious Chinese courtyard setting of the Shangri-La's **Shang Palace** are good places to be served Peking Duck in style.

Szechuan: Spicy and hot, this cuisine also has a delicious duck dish, for which marinated, smoked duck is served wrapped in pancakes with sauce and spring onions.

The hot and sour soup is mind-blowing, delicious with Szechuan fried bread. Prawns with dried chillies should not be missed. Cold lobster with fruit and may- **Tender beef steak, Chinese style.**

onnaise is an unusual starter with contrasting taste for this fiery meal.

A firm local favourite for Szechuan food is the **Dragon City** in the Novotel Orchid Singapore; for in more exotic surrounding, there's Goodwood Park Hotel's **Min Jiang** Restaurant.

Also from the northern districts of China comes **Steamboat**, or Mongolian hotpot, the Asian fondue which makes for a sociable meal as you cook fresh, raw ingredients at the table in well-flavoured stock. **Coca Steamboat** at International Building (next to Lido) served an assortment of Japanese raw cuisine as well as the usual fare for the steamboat. The dip (or chilli sauce) has a definite Thai flavour.

The South – Cantonese: An ancient Chinese proverb advises "Live in Soochow (a city noted for its refined manners and beautiful women), die in Hangchow (where teakwood coffins are made) but eat in Guangzhou (Canton)."

As more Cantonese than any other Chinese from other regions settled in the west, their cuisine is perhaps the best known of all, with its stir-fried fresh ingredients and light sauces.

Actually the Cantonese are famous for eating anything on four legs apart from furniture and anything that flies except a kite. Their menus may feature bear's paw, bird's nest, fish maw, chicken testicles, frog's leg and even live monkey's brain, as well as snakes and pigeons.

The wealth of tastes acquired by tapping nature's resources so deeply has led to simplicity of flavouring with a variety of cooking methods, steaming, frying in a wok, roasting, poaching and deep frying. In Canton, the rice bowl of China, the accompanying staple is of course, almost invariably rice.

Although the Cantonese here form only a fraction of the Chinese population, they are still the most prolific restaurateurs here.

Fatty's is perhaps the best known, a real Cantonese character dishing up delicious spring rolls, sweet and sour pork as it should be and diced chicken in black sauce.

Steamboat is a tasty experience.

A perennial Cantonese favourite is *dim sum* (literally "little heart"), a way to try countless small steamed or fried delicacies served from pretty bamboo containers brought to your table on trolleys. These little delicacies are available at most restaurants. A good place to try is the **Garden Seafood Restaurant** in Goodwood Park Hotel or the **Shang Palace** at Shangri-La Hotel.

Hakka: The "guest people", as the Hakkas were known as they came from the western border of Kwantung, use their ingenuity to make the most of every scrap of food. Chicken steamed in red rice wine and bean curd stuffed with minced meat (*yong tau fu*) served with black sauce are specialities.

Hokkien: Seafood with thick well-flavoured sauces are typical of Hokkien cuisine. But perhaps most popular of all is Hokkien mee. Thick egg noodles sauteed with pork, fish, squid, prawns and vegetables in a rich sauce is a wonderful combination. Unfried *popiah* or spring rolls, thin crepes containing cabbage, prawns, sausage and eggs are also well worth trying. **Beng Hiang** in Maxwell Road and **Beng Thin Hoon Kee** in OCBC Centre are economical ways to start on Hokkien cuisines (see Travel Tips page 276).

Teochew: Mild food, with clear broths and light seasoning is the hallmark of Teochew cuisine, one of whose wholesome recipes is fresh steamed seafood or fish. A delicate touch is evident in most dishes without any overpowering influence of unctuous sauces or sharp spices. Well-known places to try are **Ban Seng** at New Bridge Road and **East Ocean** in Shaw Centre in Scotts Road.

Hainanese: Known by the old colonials for their skills as cooks, these immigrants from the southern tropical island of Hainan have also added dishes learned from the foreigners such as breaded pork or beef cutlets to their repertoire.

The most famous of their creations is Hainanese chicken rice, with tender boiled chicken and rice steamed in the stock, accompanied by chilli, soy and ginger and garlic sauces.

Taiwanese: The island of Taiwan, a

Stir-fried mushrooms with broccoli.

bastion of traditional Chinese culture, is still ruled by Nationalists from the mainland who brought their banquet-style cuisine with them. However, the native Taiwanese, who comprise the vast majority of the population, favour a simple meal of rice or rice porridge with a selection of light, sauteed seafood and salty stir-fried vegetables.

Vegetarian: Tofu, soya bean curd, widely used in Chinese cuisine makes a protein-packed meal for vegetarians, and there are endless ways of preparing and flavouring it. Claypot dishes and a varied menu are offered at **Miao Yi Vegetarian Restaurant** in Coronation Plaza (see Travel Tips page 276). Check out **Imperial Herbal Restaurant** at Metropole Hotel for some dishes with nutritional and medicinal benefits.

Malay

A rich *rendang* or spicy stew served with "*nasi minyak*" rice, to which spices such as cardamon and cinnamon have been added, a vegetable curry and *sambal* (spicy side dishes) make up a typical Malay meal.

Malay food is traditionally eaten with the fingers, or with a fork and spoon. In deference to Islamic beliefs, pork is never served. Malay dishes are flavoured with lemon grass, ginger, garlic and shrimp paste and are usually not very *pedas* or hot in the spicy sense.

One of Singapore's all-time favourites is *satay*, small bamboo skewers of marinaded beef, mutton or chicken grilled over coals and served with onion, cucumber, *ketupat* (compressed rice) and peanut sauce. Satay Club in Connaught Drive, overlooking the sea, has open air stalls serving succulent *satay*. This is a great place for alfresco dining right in the heart of old Singapore.

Taking something from Indonesian cooking and something from the Chinese, Malay cuisine varies from one region to another. Penang with its special *laksa* (noodles in a spicy soup), *popiah* spring rolls has its devotees, as does the Portuguese influenced food of

Kon loh mee – shredded pork and chilli noodles.

Melaka, which has given its name to *gula melaka*, the traditional sago and dark brown sugar finale to a colonial curry tiffin.

Aziza's on Emerald Hill Road is undoubtedly one of the best places to sample excellent Malay cuisine in a cosy, homely atmosphere. Another is **Sukmaindra** in the Royal Holiday Inn Crowne Plaza in Scotts Road. See Travel Tips page 276 for a list of restaurants serving Malay cuisine.

Indian

The Moghul invasions, which influenced Chinese cuisine, also affected northern India giving rise to the rich Mughlai dishes. There wheat is the staple, and the *tandoor* oven is used for baking the leavened bread or *naan*, and to produce delicious marinaded fish or chicken either whole, *tandoori*, or as *tikka* (small pieces). *Kofta* or meatballs are served in rich, creamy sauces of Persian inspiration.

In the south, fiery curries are a speciality and coconut milk is widely used in the gravy. Of all foods, ghee, which is cream made into butter and then clarified, is said to be the purest. It is often used in religious ceremonies as well as in the making of *pratas*, meat dishes and desserts.

Religion plays a fundamental role in Indian cuisine. Muslims eat no pork, Hindus no beef, while Buddhists kill nothing and will not even crack an egg. As a result vegetarian cooking has reached heights of excellence unparalleled elsewhere in the world.

Indian food is often served on banana leaves, or on a *thali*, a large tray holding the staple, on which smaller bowls or *katori* are placed, filled with the accompanying dishes.

A classic Indian meal would comprise a balance of sweet, salty, bitter, astringent, sour and pungent taste and is traditionally eaten with the fingers.

In Race Course Road there are a number of restaurants such as **Muthu's Curry** and **Banana Leaf Apollo** which serve authentic Indian curries, includ-

Chapati – wholemeal unleaven bread – is an Indian staple, typically eaten with dahl (lentil curry).

146

ing fish-head curries. For more opulent surroundings for southern and vegetarian cuisine, try **Annalakshmi** in Excelsior Shopping Centre, or **Bombay Woodlands** in Orchard Road.

Moti Mahal is world famous for Kashmiri, Punjabi and Mughlai dishes. The restaurant's specially-imported wallpaper depicts a Mogul palace courtyard and garden. For wonderful northern fare in a romantic setting, **The Tandoor** in the Holiday Inn Park View is the place, where Indian musicians serenade diners every night except Mondays. See Travel Tips page 276 for other restaurants serving Vegetarian, Punjabi, Southern and Northern Indian cuisines.

Indonesian

Singapore has many Indian restaurants of unsurpassed ambience and cuisine.

This archipelago once known as the Spice Islands offers a fascinating variety of dishes hot and cold, making delicious use of the exotic fruit, nuts and vegetables which grow there. The range of dishes constituting Sumatran *nasi padang* and the Javanese use of nuts, spices and coconut cream have heavily influenced Singaporean home cooking. *Nasi Padang*, originally from the Padang area of West Sumatra, offers the chance to taste various local curried vegetable and meat dishes, served with rice. **Rendezvous** in Raffles City is one of the best.

The Dutch colonials would enjoy a wide selection of meat, fish and vegetable curries served with rice, known as "Rijstaffel", and the place to try this here is the grandly restored **Alkaff Mansion**. There 10 *kebaya*-clad beauties line up to present the diner with a feast for the eyes and palate. **Tambuah Mas** at Tanglin Shopping Centre and **Sanur** at Centrepoint, Chinatown Point and International Plaza are firm favourites with the locals (see Travel Tips page 276).

Thai

There's a distinct taste of lemon and fresh mint to much Thai food, usually served with mind-blowing *namprick*

phao paste. This is for the lovers of really hot food, as is the famed *tom yam kung* soup, the traditional hot and sour soup that really tickles the palate.

As a starter, chicken-feet salad gives a wonderful introduction to Thai cuisine – slabs of crunchy feet are mixed in a green salad soaked in a tangy sauce. Watch out for tiny scarlet *chilli padi* often used as decoration, or in dishes with the word "prik" in the name, it's extremely potent. Chicken in *pandan* leaves and pineapple rice are milder favourites. Thais have a special way of cooking seafood that is totally unique such as lobster in Thai chilli sauce and claypot crab or prawn with vermicelli (*tang hoon*).

All kinds of fresh fish and seafood may be chosen raw as at the **Chao Phaya Thai Seafood Market and Restaurant** in Ang Mo Kio and prepared whichever way you like. One good starter is fried fish-meat pancake, which has had chopped red chilli and long beans added to it. Other popular restaurants are **Siamese Fins** in Tanjong Pagar and **Tum Nak Thai**, East Coast Parkway. See Travel Tips page 276 for a listing of Thai restaurants.

Japanese

The most aesthetic food of all is Japanese, for exquisitely arranged delicacies are presented on dishes, plates and bowls of porcelain, lacquer and bamboo. Food becomes art as expertly sliced fish, vegetables and meat are combined according to colour, texture and taste.

Start with raw fish, *sashimi*, or delicate morsels of raw fish wrapped in rice and seaweed called *sushi* dipped in soy sauce mixed with green horseradish.

Watch the *teppanyaki* chef fling his knife with wild panache as he cooks slivers of beef, salmon or vegetables on a hot griddle before your eyes. You could barbecue your own *yakitori* bamboo skewers of meat and vegetables and *shabu-shabu* has all the fun of a fondue as you cook specially sliced meat and fresh vegetables in boiling broth at the table.

There has been a proliferation of Japanese restaurants in recent years.

Warm rice wine, or *sake*, served in individual flasks with tiny cups is the perfect accompaniment to the meal.

Many of the Japanese restaurants are found in hotels, for example, **Shima** at Goodwood Park, **Unkai** in ANA, **Keyaki** in the Pan Pacific; others are found at shopping complexes in the city, such as **Nanbantei** in Far East Plaza and **Kobe** in Tanglin Shopping Centre. Other Japanese restaurants is listed in the Travel Tips page 276.

Western

East-West: Several restaurants here feature an alluring combination of oriental and occidental cuisine, offering unusual dishes such as lobster with curry mango sauce or an Asian starter followed by a western main course. For the former, **The Compass Rose** at the top of the Westin, the world's highest hotel, and for the latter **The Pinnacle**, high above the Singapore River in OUB Building are tops in every sense of the word. "Crossroads cuisine" – where East meets West selection – is available at **Emmerson's Tiffin Room** located in an old shop house in Neil Road.

Continental: In Singapore you can feast on wild game dishes, slice through done-to-perfection steak and still leave room for some sinful deserts. **Baron's Table** in Royal Holiday Inn Crowne Plaza serves well-prepared continental cuisine amid a traditional hunting-lodge ambience. See Travel Tips page 276 for a list of continental restaurants.

French: Dishes like goose liver salad, pan-fried vension and fluffy lemon pancakes are availabe in most local French restaurant. **L'Aigle d'Or** located in a block of renovated shop-houses in Tanjong Pagar serves specialities such as mushroom ravioli (delicate skins encase the fresh chopped mushrooms) and the blend of proached sole and salmon as a main course. Other French restaurants are listed in the Travel Tips page 276.

English: Gordon Grill in Goodwood Park Hotel serves good olde English fare amid a romantic setting with dim

Fine French cuisine is a feast for the eyes.

light and tartan carpet. Hearty English fare is also available at **Bob's Tavern** in Holland Village.

Another good place to sample authentic English food is at the **Hubertus Grill** at the ANA Hotel. The setting is cosy with a hunting lodge atmosphere. Quiet corners provide added privacy. Selection of food include choices of game, seafood, grills and flambé dishes.

American: **Dan Ryan's** in Tanglin Road, **Hard Rock Cafe** in Cuscaden Road and **TGI Friday's** in Penang Road are popular places for generously-portioned American food served by friendly and entertaining staff.

Italian: **Prego** at the ground floor of Westin Stamford is spacious and neatly decorated in pastel colours. In the middle of the restaurant is an open bar-cum-kitchen where the chefs can be observed, lending a pleasant buzz of activity to the atmosphere. A 24-hour Italian eatery **Pasta Fresca**, located in Boat Quay, serves delicious home-made *pasta* and pizza. A list of Italian restaurants can be found in the Travel Tips page 276.

Mexican: Mexican food in Singapore ranges from "Tex-Mex" variety to traditional Mexican. In Holland Village, there are two Mexican restaurants side by side – **Cha Cha Cha's** and **El Felipe's** – both are moderately expensive – the latter serves great margaritas. Another good Mexican restaurant is **Margaritas**. Located in Jalan Lempeng, off Clementi, this restaurant has an extensive list of Mexican dishes, the atmosphere is cosy and the staff friendly.

High Tea: This has become a popular practice in Singapore – skip lunch and tuck into high tea instead. High tea has become the latest craze among young Singaporeans and modern homemakers. Most hotels' coffee houses serve high tea from 2.30pm to 6pm on weekends. Check out the **Tea Room** in Westin Stamford that serves a large spread of eastern and western fare – barbecued chicken wings, fried spring rolls, fried Hong Kong noodles, scones, puddings, mince pies and sandwiches. See Travel Tips page 276 for a listing of restaurants serving high tea.

All-American fare can be found at TGI Friday's.

Local Fruits

One tells the time of year in Singapore not by the weather, but by the fruit in season. Apart from all kinds of familiar imported fruit on sale, there is a wonderful selection of exotic local fruits to try.

Certainly the most celebrated of indigenous fruits is the thorny-shelled, strong-smelling **durian**. "Curiosity, and not the taste, first prompts the new settler to attempt the fruit," wrote Englishman James Low in 1836. "But although tasting it, as he generally does, with a prejudice against it (because of the smell), he not infrequently ends in acquiring a strong relish for it."

Native to Indo-China and Indonesia, the durian is easily recognized by its hard, green casing of protective spikes. It grows from a tree of the hibiscus family, attached to upper limbs by a thin stem, and falls when ripe, sometimes from a height of 30 to 40 metres (100 to 130ft) and usually without damage. Its dimensions are commonly 20 to 25cm (8 to 10 inches), although it may reach double this size. The rigid shell opens, albeit with some effort, along natural cleavages, revealing capsular yellow custardy arils enclosing an oval seed. The prime durian season is June to August though now they can be found all year round.

A native of India, the **jackfruit**, locally known as *nangka*, is common throughout Southeast Asia and grows all year round. Large in size, growing to about 50 by 25cm long (18 by 9 inches) across, the fruit's thick, yellow-green rind is ridged with small pointed pimples.

A cross section discloses five to six bright orange or yellow meats, each encasing a brown seed. The jackfruit's meat is fragrant and sweet when ripe, texturally akin to a lightly steamed capsicum or green pepper. As with the durian, jackfruits are sold whole on the street. And even a small one will yield 20 to 30 pieces of meat, enough for several people. A cousin to the jackfruit is the *chempedak* which is smaller, sweeter and exudes a stronger fragrant.

Refreshing offerings.

The **lychee** is native to Southern China, but great quantities, both fresh and tinned, are imported to Singapore. The tree belongs to the same genus as the *rambutan* fruit, but though it grows in the northern part of Malaysia, it strangely enough, does not bear fruit there. Lychee season usually runs from May to July.

The lychee is round and small (usually 3 to 5cm in diameter) and its leathery and knobby skin bright red colour – when picked – which soon changes to a light brown. The flesh is translucent white and juicy-sweet, smelling and tasting of roses. It is a favourite dessert, fresh or canned.

Contrary to what you may surmise, a **mangosteen** is not a kosher mango. Called *manggis* by the natives, this "seductive apple of the east" grows from a medium size tree of the *guttiferae* family, whose sap is a bright yellow colour.

There are two seasons for the fruit (at the middle and the end of the year), corresponding roughly with the durian seasons, but the mangosteen is easily upset by inclement weather. The crim-son-purple rind of the fruit is quite thick, but, having the consistency of bread-crust, easily crumbles.

Be careful of the rind's juice, however, because it stains hands and clothes and the taste is very bitter. Inside are five to eight juicy white segments possessing a sweet, astringent flavour.

Rambutan means "hairy" in Malay, and appropriately, this fruit is distinguished by many thin, plastic-like hairs protruding from a bright red rind. Commonly 3½ by 5 cm, it grows in bunches from a tall, bushy tree.

Open the *rambutan* by inserting a thumbnail into its mid-section and prying apart the halves of its shell. Its iridescent white pulp is thereby revealed and may be easily popped into the mouth. The interior seed is firmly attached to the flesh, and must be scraped from it with the incisor teeth. The *rambutan*'s taste is juicy-sweet, akin to that of tinned pears.

The **papaya** plant has many unusual properties. Botanically it is more herb than tree; the trunk is hollow, soft and fibrous. The papaya is native to Central

Fruity delights in Chinatown.

America, having been brought to the Philippines by the Spanish and then propagated throughout Southeast Asia during the 16th century. It matures quickly, bearing fruit from seeds within a year, and continues to produce the year round at a rapid pace.

Papayas vary greatly in size, colour and taste. Local varieties tend to be about a foot in length (and about half as wide), yellow outside, and bright orange within. The taste is smooth and bland, the best ones being quite sweet and juicy. The flesh is high in vitamin A and calcium, and its properties aid digestion because of the presence of the enzyme papain which breaks down the amino acids into protein (and therefore is commonly extracted and sold as a meat tenderiser).

Native to Java, the **starfruit** is known there by the Jelliflous name *blimbing*. Its English appellation derives from its pentagonal shape, formed by fluting or wings running from the base to the apex. It is a curious-looking object indeed, with waxy skin that is first green and then ripens to a translucent yellow. The texture is crisp and the flesh juicy, like an apple. The best starfruit have a strong acidic taste, being very high in ascorbic acid or vitamin C.

"Nature," wrote M. Poivre in the 18th-century treatise, *Voyages of a Philosopher*, "seems to have taken a pleasure in assembling in Malayan countries its most favourite productions."

Beverages

Singapore's home-made beers like Tiger, Anchor and the new Raffles Light are excellent accompaniment to Asian food. Wines and spirits of all kinds are widely available, with longer lists in the better restaurants. And you shouldn't leave the island without trying a Singapore Sling cocktail. Or try the original recipe at home: 2 ozs Gin juice, 1 lemon, 1 teaspoon powdered sugar. Pour over ice in a highball glass. Add soda water, ½ oz Cointreau, ½ oz cherry brandy, stir and decorate with a slice of lemon.

TRIAL FOR ASSE

The purpose of thi

cultivars for garde

general appearanc

SSMENT OF ANN

trial is to assess se

s in Singapore. Six cu

floriferousness, pest/

The "Green" Scene: Exploring Nature

Once a colonial outpost where tigers accounted for 300 deaths a year and crocodiles roamed the river banks, Singapore is now much tamer, with only the occasional python slithering along a storm drain and the ubiquitous geckos or "chick-chaks" on the walls and ceilings as reminders of the tropical environment. But there is still plenty of nature on view, especially in the central and northern parts of the island where large tracts of tropical forest, mangrove and swamp endure. In fact, getting close to nature is as much a part of Singapore life as eating and shopping.

Despite its highrise reputation, Singapore has more green space then any other major city in Southeast Asia and a growing conservation movement insures that parks and gardens will be there for many generations to come. The rising standard of living has actually contrib-uted to this environmental conscious-ness, as Singaporeans realize that nature is an indispensable part of a better standard of living.

The Botanic Gardens: Singapore's oldest national park lies just outside Orchard Road, one of the world's busiest shopping areas. Set up by the Singapore Agri-Horticultural Society in 1859, it is known worldwide as a living museum of tropical plants. Spacious and beautifully landscaped, with well-paved walkways winding around the luscious greenery, the Gardens are popular for family picnics, jogging or strolling. The cultured orchids and other tropical plants are famous, but the many varieties of birdlife are unknown to most. A walk at dawn, when it is cool, quiet and uncrowded, with eyes opened and ears attuned to the birds, is an enriching experience.

Long-tailed Macaques whose antics formerly provided amusement for visitors, have all gone, removed by the authorities when they became a problem to humans. The Gardens, however, are not devoid of animal life. The Plan-

Preceding pages: Sunning on a sign; lake tranquility in the Botanics, which is famous for its extensive orchid collection (below).

tain and Slender Squirrel as well as the Common Treeshrew can still be found. Reptiles such as the Green Crested and Changeable Lizard and the Common Flying Lizard are still common, while the Reticulated Python is occasionally sighted in the culverts and drains along the boundary.

The birdlife of the Gardens is interesting. Surprisingly, a wide variety of species is found in such a small area, which measures about 23 hectares (57 acres), excluding the newly-acquired land bordering the campus of the Institute of Education. Since the early decades of the 20th century, 80 species of birds have been recorded within the Gardens, of which 67 are Singapore residents. At least half of the resident species have nested regularly or, at one time or other in the Gardens, although 13 species are no longer found.

The "greening" of Singapore has resulted in many scenic spots.

Most of the species that have gone required large tracts of undisturbed forest in order to survive. With the whittling down of the Botanic Jungle, it is inevitable that forest species suffered.

Despite its reputation as the second patch of primary forest left in Singapore – Bukit Timah Nature Reserve is the other – the Botanic Jungle is unfortunately in a degraded state. It is becoming less and less dense as the old giants topple over. Reclusive forest birds are most vulnerable to this degradation. One common flowerpecker, the Orange-bellied Flowerpeckers have been reduced and replaced by their cousin, the Scarlet-Backed Flowerpecker.

Nevertheless, the Botanic Jungle still harbours small numbers of some forest species. The Banded Woodpecker, Striped Tit-babbler, Abbott's Babbler and the Greater Racket-tailed Drongo are still in evidence as they were decades ago. These birds have survived by moving beyond the confines of the Jungle to forage for food. Banded Woodpeckers can be seen pecking at the ants on old Tembusus (*Fragraea fragrans*) at the fringe of the jungle, while Racket-tailed Drongos rule the shadowy groves of the Albizias (*Albizzia falcataria*) along Tyersall Avenue. Abbott's and

Striped Tit-Babblers venture out of the Jungle into the denser hedges and appear in the gardens of neighbouring bungalows. As in the days of Bucknill and Chasen, joint authors of the first book on Singapore birds published in 1927, the visitor can still see flocks of Long-tailed Parakeets and Pink-necked Pigeons flying in to land on fruiting trees. A couple of Hill Mynas can also be seen perched in the morning hours, as in colonial days, on the topmost points of the Jungle canopy and whistling away in their loud, clear voice.

After Independence, as Singapore embarked on its course towards modernisation, the Botanic Gardens was caught up in the relentless development initiated by the new government. A general campaign to clean and spruce up Singapore to fit its modern, progressive image was started. Wastelands and roadside zones were cleared of their wild native vegetation and replaced with neat grasses and instant stands of rain trees (*Samanea saman*), Angsana (*Pterocarpus indicus*) and exotic palms – all planted in an orderly pattern.

For the comfort of visitors, the edges of the main lake were cleared of reeds and shrubs and cemented all around and the swampy corner at the northern end was tamed. The sprucing campaign caught up with the corner at the northern end of the Gardens, a wild patch hedged in by Tyersall and Cluny roads. The marshy ground here was curtailed, and a second lake with a prim and proper look created. The thick hedges, consisting mainly of ferns, fishtail palms (*Caryota mitis*), wild cinnamons (*Cinnamomum iners*) and creepers such as passion fruits (*Passiflora laurifolia*) and wild water lemons (*Passiflora foetida*), growing in riotous profusion around ageing oil palms (*Elaeis guineensis*), were largely cleared. Species, such as the Yellow-vented Bulbul, that depend on these dense hedges for nesting, breeding and foraging decreased although this species still are one of the more common garden birds in Singapore.

A sad and poorly understood episode in the avian life of the Botanic Gardens,

The Pink-necked Pigeon has adjusted to urban habitats.

160

as well as the entire main island, is the disappearance of the Magpie Robin. A handsome black-and-white thrush with sprightly habits and sweet melodious voice, the Magpie Robin is a popular cage-bird among the Chinese people. Several pairs of them can still be seen here, but they are the survivors of the population introduced several years ago by the authorities. In the days of the Straits Settlements, Magpie Robins were so ubiquitous that the British colonialist called them the "Straits Robin" in nostalgic memory of the little Robin of their homeland. As late as the 1960s, Magpie Robins could still be seen in great numbers hopping on the lawns of the Gardens as they foraged for worms and insects and retreating into the dark shadows of the hedges when people streamed in with the advancing day.

The decline was dramatic for, by the late 1970s, they were practically gone from the Gardens and suburban areas. In the 1980s, they had disappeared from the main island. The cause for the demise of the Magpie Robin is still wrapped in controversy. The loss of suitable nesting and roosting sites, as a result of the clearing of wasteland vegetation and hedges, is probably a significant contributory factor, if not the decisive one.

In its present more civilised appearance, the Gardens favour species that are adapted to a parkland habitat. Most of all, the White-vented Myna proliferated – a species introduced to Singapore from Java probably in 1920. Unlike the Magpie Robin, it can nest and breed in almost any habitat. The Spotted Dove is generously represented and can now be seen ambling on every lawn and road. Richard's Pipit and the Scaly-breasted Munia appear on the grassy patches. The Black-naped Oriole, which invaded Singapore in the 1930s from Indonesia, and the Pied Triller, not present in the days of Bucknill and Chasen, are now numerous. The Dark-necked Tailorbird, so common at one time, has been replaced by the Common Tailorbird, whose vociferous chirping can now be heard in almost every Singapore garden.

The Gardens have proven attractive

The Yellow-vented Bulbul is found anywhere in the region.

to some species such as the Collared Kingfisher, Brown-capped Woodpecker and the Brown-throated Sunbird that were originally more at home in a mangrove or coastal habitat. The Collared Kingfisher thrives by being more flexible in its diet – eating lizards, frogs, insects as well as fish – and has become as adaptable away from the coasts as has the White-throated Kingfisher. The Brown-capped Woodpecker survives on ants crawling on trees. The Brown-throated Sunbird, like the more common Olive-backed, enjoys the nectar of the exotic plants such as canna (*Canna orientalis*), common hibiscus (*Hibiscus ross-sinensis*) and Indian coral tree (*Erythrina variegata*).

The most amazing adaptation to an increasingly humanised Gardens is that of the White-breasted Waterhen. A wetland species, this bird can be seen on the lakes, walking with long-toed feet on the leaves of the water-lily and cocking its tail up and down. It can also be seen in odd situations, trotting leisurely on neat lawns or even along roads and scampering away into the shrubs only when approached too closely. Feeding on insects, seeds and snails, it survives wherever there is some wet ground or ditch, no matter how insignificant. Its raucous calls have become as familiar to Singaporeans as the fluty whistlings of the Black-naped Oriole.

Despite the changes over the past decades, the Botanic Gardens still hold surprises for birdwatchers. The rare Red-legged Crake has been heard calling in the woods along Tyersall Avenue, where some Rufous-tailed Tailorbirds have also been spotted. The Grey-rumped Treeswift can be seen nowadays circling above the trees. A flurry of excitement swept through the local birdwatchers community in 1987 when a pair of Crested Goshawks nested in a conspicuous tree, moving in and out of the nest in clear view of visitors walking below. This is the first nesting record for the species in Singapore and the third for the whole of the Malay peninsula.

Especially in the evenings, the metallic "*tonk tonk*" notes of the Coppersmith

Atop its flowery perch – a Brown throated Sunbird.

Barbet can be heard. This is another colourful bird which, with the opening of the forest, invaded Singapore and the entire Malay peninsula only 50 years ago. While the visitor from northern countries looks on this bird and colourful kingfishers as desired exotic species, it should be remembered that they do not really represent the avifauna typical of the region's natural habitat.

Linger into the twilight hours until complete darkness sets in. Large-tailed Nightjars will come out, their *"tock, tock"* calls issuing from almost every tree when the night is clear and fine. Some sit on the warm tarmac and when disturbed, take off in soft, silent flight. Although the Brown Hawk-owl can no longer be heard, the lilting hoots of the Collared Scops Owl is guaranteed. The Collared Scops, originally a forest species, is becoming common in suburban areas, wherever there are patches of trees. The most awe-inspiring call in the night comes from the rare Spotted Wood Owl whose call is a sequence of booming coughs, sounding like the deep barking of a giant dog. Reverberating throughout the Gardens, it sends chills down the spines of lovers in the night.

The Gardens received a big boost when a stretch of land on the other side of Cluny Road was acquired recently, extending the boundary right up to Bukit Timah Road. Unfortunately, the cleaning and sprucing habits surfaced once again. Marshy patches, where snipes and rails love to haunt, were filled up. Beautiful and intriguing old hedges that grew uncontrolled in luxuriant variety were totally wiped out, and in their place, orderly rows of several ornamental species appeared. The area now has a clinical look and is certainly dull because lack of the variety in plant and animal life that is typical of old natural hedges and marshy grounds.

The Botanic Gardens continues to provide a haven for many varieties of birds. Although many species, unable to adapt, have disappeared, some are clinging on tenaciously, while others have proliferated in the more humanised landscape. For the Gardens to continue to

A pair of Black-naped Orioles.

nourish its birdlife, it is best that as much as possible of the local vegetation be retained. Developments, especially the construction of buildings, should be minimised, not only within the Gardens; but also at periphery. Only then can a rich and multi-faceted appreciation of nature be wholly sustained.

Singapore Zoological Gardens: Mandai Lake Road. Tel: 2693411. Hours: 8.30am to 6pm. Admission: Adult S$7; Child: S$3. The Singapore Zoo stands out in nearly every category by which animal collections are judged: variety of wildlife (more than 200 species), handsome open-air enclosures that present animals in their natural environment, captive breeding of endangered species and attractive landscaping. But where the zoo really excels is melding education and entertainment into a delightful combination that reaches out to both adults and children.

It would be hard to find a zoo with a more creative approach to wildlife display. Modern glass enclosures offer visitors an underwater view of crocodiles and pygmy hippos in their riverine environment, while polar bears swim in true arctic conditions. Spider monkeys and gibbons leap lithely through the trees, as rhino share space with antelope in a stunning recreation of the African plains. The zoo also boasts the world's largest captive orangutan colony, the result of a special breeding programme.

Animal shows are performed several times each day at the zoo's open-air amphitheatre. One features reptiles and primates (orangutans, chimps and gibbons) while the second showcases the considerable intelligence of elephants and sea lions. Feeding times of the various animals are posted near the park entrance, with the most spectacular feasts at the polar bear and lion habitats.

One of the newest features is **Children's World**, where kids can have close encounters of the animal kind with domesticated beasts – camels and cows, donkeys and llamas, ducks and chickens. You can stroke or cuddle the animals, see baby chicks hatch from their eggs, watch an Aussie sheep dog at **Showtime at the Zoo.**

work or take a ride on a miniature train.

In 1994, the zoo unveils its newest feature, the long-awaited **Night Safari** with 1,200 nocturnal animals in 47 different habitats including a Nepalese river valley, Malayan rainforest, Himalayan foothills and African plains. The first of its kind in the world, Night Safari will feature after-hours hunters like tigers and lions, as well as lesser known creatures like the Himalayan tahr mountain goat, babirusa pig, one-horned rhino and barasingha swamp deer. Night Safari will be open 6.30pm to midnight; admission prices will be the same as those for the regular zoo.

Mandai Orchid Gardens: Mandai Lake Road. Tel: 2691036 Hours: 9am to 5.30pm. Admission: Adult: S$2; Child: S$0.80. Not far from the zoo, on a hillside covered with a riot of glorious colour, is one of the world's finest displays of orchids of all shapes and sizes. Growing in a mixture of charcoal and brick, orchids clamber up poles in banks of vivid profusion, while others hang in delicate sprays from suspended pots.

Brilliant and long-lasting, the orchids are exported all over the world from here.

Visitors can make their selections to take away, ready-boxed for the flight. In cool climes, the blooms can last up to two months if the stems are regularly trimmed and the water changed. Arachnis, Renanthera, Vanda, Dendrobium and Oncidium are some of the genera on view, and each year, new hybrids increase the variety of these exotic plants.

Bukit Timah Nature Reserve: This Reserve is in the geographic centre of Singapore, only a few kilometres from the bustling city, easily reached by taxi, once the driver has understood that the reserve is where he is supposed to go, not Bukit Timah, part of the town. After turning off from busy multi-lane Upper Bukit Timah Road, the reserve's heavy, moist and dark green quietness, overlaid by the uninterrupted buzzing of cicadas, is somewhat unreal, an isolated patch of land showing how the region would look like if man had not intervened.

The reserve includes Singapore's highest hill, Bukit Timah (163 metres/

Orchids are the national flower of Singapore.

535ft), and protects, on 71 hectares (175 acres), the nation's only virgin lowland rain forest. Towards the east, the reserve is contiguous with the protection forest of the water catchment area, 25sq km (9sq miles) of ecologically valuable secondary forest.

Subsequent to intensive logging of the forests of Singapore in the middle of the last century, Bukit Timah was declared a forest reserve as early as 1884 in response to research on climatic changes after deforestations. Already at that time people observed locally a danger that is feared globally today. Over the past 100 years, boundary changes have reduced the size of the reserve, and poaching of timber and animals reduced its ecological diversity. Today, most large mammals including tiger (last shot in 1924), leopard, Sambar Deer and Barking Deer are extinct in Singapore as are ecologically sensitive birds such as hornbills, trogons and broadbills. It is to be hoped that today's legal protection, the increasing age of the adjoining secondary forest and people's growing

ecological consciousness will help stop the extinction process.

The reserve has a small parking lot, where a ranger sells from a little wooden outlet trail maps of the reserve. At the entrance, there is normally a large troop of Long-tailed Macaques demanding, rather than begging, to be fed. They pay no attention to the various notices informing that littering is an offense and empty garbage bins in search of food.

To explore the reserve follow the asphalted road from the parking lot to the hilltop. Many trees along this road are labelled with English and scientific names and give the newcomer to the tropics a feeling for the enormous diversity of plant species. Bukit Timah and the Singapore Botanic Gardens are two of the very few places in the region where the visitor can improve his skill in identifying at least a small fraction of the several thousand tree species found in Southeast Asian forests.

Singapore is home to a rich variety of beautiful tropical birds that occur in all parks and gardens. However, their na-

Left, long-tailed Parakeet. Right, crimson Sunbird.

tive home is not the forest that occurred naturally in the region and consequently they are missing from Bukit Timah. The Olive-backed Sunbird is replaced by the Crimson Sunbird, the Scarlet-backed Flowerpecker by the Orange-bellied Flowerpecker, the Common Tailorbird by the Dark-necked Tailorbird, the Yellow-vented Bulbul by the Cream-vented Bulbul and the Pink-necked Pigeon by the Green-winged Pigeon.

Some secretive birds of the undergrowth are best found by knowing or at least guessing the nature of their calls, such as the "chongchongchong" of the Striped Tit-Babbler, the fine whistling song of the Short-tailed Babbler or the scolding of the Little Spiderhunter. Also, Greater Racket-tailed Drongo and Asian Fairy-bluebird may be localized in the lower canopy through their cackling and whistling calls.

Very few mammal species have survived, but the frequently heard hissing identifies members of large populations of Slender Squirrels and Plantain Squirrels. Another squirrel-like mammal with

The Chestnut-bellied Malkoha is related to the cuckoos.

a long pointed nose is the unrelated Common Treeshrew.

The more adventurous hiker may leave the road and turn right onto the Rock Path which winds its way over slippery steps and rocky outcrops through a beautiful setting of large trees, which holds nests of the White-bellied Sea-eagle, and which are home to Singapore's only common forest woodpecker, the Banded Woodpecker. Another attractive trail, leaves the main road to the left and leads to Humpstead Hut, one of about 10 rain shelters on the reserve. This is the best place in Singapore to find the Blue-rumped Parrot. Listen for its jingling call. Or try to spot the source of the deep cooing calls in the canopy. It is the Red-crowned Barbet, one of Singapore's two members of a beautiful family of tropical birds. The shadow that races along a tree top branch may be a Chestnut-bellied Malkoha, a tropical cuckoo that prefers to run rather than to use its wings.

The hilltop is a perfect place to wait for White-bellied Sea-eagles or Brahminy Kites, and the besotted birdwatcher

can meet the challenge of identifying at least 12 species of swifts and swallows. The magnificent view over the protection forest of several water reservoirs makes the visitor forget that he is in one of the world's most densely populated countries. Unfortunately, no easily identifiable trail connects Bukit Timah with that area, and, to explore it, the visitor must enter from the east, MacRitchie Reservoir, for example. For those who have time, it is worthwhile exploring this vast secondary forest, which holds even more animal species than Bukit Timah, in spite of its loss of plant diversity. And, because this forest is becoming older, rare resident and vagrant birds such as Thick-billed Pigeons may establish larger populations.

Like several nature reserves of the region, Singapore's forests can be considered an interesting experiment on the fate of ecological islands in the middle of a sea of man-made landscape. Is wildlife cut off or will it eventually recolonise the area once the habitat improves? Can any particular species maintain a viable population over long periods of time, or is extinction programmed due to the small size of the ecosystem?

In the evenings, the sun often disappears behind thunderstorm clouds that regularly build up over Sumatra, 100km (62 miles) to the west. The chorus of cicadas changes as Brown Hawk-owls, Collased Scops Owls and Large-tailed Nightjars raise their voices and bats dive through the light of the street lamps hunting insects of the night. Just as in any rain forest, you will feel sweaty and probably be bitten by ants and mosquitos. If you enjoyed the Bukit Timah experience, consider yourself fit for the national parks of Malaysia and Indonesia. However, if you found this forest excursion bothersome, this is your chance to change plans. Probably, resorts such as those on Pulau Tioman or Langkawi will provide sufficient comfort while allowing for some proximity to nature.

Beyond the bright lights: Most visitors to Singapore, famous around the world for its clean roads, bright lights, elegant

The Common Treeshrew is distinguished by its pointed snout.

skyscrapers, shopping centres and efficient airport, are invariably trapped within the cosmopolitan city, leaving after a sojourn of a few days or weeks with the impression that they have seen all there is to this small island republic. There is, however, more to Singapore than meets the eye. Nature lovers and adventurous types will be pleased to know that a sort of hinterland exists in this small country – untrodden even by locals and waiting to be explored.

This so-called hinterland is a stretch of rural and semi-rural landscapes just to the north of the city, beyond the Pan-Island Expressway. Most of these areas are ideal for visitors who need to get away from the hustle and bustle of city living for a half-day or one-day immersion in a quiet, soothing, green environment. Here is a world of mangroves, orchards, coconut and rubber plantations, fish ponds and farmlands – all were integral features of the old Singapore. For those keen on birdwatching, some areas provide ample satisfaction in search of rarities that would not be as easy to come by, even north of the Johore Causeway. In addition, a visit to the **Jurong Bird Park** is a must for all bird lovers. Check out the chapter *Sentosa and the West Coast* page 218 for more information.

One for the birds: The **Sungei Buloh Bird Sanctuary**, consisting of approximately 85 hectares (210 acres) of orchards, ponds and mangroves, is on the northwest coast of Singapore, flanked on the west by Lim Chu Kang Road and on the east by Sungei Buloh. The area was proposed as a bird sanctuary by the Malayan Nature Society in 1987 and was immediately agreed upon by the government. The sanctuary, which consists of a variety of habitats within a small area, is remarkable for the abundance and diversity of its birdlife. It is estimated that more than 126 species of birds – resident, visiting or transient – can be seen.

A visitor centre, a carpark and a bridge across the Sungei Buloh are planned for the near future and will provide easy access into the sanctuary from the Kranji

Many species of shorebirds arrive from Siberia to spend the winter months in Singapore.

Dam, where there is a picnic area. Meanwhile, visitors are advised to enter the area along the track opposite the bus terminus canteen at the end of Lim Chu Kang Road.

Entering from the west, the visitor first encounters a series of small freshwater ponds, green with algae and surrounded by shrubs and mangroves. These ponds were formerly used for breeding aquarium fish. Some of the fish still thrive, and with the owners gone, birds have a heyday. Collared as well as White-throated Kingfishers sit on the low stakes by the bunds, waiting to swoop. Cinnamon and Yellow Bitterns stalk along the reedy edges, bursting into the air in alarm as visitors pass. During the migrating season, White-winged Terns in their white plumage, gather above, swooping down now and then to skim over the placid surface of the water for insects. The patches of woods and clumps of fruit trees are alive with resident birds – Yellow-vented and Olive-winged Bulbuls, Black-naped Orioles, Common Goldenbacks, Pied Fantails, Spotted Doves and Pink-necked Pigeons.

To enter the main part of the sanctuary, cross the ponds along the northern end of the bund and cut through the wall of mangroves on a wooden bridge crossing a charming little river. Beyond the bridge is a series of large ponds fringed by shrubs and tall grasses which provide excellent cover for close observation of wading birds feeding on the exposed mud-beds.

It is these migrating waders, of which more than 20 species have been sighted, which are the stars of Sungei Buloh Bird Sanctuary. From as early as September to as late as April, large flocks of plovers, sandpipers, stints, curlews, godwits, and egrets gather to feed on the mud exposed by the ebbing tide. Whimbrels, Curlew Sandpipers, Mongolian and Lesser Golden Plovers dominate the scene. Asiatic Dowitchers, a very rare wading species, have been regularly spotted. Great and Little Egrets grace the scene as they wade in the shallows or fly gently across the ponds to roost in the mangroves.

A Monitor patrols its mangrove habitat.

Local herons, such as the Grey, Purple and Little, are also conspicuous. With the rapid reclamation of coastal areas in other parts of the Republic, the sanctuary now stands out as Singapore's last significantly sizable feeding ground for migrating wading birds. The ornithological importance of the site is underlined by the fact that Singapore is the last stop over in the migration path down the Malay peninsula before the thrust to regions further south.

The best time to watch the waders is when the tide moves into the ponds. During low tide, most of the waders feed at the coastal mudflats, especially at the estuary of Sungei Mandai, just east of Kranji Dam. When the incoming tide sweeps over these, the waders retreat inland and swell the crowds at those ponds where the mud is still exposed. When these mudbeds are in turn flooded, the waders retreat to the islets within the ponds and to the bunds crisscrossing the area, where they can be seen as a dense, agitated community. Their shrill cries as they circle in spectacular flocks searching for roosting sites make this an exciting place for birdwatchers and photographers. Landing in unison on any available piece of exposed mud, they stand shoulder to shoulder like sardines, jittery and twittering. The slightest disturbance causes an eruption like exploded confetti as they burst into the sky and circle the ponds in nervous agitation.

Those wishing a diversion from watching-wading birds will enjoy exploring the mangroves fringing the irregular coastline to the north. Large Monitor Lizards prowl on the mud and scramble and splash into the seawater when disturbed. When the ponds were in operation, the owners showed these creatures no mercy, killing and even eating them as a local delicacy, believing that they were the predators of the fish and prawns in their ponds. Nowadays, with the owners gone, they seem to be slower in taking flight.

Large-billed Crows gather in large flocks in the trees. Dollarbirds sit, quiet and motionless, on the more prominent points. Watch out for mangrove birds, such as the Mangrove Whistler, Brown-capped Woodpecker, Ashy Tailorbird, Pied Triller, Common Iora, Laced Woodpecker, and Copper-throated Sunbird. The last named, a rare species in Singapore, are readily spotted as they flit about feeding on the nectar of mangrove flowers.

On the eastern side of Sungei Buloh, mangroves extend all the way along the coast to the Kranji Dam. This stretch of mangroves has scarcely been studied or explored and may yield interesting sightings to those who are venturesome. The mangroves here are dense, especially on the landward side, where they are entangled with an encroaching belt of grand, old sea-hibiscus, providing attractive roosting sites for mangrove birds. A plan exists to build a wooden walkway, near the projected visitor centre, across the mangroves to the sea. Unfortunately, this stretch of mangroves, from Sungei Buloh to Kranji Dam, is out of the boundary of the sanctuary. It is, however, worth preserving because this type of habitat has already become a rarity in

A Singapore rarity: the Greater Painted-snipe.

Singapore, and is of vital importance in maintaining the diversity of mangrove species within the sanctuary.

The Sungei Buloh Sanctuary is a success story for the Malayan Nature Society and nature lovers in Singapore. It is significant in that it is the first sizable piece of land to be established as a nature sanctuary in this economically booming nation since the departure of the British colonial government – a sanctuary resulting from the co-operation of a public organisation and the state.

Kranji Bund: Kranji Reservoir lies to the southeast of the Sungei Buloh Bird Sanctuary. The reservoir was created in 1975 by damming the Kranji River at the mouth and is now managed by the Public Utilities Board (PUB). The adjacent farmlands are intact and traditional vegetable farming is still practised. Scattered around the various coves and inlets of the reservoir are some of the most extensive freshwater marshes in Singapore – a relatively rare type of habitat in the Malay peninsula.

Freshwater life flourishes in these wetlands. A remnant population of Estuarine Crocodiles, much-maligned and persecuted by the local people even to this day, still holds out in the less accessible parts of the reservoir. The elusive reptiles hide in the marshes during the day and come out at night to prey on fish in the deeper waters. Monitor Lizards are abundant. Tomans and Aruans – two species of Snakeheads – lurk in the open water of the hyacinth beds.

The most accessible marsh is located near the PUB water-refining plant at the end of Neo Tiew Lane. Park your vehicle in the open space near the plant's gate. A good time to visit the area is the few hours just after dawn and in the evening before darkness sets in. White-breasted Waterhens are abundant along Neo Tiew Lane and the visitor has plenty of opportunities to watch these dainty-looking birds up close as they trot a short distance ahead before scampering into the grassy edges. From the shrubs and fruit trees of the adjacent farms come the vociferous chirpings of the Common Tailorbirds. The nests of the

A Brahminy Kite swoops in for the kill.

Baya Weavers – curvaceous, bulbous structures made of reeds – can be seen pendulating from the fronds of the coconut trees near the water-refining plant.

Walk along the bund which runs towards the north. It was created by the PUB in order to form the canal on the left which channels the waters of the reservoir to the refining plant. Water hyacinths proliferate in the canal and require to be cleared regularly. Beyond the canal is a stretch of reeds and grasses, where large flocks of Baya Weavers scramble and hop over one another as they forage for seeds. To the right is the open water of the reservoir where Little Terns fly around, now and then hovering with fluttering wings before diving for fish. During the migrating season, the reservoir teems with White-winged Terns cruising over the water while Brahminy Kites circle overhead, and an Osprey may flap by low over the water.

Move along the bund and, Cinnamon and Yellow Bitterns burst out from the reedy edges of the canal and fly away to land further up. In the migrating season, Great and Black-browed Reed Warblers lurk nervously in the thick clumps of grasses, scolding away in squeaky voices. Richard's Pippits run along the dusty track, and are accompanied, during the migratory season, by Yellow Wagtails in their dowdy winter plumage. Zitting Cistcolas and Scaly-breasted as well as Chestnut Munias scatter from the grasses on the bund when disturbed.

Look out for the White-bellied Sea Eagles and Ospreys that regularly use the crossbars of the towers of the British Broadcasting Corporation on which to tear up and gobble up their catch. During the migrating season, a few Greater Spotted Eagles can be seen circling high in the sky above this area.

Immediately beyond the BBC towers, to the left and right of the bund, is an impressive stretch of marshland crowded with reeds, simpoh shrubs and ferns and with water hyacinths carpeting the water. Here, water birds abound. Purple, Grey and Little Herons stand conspicuously at the edges of the reedy clumps or by the rocky slopes of the bund, waiting patiently for a fish to spear. Eye-browed

and Ruddy-breasted Crakes stalk on the hyacinth beds. Common Moorhens swim in the open pools and gangling Purple Swamphens, with reddish frontal shields, bills and legs, are obvious as they forage in their slow clumsy manner on the denser masses of hyacinths.

A stroll to the end of the bund may be rewarding because of the Grey and Purple Herons which gather regularly here in large numbers. They are not shy and can be closely approached. At dawn, poachers busy with their rods or carrying their catches – some of which are as thick as a man's thigh – may be encountered.

It has to be hoped for that the marshes around the Kranji Bund will be preserved, for they constitute an extensive, easily accessible quiet corner of Singapore with an abundance of life-forms that have adapted to a freshwater wetland habitat. A morning or evening spent here is a refreshing experience. The open skies and the absence of tall buildings impart a sense of space and just for a while, it's difficult to image that this is really Singapore.

A Yellow Bittern.

SPORTS

Singapore's prosperity has lead to a greater appreciation of leisure time and a drive towards better health through exercise. As a result, the island is slowly turning into a nation of sports fanatics. The Sports Council says that 65 different sports are now played in Singapore. The most popular are walking and jogging, with more than a quarter million regular participants. Other top sports are swimming, badminton, soccer, basketball, tennis, squash, cycling and golf.

Big international sporting events are held at the National Stadium (where Singapore's national soccer team plays) and Singapore Indoor Stadium at Kallang. Check the *Straits Times* sports pages for forthcoming events. The best place to watch old colonial games like cricket and rugby is at the Padang in the middle of town.

Bowling: Ten-pin bowling has been popular in Singapore since the 1950s.

At virtually any time or day, or night, someone will be energetically hurling a bowl towards the pins at any one of Singapore's popular bowling alleys. There are about a dozen bowling alleys spread across the island, many of them in the suburbs. Shoes are available for hire if you haven't packed your own, and charges are reasonable. Remember to book a lane before you go, especially on weekends. Expect to pay between S$2.60 and S$3.80 per game.

Jackie's Bowl: 542B East Coast Road. Tel: 2416519.

Kallang Bowl: 5 Stadium Walk. Tel: 3450545.

Orchard Bowl: 8 Grange Rd. Tel: 7374744.

Superbowl: 15 Marina Grove, Marina South. Tel: 2211010.

Victor's Superbowl: 7 Marina Grove, Marina South. Tel: 2237998.

Golf: Singapore is the undisputed king of the greens in Southeast Asia and the island is said to have more golf courses per capita than any other place on earth. Many of these are designed by leading

Preceding pages, Singapore's coastal conditions make it ideal for sailboarding. **Below,** rugby on The Padang.

course architects. Many of the clubs welcome non-members. Green fees range from as little as S$80 on weekdays to as much as S$220 on weekends when nearly every course in Singapore is crowded. Caddies cost S$15–30.

Changi Golf Club: Netheravon Rd. A 9-hole, par 68 course open to visitors on weekdays (S$80). Tel: 5455133.

Keppel Club: Bukit Chermin. An 18-hole, par 72 course. The front nine is over rolling hills, while the back nine cuts across wooded flatlands. Open to visitors both weekdays (S$120) and weekends (S$180). Tel: 2735522.

Raffles Country Club: Jalan Ahmad Ibrahim. Offers a choice of two 18-hole courses, the tree-shaded Palm Course or the picturesque Lake Course. Open to visitors weekdays (S$100) and weekends (S$220). Tel: 8617655.

Seletar Country Club: 3 Park Lane. This old RAF course welcomes visitors on Tuesday to Friday only (S$80). The SCC will abandon this course in 1994 with the completion of a new 18-hole facility at Sungei Seletar. Tel: 481 4745.

Sembawang Country Club: Sembawang Rd. A par 72, 18-hole course that welcomes visitors both weekdays (S$100) and weekends (S$120). Tel: 2570642.

Sentosa Golf Club: two 18-hole courses near the new Beaufort Hotel. Serapong Course is currently open, but Tanjong Course is undergoing renovation and reopens in 1994. Visitors are welcome weekdays only (S$200). Clubs can be hired for S$15. Tel: 2750022.

Singapore Island Country Club: Upper Thompson Rd. One of the world's most beautiful places to tee off, set amid parkland and jungle on the shores of MacRitchie Reservoir. Many of the world's top golfers including Greg Norman, Fred Couples and Nick Faldo have played here. Four 18-hole courses are open to visitors, but only on weekdays (S$200). Tel: 4592222.

Warren Golf Club: 50 Folkstone Rd. A par 70, 9-hole course that's open to visitors on weekdays (S$70). Tel: 7776533.

Singapore has two driving ranges.

Golf is the unofficial religion in Singapore.

Parkland Driving Range on East Coast Parkway charges S$6 for 90 balls. **Marina Bay Golf & Country Club** offers a three-storey driving range with all the latest high-tech gadgets and a 9-hole putting green. Charges S$10 for 112 balls.

Horse racing: One of the most popular spectator sports is horse racing. The sport of kings has been around since 1843 and the current venue is **Bukit Turf Club** on Dunearn Road. Bukit is one of the world's most picturesque tracks, two grass ovals surrounded by luxuriant tropical vegetation. But Bukit isn't just a pretty face: it has all the high-tech gadgets that one associates with modern horse racing, from giant replay screens to close-circuit reports from other major tracks in the region.

Bukit Turf Club has been at its present site since 1933. Before racing came on the scene, the grounds were used as a rubber plantation, rifle range, polo field, golf course and aerodrome. The first plane to touch down in Singapore landed here. The races are run 32 weekends each year. Call the Bukit Turf Club information number (Tel: 4693611) or check the *Straits Times* for exact dates. Race programmes usually start at 1.30 on Saturday or Sunday afternoons. You can come on your own – Bukit Turf Club is easy to reach by taxi or public bus. General admission to the grandstand is only S$5.

The most important meets of the year are the Singapore Derby (March), the Singapore Gold Cup (in June or July), the Lion City Cup (October) and the Queen Elizabeth Cup (in October or November). The track also features a wide variety of food and beverage outlets. **Rasa Singapura** offers hawker stalls with local dishes like *satay*, chicken rice and *laksa*. The Derby upstairs is both a sports bar with in-house video coverage and a modern air-conditioned restaurant with Western and Asian cuisine. And don't forget that the members' enclosure has a strict dress code: no jeans, collarless shirts, shorts or open-toed shoes are allowed.

Polo: Another vestige of the British Empire is polo, which is played from

And they're off! Equine action at the Turf Club.

178

February to November at the **Singapore Polo Club** on Thompson Road. The tropical setting is exquisite and the action is often fast and furious as visiting teams come in from around the globe.

There are four important polo events each year: the Cartier Polo Tournament (April), the Rolex International Tournament and Rolex Cup (August) and the Mercedes Tournament (November). The matches normally begin about 5pm to take advantage of the late afternoon cool. Non-members are welcome to watch and drink at the bar. Tel: 2564530.

Racquet sports: Many hotels offer **tennis** courts. Otherwise, the island offers a number of other courts. Try the **Singapore Tennis Centre** on East Coast Parkway (Tel: 4425966) which charges S$8 per hour on weekdays and S$12 on weekends, or the **Tanglin Tennis Centre** on Sherwood Rd (Tel: 7340707) which charges S$5 per hour both weekdays and weekends.

Squash has grown in popularity in recent years. Two of the best places to play are **East Coast Recreation Club**

(tel. 449 0541) and the National Stadium (Tel: 348 1258). Hourly fees range from S$5 to S$8.

Badminton is extremely popular in Southeast Asia, but most courts are located at school campuses and private clubs. For information on where visitors can play, call the Singapore Sports Council (Tel: 354 7111).

Water sports: Fancy a swim? Singapore is one of the few places where you can walk out the door of the airport terminal and be on a beach in less than ten minutes. The same can be said of windsurfing, sailing and canoeing. You can also water ski, snorkel and even scuba dive in the tropical waters that surround Singapore.

Sentosa island and **East Coast Park** are the most obvious choices for a day at the beach because of easy access and variety of activities. There are small food stalls directly behind the beach at both places, or you can cook your own meal at one of the barbecue pits.

The waters along the East Coast and the lagoons at Sentosa Island are both

Singapore is one of the top waterskiing nations in the region.

safe for canoeing, even for the inexperienced. Canoes can be hired (minimum S$3 an hour), along with lifejackets at both beaches.

East Coast Sailing Centre: offers windsurfers (S$10 an hour) and small sailboats (S$20 an hour) for hire. Two-day (S$90) and four-day (S$300) courses are also available. Tel: 4495118.

William Water Sports in Punggol offers waterski boats, drivers and gear for hire at about S$60 an hour. Tel: 282 2679. Tel: 2833495.

Trail sports: Singapore is a great place for hikers, bikers and runners. The island is essentially flat, which means it's almost perfect for beginners. However, at the same time, there is enough rugged topography for those who crave challenge.

The island's longest jogging and biking path runs through **East Coast Park**, a total length of 10km (6 miles) between Fort Road and Sungei Bedok. The route winds along the edge of the Singapore Straits through coconut groves, spacious lawns and tropical gardens. Those who don't bring their own food and drink can stop along the way at places like the UDMC Seafood Centre and its famous open-air restaurants.

You can ride or run offroad in the adjacent reclamation area, a triangle of vacant land bounded by East Coast Parkway, Marina Bay and Singapore's bustling outer harbour. Numerous trails lead through pine forest and open grasslands to several secluded beaches.

Singapore's best place for offroad running and riding – and also one of the best places for a walk in the jungle – is the **Catchment Area**, a huge nature reserve in the middle of the island that centres around MacRitchie, Peirce and Seletar reservoirs. The area is especially popular with mountain bikers and bird watchers.

Much of the Catchment Area is inaccessible without a local guide, but easy places to enter are the parking lot at the end of Rifle Range Road (near Bukit Timah) and the parking lot at the foot of MacRitchie Reservoir. You can also enter from the parking lots at Lower Peirce

Getting to grips with nature on Pulau Ubin.

and Upper Peirce dams, both off Upper Thompson Road. A network of unpaved roads and trails leads through secondary rain forest, swampland and around the edge of scenic lakes. Monkeys frolic in the jungle canopy and you can spot many different types of tropical birds.

Several other areas have paved biking and hiking routes: **Sentosa Island** in the harbour, **West Coast Park** near Jurong, and **Bishan Park** off Upper Thompson Road. All three have well-marked bicycle routes and adjacent paths that can be used for walking or jogging.

An alternative offroad venue is **Pulau Ubin** island, a veritable paradise for bikers and hikers with a maze of country roads that wind through old rubber and rambutan plantations. Pulau Ubin can be reached by ferry from Changi Point at the eastern end of Singapore.

Other popular walking and running spots include the Botanic Gardens on Tanglin Road, Labrador Park at the foot of Alexandra Road, Kent Ridge Park near the university, and Bukit Batok Park near the town of the same name.

The biggest boon for bikers, hikers and joggers is 300-km (186-mile) of green corridors that will materialize over the next 30 years, linking existing parks and nature reserves. The first phase of the project, a leafy path between Bishan Park and Braddell Road, opened in 1992.

You don't have to bring your own wheels to Singapore. Bikes can be rented from several places in East Coast Park and Sentosa for around S$5 an hour.

Other Sports: Take to the air with the **Singapore Flying Club** (Tel: 4810502/0200) at Seletar Air Base. Prices range from S$245–285 excluding a visiting membership fee of S$65. Hit a bull's-eye with the **Archery Club** (Tel: 2581140). Or hustle a game at **King's Snookerium** in the Amara Hotel Shopping Complex (Tel: 2246424/4488). **The Singapore Cricket Club** (Tel: 3389271), holds regular weekend matches from March until October. Access to the club is restricted to members, but visitors can watch games every Saturday at 1.30pm and Sunday at 11am on the Padang

Weekend traffic at the East Coast.

NIGHTLIFE

Singapore is no naughty night spot, nor is it the risque port of the turn of the century. Singapore has cleaned up its act, but there's plenty to do after sundown nevertheless. There's no need to feel that all the place has to offer is government-sponsored anti-smoking parties in Orchard Road and tea dances.

In fact the clubs and discos are humming and springing up in unusual locations. **Zouk** is a Mediterranean-style hang-out which has everything from boutique, cafe, wine-bar to disco and restaurant housed in what was once three different warehouses on the Singapore River. As its name suggests, **The Warehouse** is in a similar location, a huge spacious place where 1,100 people can dance the night away.

One of the hottest place in town is **Fire** in Orchard Plaza, a double disco, with a huge dance-floor downstairs while up in The Party Pub one of the best local bands plays for the less active crowd.

The **Hard Rock Cafe** has them queueing up outside and down under the Hyatt, **Brannigan's** is always packed. Jazz fans hang out at the **Saxophone** in Cuppage Road, where musicians play on the bar and tables spill out onto the pavement. The same is true of Somerset's at Westin Stamford.

The latest craze in Singapore is *Karaoke*, a Japanese invention, where you take the mike yourself and belt out the blues, showing the world what only the bathroom mirror has ever seen and heard. Choose a song, and the sound track will be played on disc while a video clip with the lyrics appear on the screen and then off you go!

Java Jive in Holland Village is one of the most popular karaoke pubs. **Gazers** in Armenian Street and **Limelight** in the Novotel Orchid are also popular and if you want to experience karaoke on a large scale drop by the **Lido Palace** in the Concorde Hotel Shopping Centre or **Kabuki** in Orchard Building on Grange Road. **Singsation** at the Plaza Hotel has

Preceding pages: Lights out – The historic Cricket Club is dwarfed by more modern monoliths; nights out – al fresco at Peranakan Place. **Below**, karaoke is often a team sport.

private theme karaoke rooms, like The Airplane which has real cabin seats.

The newly renovated area of **Tanjong Pagar** (see chapter *Chinatown and Financial District* on page 206 for more details) is chock-a-block with pubs and restaurants of all styles and nationalities. The **Flag & Whistle** is worth crawling to, and on to **Elvis' Place** to touch base with the King of Rock n Roll. Old shophouses have been converted into cosy restaurants, like **Siamese Fins** and **Pasta Brava**.

You could always take a trip around the Southern Islands to enjoy the tropical sunset and balmy night and be pampered on board one of the evening cruises listed in the Travel Tips.

On the island of **Sentosa** some attractions stay open late, and the **Musical Fountain** is an audio-visual treat. There's also a *Pasar Malam*, night market with stalls of clothes, crafts and curios. Check out the chapter *Sentosa and the West* on page 218 for more information. All over town the shops are open late, making evening shopping

a cool alternative. Over in Toa Payoh there's a night market on Mondays, Tuesdays, Thursdays and Fridays.

If you fancy being guided to several different venues in one night, evening tours are perfect. You might like to be pedalled around in a trishaw or take a bumboat ride down the river. There are organised visits to hawker centres as well as the chance to be tempted into trying the world-famous Singapore Sling cocktail. Cultural shows are a fascinating and relaxing way to learn about Asian customs and dances.

Down in the city, in Robinson Road, not everyone goes home at night. There's **Oscar's**, a brasserie down in the basement of Tuan Shing Towers for *Apres le Grind* relaxing and great food at low prices. Just opposite is a kaleidoscope of colourful activity, music, food and drama under lacy Victorian iron arches of the octagonal **Festival Market Telok Ayer** (see chapter *Chinatown and Financial District* on page 206 for the write-up).

A favourite lunch spot for city slickers,

The King is alive – and living in Singapore.

this lively shopping cum entertainment centre cum food market stays open in the evening with festive shopping from colourful trolley carts. The whole place is buzzing with activity as Boon Tat Street closes after 7pm and tables spill out into the streets so that the people can watch the world go by. At weekends Petticoat Lane comes to Singapore with an informal flea market, a noisy, fun way to look for bargains and rummage for the unusual souvenir.

The **East Coast Parkway** has a line of delightfully informal seafood restaurants where only the freshest catch is served all prepared in true local style. **Newton Circus** is not to be missed, a hive of activity next to a flyover, where local food of every kind is freshly prepared by hawkers in a carnival atmosphere of shouting, tossing, chopping and exuberant showmanship and then eaten out under the stars.

The gourmet will not be disappointed in Singapore. There's **Maxim's** in the Regent and **Latour** in the Shangri-La for incomparable elegance and fine din-

ing. Relative newcomer **L'Aigle d'Or** at the Duxton is fast becoming recognised as one of the best French restaurants in town. **Nutmegs** in the Hyatt Regency has excellent American food. For fine Asian dining, try the **Ru Yi** at the Hyatt or the **Li Bai** at Sheraton Towers.

Food Alley is fun to explore for different local food and all around Emerald Hill and Cuppage Road are restaurants and bars as well as the chance to sit in the street cafes and watch the action.

Try any of the Asian restaurants with cuisines from far flung areas of China, Thailand, Malaysia, Korea or Vietnam. It's easy to relax in any of the coffee shops. Either join the locals in a *Kopi Tiam* or go to the hotels, where the coffee house may well be open 24 hours and there's something on the menu for everyone, many of them open 24 hours. For more "eating" suggestions, turn to the chapter on *Food* page 138.

Go back in time to the elegant **Alkaff Mansion** perched high upon Mount Faber Ridge. Surrounded by glorious

Dining options abound – from chic (below) to simple (right).

gardens, this is the place to experience colonial living in style. Lovely maidens parade in *sarong kebayas* gracefully serve the famous Indonesian Rijstaffel.

For the ultimate in nostalgia it has to be **Raffles Hotel**, recently restored and perfect for a romantic evening in the gracious, relaxed atmosphere of the 1920s. The Raffles Grill with its Chippendale furniture, oil paintings, original prints and display of the antique silver used over the years in Raffles Hotel is the setting for elegant dining in true old-fashioned style. After dinner, sip a nightcap on the verandah overlooking the famed Palm Court. Or proceed to the Long Bar or the Bar and Billiards Room.

Relax over a sundowner with a view right over the island as the sun sets in glorious tropical colours. **The Compass Rose** is 70 stories up the Westin Stamford and for more of the highlife, dine next door. Another suggestion is to relax and enjoy dinner as you slowly revolve high above Orchard Road in the **Top of the M** at the Mandarin or watch Singapore's bustling harbour far below from **Prima,** a revolving restaurant which is situated on top of a grain storage elevator on Keppel Road.

For lovers of lower things, **Bugis Street** is back. That notorious nightspot has returned, rebuilt and cleaned up. The beer garden and hawker stalls are at the centre of things and street eating is the order of the night. Those who just like to watch can do so in air-conditioned calm upstairs.

Pub-crawl: Almost all major hotels have bars, many fashioned after English pubs, others simply called pubs but are really cocktail lounges.

Anywhere, Tanglin Shopping Centre (Tel: 2351041). One of Singapore's favourite bands, Tania, entertains. Relaxed setting, and a good mix of tourists, expats and locals.

Bar & Billiard Room, Raffles Hotel (Tel: 3371886). Relives the atmosphere of Singapore in the 1930s. Ask for the famous Singapore Sling.

Bob's Tavern, Holland Village (Tel: 4672419) is an olde British pub with a friendly atmosphere.

Brannigan's, Hyatt Regency (Tel: 7331188). A large, lively nightspot which is popular with the US and British fleets when they hit town.

Captain's Bar, The Oriental Singapore (Tel: 3380066).

Cheers, Novotel Orchid (Tel: 2503322). Arty and colour-coordinated, with top local bands performing.

Clipper Bar, Mandarin Singapore (Tel: 7374411).

Club 11, Mohamad Sultan (Tel: 7388583). This restored shophouse makes for a cozy bar with karaoke.

Elvis's Place, Duxton Hill (Tel: 2278543). Music from the King and from the '50s and '60s.

Europa, Changi Village (Tel: 5425617). A great place to relax and listen to great music despite the fact that this place is way out in the east coast.

Flag & Whistle, Duxton Hill (Tel: 2231126). A typical English pub. Drink and be merry or try your hand at darts or skittles.

Front Page, Mohamad Sultan (Tel: 2357013). A restored shophouse deco-rated like a Peranakan home where journos and advertising execs hang out. Music from the '60s and '70s.

Hard Rock Cafe, Cuscaden Road (Tel: 2355232). Especially popular with the younger crowd. Enjoy the easy going atmosphere and the great music from the good ol' rock-n-roll days.

Harry's, Boat Quay (Tel: 5383029). Popular with bankers at happy hour but loosens up later. Great jazz jam session on Sundays from 6pm.

Java Jive, Holland Village (Tel: 4684155). A small but popular karaoke club where there's dancing on Thursday and Saturday nights as well as on the eves of public holidays.

JD's Pub & Bistrotheque, Peranakan Place (Tel: 7326966). A club atmosphere, with an entertaining programme of local performers.

JJ Mahoney, Duxton Road (Tel: 2256225). Another typical English pub-cum-karaoke club. Request a song and the deejay will pass you the mike.

Next Page, Mohamad Sultan (Tel: 2356967). Decorated like a Chinese **An American icon.**

home; the two deejays here spin reggae, blues, funk and soul.

Oran Utan, Zouk (Tel: 7382028). Singapore's first brew pub where the beer flavours are always changing.

Saxophone, Cuppage Terrace (Tel: 2358385). Jazz rules in this quaint little shophouse.

Somerset's, Westin Plaza Hotel (Tel: 3388585). A classy jazz lounge decorated in Old Singapore motif.

The Carriage Bar, York Hotel (Tel: 7370511). Cosy bar, with pictures of carriages lining the wall.

The Bar, The Regent Singapore (Tel: 7338888). Great place for a quiet relaxing evening.

The Long Bar, Raffles Hotel (Tel: 3371886). The peanut-throwing tradition lives on in this lovely bar.

Where Else, Cairnhill Place (Tel: 7381113). Singapore's singles bar for professionals.

Yesterday's, United Square (Tel: 3550629). Take a trip down memory lane. The theme is oldies but goodies.

Zouk, Jiak Kim Street (Tel: 7382988).

Overlooking the disco, this pub is the only one in town with an MTV (Music Television) video channel.

Discos: The disco spirit has certainly taken over in Singapore. Ask a young Singaporean what to do on a Saturday night, and he or she will take you to dinner and then to their "fave" disco. Most of the places are outfitted with expensive light and sound equipment. And despite the persistent use of the term "disco" the music is fairly up-to-date, if a little on the pop/mainstream side. Many of the clubs are styled after the European model, requiring a high cover charge and a dress code that is more young/formal than far out.

Unfortunately, most of the good discos here are equated with expensive discos. Most discos have a cover-charge ranging from S$15 upwards, and more on weekends. However, many of these places have regular "Ladies Nights", when cover charge will be waived for the ladies.

Caesar's, Orchard Towers (Tel: 2532840).

Serious "zouking" occurs at Zouk nightly.

Chinoiserie, Hyatt Regency (Tel: 7331188).

Ding Dong A-Go-Go, Bugis Street (Tel: 3391026).

Fabrice's, Dynasty Hotel (Tel: 7388887)

Fire, Orchard Plaza (Tel: 2350155).

Heartthrob, Melia At Scotts (Tel: 7323969).

Kasbah, Mandarin Hotel (Tel: 7374411).

Reading Room, Marina Mandarin (Tel: 3383388).

Ridley's, ANA Hotel (Tel: 7321222).

Scandals, Westin Plaza Hotel (Tel: 3388585).

Subway, Plaza Hotel (Tel: 2980011).

TGIF, Far East Plaza (Tel: 2356181).

The Library, Mandarin Hotel (Tel: 7374411).

The Warehouse, Havelock Road (Tel: 7329922).

Top Ten, Orchard Towers (Tel: 7323077).

Xanadu, Shangri-La Hotel (Tel: 7373644).

Zouk, Jiak Kim Street (Tel: 7382988).

Lounges: For those to whom relaxation means soft music in the background, and company to while the night away, most major hotels have lounges open till the early morning.

Act 1, Mandarin Singapore (Tel: 7377411).

Atrium Lounge, The Oriental Singapore (Tel: 3380066).

Canopy Bar, Hyatt Regency (Tel: 7331188).

Clemenceau's, Holiday Inn Park View (Tel: 7338333).

Fountain, ANA Hotel (Tel: 7321222).

Highland Bar, Goodwood Park Hotel (Tel: 7377411).

Kangxi, Allson Hotel (Tel: 3360811).

Lido Palace, Glass Hotel Shopping Centre (Tel: 7328855).

La Rendezvous, Le Meridien Singapore (Tel: 7338855).

Lobby Court, Shangri-la Hotel (Tel: 7373644).

Lobby Court, Westin Stamford (Tel: 3388585).

Lotus, Le Meridien Changi (Tel: 5456632).

Beaded, braided and belting out a number at a local bar.

Palm Grill Bar, Westin Plaza (Tel: 3388585).

Tea Lounge, The Regent Singapore (Tel: 7338888).

The Bar, Royal Holiday Inn Crowne Plaza (Tel: 7377966).

The Club Bar, The Beaufort Sentosa (Tel. 2750331).

The Lounge, Crown Prince Hotel (Tel: 7321111).

The Pavilion, The Beaufort Sentosa (Tel: 2750331).

Theatre restaurants and floorshows: Theatre restaurants, a combination of restaurant, bar and dance hall with nightly floor shows used to be highly popular with Chinese businessmen who taking their clients out for entertainment. In recent years, however, their popularity has waned. The **Neptune** (Tel: 2243922) is one of the last remaining. Billed as the largest of its kind in Southeast Asia, it has a two-storey Oriental Pavilion and revolving stage.

What's a holiday without a cultural performance? In Singapore you can catch a 45-minute **Instant Asia** cultural performance staged for diners at the Singa Inn at the East Coast Parkway. Or at a nightly poolside show **Asean Night** at the Mandarin Hotel featuring music, song and dance from Singapore and its neighbouring countries – Malaysia, Indonesia, Thailand and the Philippines. Alternatively, you can attend the cultural show at the **Cockpit Hotel** on Oxley Rise and get to taste the famous **Singapore Sling**, that comes free for adults. Otherwise, catch the **Tropical Night Experience** cruise on the *Island Jade* with show included.

Wayangs: Streetside operas, like blue papered funeral hearses, streaming Hindu temple processions and musical Malay wedding parades, are jarring reminders that if Singapore is a "cultural desert", it is studded with many a brilliant oasis. Stages on stilts decorated with bright lights and painted dragons illuminate small streets.

Wayangs are staged all year, but are more frequently seen from August to September during the Festival of the Hungry Ghosts.

Come to the cabaret, old chum, come to the Neptune Theatre.

WALKING WITH THE PAST

More than 170 years after Raffles first set foot in Singapore, the island is still governed from the colonial nucleus he established on the north bank of the Singapore River. As well as being the hub of government, the **Colonial District** is also the location of Singapore's most famous landmark.

Nearly everyone who comes to Singapore ends up at **Raffles Hotel** at one point or another, usually for a drink at the Long Bar or a walk through the lush gardens. Enter through the wonderfully ornate cast-iron portico, which leads into the lobby with its range of Persian carpets. You might have a drink and a game or two in the billiard bar and perhaps a curry lunch at the Tiffin Room. Or wait till evening for a sundowner at the Long Bar, before a romantic dinner in the elegant Raffles Grill. And don't forget to try the world famous Singapore Sling, a cocktail invented at Raffles in 1915.

Raffles underwent a major facelift in the early 1990s to restore the hotel to its colonial splendour. Sensitively done, the restoration involved tracking down original plans and finding skilled craftsmen to repair and recreate the original fittings. The result is a resounding success and Raffles can take her place among the great hotels of the world once again. Opened in 1887 by the Sarkies Brothers, the "Grand Old Lady of the East" has seen its fair share of kings and queens, presidents and prime ministers, movie actors and lions of literature, as well as millions of ordinary people who are attracted to this paragon of tropical elegance and style.

Raffles City: Towering above the hotel is a silver monolith called **Raffles City**, one of the island's largest retail, office and hotel complexes and a busy hub of the Mass Rapid Transit (MRT) network. One of the office blocks houses the headquarters of the Singapore Tourist Promotion Board (STPB) with a tourist information office on the ground floor

Preceding pages, for over 100 years, The Raffles has been a welcome sight for discerning travellers. **Below,** dotted route on map is only a suggested itinerary to follow.

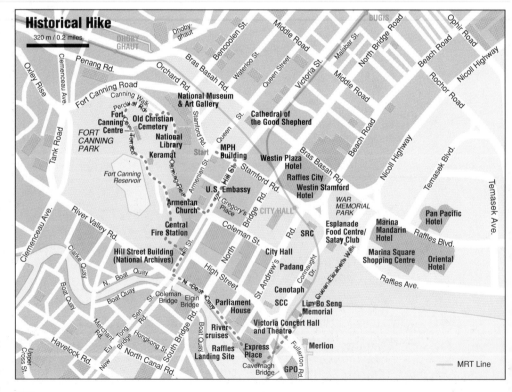

Historical Hike

320 m / 0.2 miles

— MRT Line

facing North Bridge Road. The **Westin Stamford** is the world's tallest hotel, with panoramic views offered from the penthouse Compass Rose restaurant.

War Memorial Park, dedicated to civilians from the four main ethnic groups who suffered and died in Singapore during World War II, lies just in front of Raffles City. On the opposite side of the park are two huge developments on reclaimed land that was once part of the sea. **Marina City** is the island's largest shopping centre, a huge American-style mall with hundreds of shops. Next door is a massive convention and hotel complex called **Suntec City**, scheduled for completion in 1994.

The spire of **St Andrew's Cathedral** rises up from a green mantle of trees to the south of Raffles City. The church owes its sparkling white surface to the strange plaster used by the Indian convict labourers, called Madras *chunam*, made of egg white, shell, lime, sugar, coconut husk and water.

This is the third place of worship on the premises. The original was the Church of St Andrew, designed in Palladian style by George Dromgold Coleman, superintendent of Public Works from 1828 to 1841 and the architect responsible for shaping much of British colonial Singapore. The second, including the current spire, was twice struck by lightning and demolished in 1855. The present cathedral, in the style of an early Gothic abbey, was consecrated in 1862. The stunning white exterior contrasts with the dark pews inside, and sunlight gently filters through the coloured stained glass windows making dappled patterns beneath the cooling fans.

Singapore's most important government buildings cluster at the southern end of a long green space called the **Padang**. Known as the Esplanade in colonial times, this is where the ruling class took a turn in the cool of the evening, exchanging the latest gossip at Scandal Point. After the Japanese had taken Singapore in 1942, European civilians were rounded up on the Padang and marched to Changi prison.

Overlooked by the **Singapore Cric-**

St Andrew's Cathedral – splendid and serene.

ket Club at one end and the **Singapore Recreation Club** at the other, the Padang is now a venue for National Day Parades and various sporting events including cricket, rugby and softball.

The **Supreme Court** (1927) with its stout Corinthian columns and green dome sits on the site of several earlier structures. The first was a private house designed by Coleman. This made way for the Hotel de l'Europe which was demolished in 1900 to make room for the Grand Hotel. This in turn made way for the present building.

The adjacent **City Hall** was completed in 1929, with a facade of Greek columns and a grand staircase. It was on these very steps that Lord Louis Mountbatten accepted the surrender of Singapore by the Japanese General Itagaki on 12 September 1945. Lee Kuan Yew declared Singapore's independence from Britain on the same spot 14 years later, in 1959.

Next along is Singapore's **Parliament**, rather modest by world standards, but impressive nonetheless. To be

fair, Coleman never intended the building to house a national government. It was built in the late 1820s as the private home of a British merchant and later served as a court house and various government offices before it became the house of Parliament.

The colonial structure directly to the east of Parliament are **Victoria Concert Hall and Theatre**, built in the 1880s to commemorate Queen Victoria's Diamond Jubilee. As home base of the Singapore Symphony, the building has long been the island's premier venue for opera, ballet and classical music.

Empress Place Museum: 1 Empress Place. Tel: 336 7633. Hours: 9am to 7.30pm daily. Admission: Adult: S$6; Child: S$3. The Empress Place Building is one of the oldest in Singapore, having gone through several transmutations until it was eventually turned into a stately museum. The neo-classic facade was first unveiled in 1854 as a courthouse. Later the building housed Singapore's legislative assembly, but by the 1960s it had been reduced to a

The Victoria Theatre is a cultural oasis.

hotchpotch of various government offices. By the early 1980s, Empress Place was somewhat faded and grey, a building that had seen better days. There was talk of demolition. But the tourist board poured S$25 million into renovation.

The rejuvenated Empress Place was introduced to the public in 1989. The ground floor is given over to a private art gallery, souvenir shops, cafe and restaurant, while the top floor has been fashioned into a world-class museum of Chinese artefacts – many of them never before seen outside China.

Directly behind Empress Place is the **Singapore River**, which meanders down from near the middle of the island, pouring into Marina Bay beyond **Cavenagh Bridge** (1869) and **Anderson Bridge** (1910). A walk along the banks affords stunning views of the downtown skyline, or you can hop aboard a bumboat for a one-hour river tour (S$6 for adults and S$3 for children). The whitewashed **Raffles Statue** stands on the spot where Raffles first set foot in Singapore in 1819.

Follow the river past Elgin Bridge, to where it intersects, which busy **Hill Street** is. The **National Archives** dominates this corner, a grey Moorish-style building with delicate horseshoe arches that is often overlooked as one of the city's premier examples of British colonial architecture. Further along is **Clarke Quay**, a massive historic renovation project that aims to transform an old warehouse district into a shopping, eating and entertainment district. Clarke Quay will eventually embrace more than 200 retail outlets, bars and restaurants.

North along Hill Street, past the old red and white fire station, is the exquisite **Armenian Church**, also called **Saint Gregory the Illuminator**. Built in 1835 and designed by Coleman, this is the oldest church in Singapore. A cemetery in the church grounds is the final resting place of some eminent Singaporeans, among them George Coleman, the Sarkies brothers who founded Raffles Hotel, and Agnes Joaquim, after whom Singapore's national flower, Vanda Miss Joaquim, is

Elgin Bridge spans the Singapore River.

named. Agnes discovered the Vanda Miss Joaquim orchid in 1893 in a bamboo grove behind her home. She took the purple bloom to the Henry Ridley at the Botanic Gardens who identified the plant as a rare natural hybrid.

Rising up behind Hill Street and Stamford Road is a tree-covered bluff that was once known as **Bukit Larangan** ("Forbidden Hill"). In the early years of Singapore's history, this strategic location was the site of grand palaces protected by walls and swamps. The Majapahit princes who ruled Singapura in the 14th century were buried there and it was rumoured that their spirits haunted the place. Raffles, undeterred by such superstition, built his residence there and renamed it Government Hill.

In 1860 the British built a fort atop the hill, from where dawn, noon and dusk were announced each day by way of cannon fire. Now called **Fort Canning Park**, this lovely oasis of green is a cool retreat from the tropical heat and humidity. The park still contains the island's first Christian cemetery as well as a much older tomb purported to contain the remains of Iskandar Shah, the last king of Singapura. The lookout point affords an interesting view over the city and the Colonial District. Fort Canning is also the home of avant-garde stage in Singapore, with productions at both the **Drama Centre** and the **Black Box Theatre** by Theatreworks and other prominent local groups.

National Museum and Art Gallery: Stamford Road. Tel: 337 7355. Hours: 9am to 4.30pm daily. Admission: Adults: S$1; Child: S$0.50. Opened in 1887 as the Raffles Museum, the exhibits trace Singapore's heritage and offer insight into the rich cultures of Southeast Asia. Two highlights of the museum are a hall with 20 dioramas on local history and the Sireh Gallery with its vivid depiction of Straits Chinese life in the 19th century. The gallery stages regular exhibitions of Oriental and Western art and the shop sells interesting cards and books on old Singapore.

The museum looks out over **Bras Basah Park** where many trishaw driv-

The Armenian Church, Saint Gregory the Illuminator is the oldest church in Singapore.

ers gather during the day. There are a number of historic buildings in the park environs including the Roman Catholic **Cathedral of the Good Shepherd** and the former **St Joseph's Institution** which is slated to become an art and culture centre. **Maghain Aboth Synagogue** is on Waterloo Street.

Orchard Road starts at the top of the park, at the big intersection dominated by Cathay Cinema. **Plaza Singapura** and **Park Mall** are the first of the big shopping centres that have given Orchard Road its international reputation. But the shopping's gain is history's loss, for most of the Victorian buildings that once lined this street were bulldozed to make way for the malls. Still, history endures in bits and pieces.

Just beyond Plaza Singapura is the **Istana**, the official workplace and residence of Singapore's president. The palace and its lavish garden are strictly off-limits to the public, except on National Day and certain public holidays when the gates are thrown open to thousands of curious sightseers, most of them lo-

Modern art fronts the entrance to the Singapore Museum.

cals. The Istana was built in 1869 on the grounds of an old nutmeg plantation and it served as the residence of the British governor until the island became self-governing in 1959.

Further up Orchard Road is a charming old building called **Peranakan Place** which has been transformed into a showcase for local food and culture. There is a sidewalk cafe on the ground floor where you can sip ice lemon tea beneath swaying palm trees, and a heavily wooded bar upstairs (where happy hour starts at 3pm) But the main attraction here is the **Peranakan Showhouse Museum** dedicated to the life and times of the Straits Chinese, a restored house with authentic 19th-century furnishings, clothing and other artifacts. The museum is open Monday–Friday from 10.30am to 3.30pm. Admission: Adult: S$4; Child: S$2.

There are also some lovely old Peranakan homes around the corner on **Emerald Hill**, and a row of restored shophouses along **Cuppage Terrace** including several that have been turned into bars and sidewalk cafes.

CHINATOWN AND FINANCIAL DISTRICT

The area south of the Singapore River comprises two distinct neighbourhoods – Chinatown and the Financial District (also called Shenton Way after its main street). They mesh and intermingle along some streets, but for the most part Chinatown comprises lowrise shophouses set against a backdrop towering banks and office buildings, the tallest skyline in Southeast Asia and one of the most impressive in the world.

It may seem strange to have a Chinatown in a place that's over 70 percent Chinese, but the oddity can be traced back to Raffles who subdivided his new town into various districts in the early 1820s. The marshy area at the mouth of the Singapore River was designated a commercial area while the area directly west was given to recent Chinese immigrants who did much of the manual labour in those days. More than 170 years later, the neighbourhoods endure as a tribute to Raffles' vision.

Chinatown: Narrow, noisy streets and shophouses huddle on the south bank of the Singapore River, stretching inland as far as Cantonment Road. The old neighbourhood is hemmed in by highrise now, but Chinatown is still dominated by exotic sights and smells – dried fish, fried noodles, funeral offerings, incense sticks, wooden clogs, paper umbrellas and mountains of gaudy tourist tat.

Frogs and turtles await the chopper in the local wet markets, while sharks' fins and birds' nests are spread along the pavement. In the medical halls, there are pearls to be ground, snakes to be boiled and ginseng roots to rejuvenate the aged. And at certain times of year the pungent aroma of durian permeates everything, as people flock from all around Singapore to buy the spiky green fruit. It's as if nothing has changed in a hundred years, a place lost in time, somehow disconnected from the get-ahead, technocratic Singapore.

The heart of Chinatown is an area off

Preceding pages: doors at Thian Hok Keng, the Temple of Heavenly Happiness; busy Chinatown bazaar. Below, dotted route on map is only a suggested itinerary to follow.

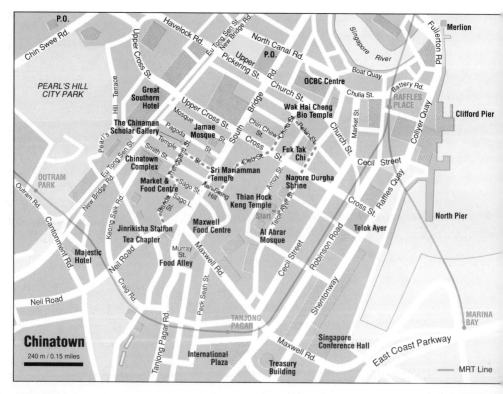

South Bridge Road that embraces Pagoda, Temple and Trengganu streets. Many of the old trades are still alive, although this may be the last generation for some. Look out for barbers snipping on the sidewalks and idol carvers who bring temple figures to life. The calligrapher sits and reads letters and then writes replies for his illiterate clients.

Upstairs at 14B Trengganu Street is **The Chinaman Scholar Gallery**, a haven of peace above the fray. This is a reproduction of a typical 1920's middle-class Chinese home, a cornucopia of chinoiserie, embroidery, opium pipes and pillows and all kinds of musical instruments which owner, Vincent Tan can play. Nearby **Sago Lane** was once known as the "Street of the Dead" as it was here that Chinese families brought their aged to die.

The basement of **Chinatown Complex** is worth exploring for the extraordinary ingredients on sale – from live fish, reptiles and poultry to a range of bean curds and glorious fresh fruit, flowers and vegetables. Culinary bargains of all kinds can be had here – if you know how to barter. Just across New Bridge Road is **People's Park**, which offers similar bargains in terms of electronics, watches, gold, costume jewellery, clothing and toys. Another good place to shop in the neighbourhood is a huge blue building called **Chinatown Point** at the corner of New Bridge Road and Cross Street, a complex that includes the **Singapore Handicraft Centre** with its numerous shops selling arts, crafts, souvenirs and antiques.

Chinatown has its fair share of Buddhist temples. But one of the most curious things about the neighbourhood is the fact that it harbours some of the island's best Hindu and Muslim shrines.

Towering above the shophouses are the brightly painted figures on the *gopuram* entrance of the **Sri Mariamman Temple on South Bridge Road**, the oldest Hindu shrine in Singapore. Brightly clad devotees perform *pujas* amid gaudy statues and vivid ceiling frescoes. Built during the 1820s, this is the annual site of Thimiti – the fire walk-

Red lantern day in Chinatown.

ing festival – a ritual dedicated to the goddess Droba-Devi, when the faithful work themselves into a trance and walk over burning embers to fulfil their vows.

A block away is the lovely **Jamae Mosque**, painted a creamy green with white trim. The pagoda-like minarets are rarely seen in mosque construction, and reflect strong Chinese design influence. The mosque was built in the early 1830s by Muslim immigrants from southern India.

Between South Bridge Road and the Financial District is a maze of tiny streets, each with its own story. **Club Street**, where the clan associations had their headquarters, was home away from home for early Chinese immigrants, as it was the clans who helped out in times of need. Workshops in **Ann Siang Hill** produce papier mache lions' heads for the traditional dances of celebration at Chinese New Year, official openings, festivals and ceremonial occasions. Here too, all kinds of consumer goods are made in paper and cane, to be burnt in honour of the deceased for their use in the afterlife.

A row of shophouses on Erskine Road has been turned into **The Inn of the Sixth Happiness** – named after the 1958 Ingrid Bergman film. This small hotel is unabashedly Chinese, from the tearoom in the lobby to the rosewood furnishings. Many of the rooms have special themes, like the Honeymoon Suite with its Ming chairs and 200-year-old elmwood wedding bed. There was a Chinese graveyard on the site until the 1860s, when the current structures were built. They were used as carriage houses, horses on the ground floor and drivers above. Across the street was a thriving open-air market where silk, spices, gold and opium were sold.

Telok Ayer Street once ran along the waterfront, but today the road is blocked from the sea by a wall of gleaming skyscrapers. It was here that seafarers and immigrants from the Fukien Province set up a joss house in gratitude for their safe arrival after their long sea voyage from China in the early 1820s. The little joss house eventually became **Thian Hock Keng Temple** (Temple of

Roof adornments add colour to a Hindu temple (below) and its Chinese counterpart (right) in Chinatown.

Heavenly Happiness) dedicated to Ma-Chu-Po, Goddess of the Sea, who reputedly to calm the waters and rescues those in danger of drowning.

Completed in 1842, the temple was built without the use of a single nail. Dragons, venerated for protection on sea voyages, leap along the roof and curl around great granite pillars. Incense wafts from great brass urns in front of altars laden with fruit offerings. There's always plenty of activity, from worshippers clasping incense sticks and bowing in prayer to noisy bargaining for souvenirs.

Further along the road is **Nagore Durgha Shrine**, also called Masjid Chulia, an architectural companion to the mosque on South Bridge Road. Notice the Doric columns and Palladian doors on the facade. Built by Muslims from southern India in 1830, the mosque is another example of the ethnic and religious variety found in Chinatown.

Fuk Tak Chi Temple (Temple of Prosperity and Virtue) is two blocks further north, near the intersection of Telok Ayer and Pekin streets. Dating from 1825, the shrine belongs to a small religious group called the Shenist sect which combines aspects of Buddhism and Confucianism. Nearby is a fascinating shop selling incense and "hell money" which will be burnt in the temple as offerings to the gods and ancestors.

The dusky, incense-filled **Wak Hai Cheng Bio Temple** is tucked away on Phillip Street beneath the towering banks. The temple combines Buddhism and Taoism, a delightful old structure that was built in the 1850s with an ornately decorated roof that depicts Chinese village life including ceramic shops, opera stage and houses. In the courtyard is a furnace where paper money is burned to assist the deceased in their journey to the "west".

Tanjong Pagar: Once a dingy and decrepit part of town, the Tanjong Pagar district on the southern fringe of Chinatown has been lovingly restored into a haven for all kinds of arts and crafts, as well as cosy restaurants and pubs.

The area has a long and interesting

history. Tanjong Pagar ("Cape of Stakes") was a Malay fishing village in the early days. Legend has it that this part of the coast was afflicted by schools of garfish which attacked people on shore. The Sri Maharajah, on the advice of a young boy, built a barricade of plantain stems along the coast, trapping the garfish and allowing their slaughter.

The 1830s saw the start of the agriculture craze in Tanjong Pagar. The area was deemed especially suitable for the cultivation of nutmegs because of the soil and the undulating ground. As a result, many of the shophouses in the area were used as meeting places for Chinese societies or workers' quarters. By the 1960s the neighbourhood had fallen into disrepair and it may have been knocked down if the government had not started its big building conservation drive. As a result, Tanjong Pagar became both an archetype and a testing ground for how the remainder of historic Singapore would be restored.

The 200 shophouses have been gradually renovated for "adaptive re-use" as restaurants, shops and offices, including an old rickshaw station at the eastern apex. The first units were put up for tender in 1987 and almost overnight Tanjong Pagar became a haven for interior designers, architects, photographers and other creative people in search of office space. At the same time, merchants have flocked to the neighbourhood.

The array of restaurants is astounding for such a small area: from upscale European eateries like D'Paolo and Pasta Brava, to modest noodle and sandwich shops. The two-storey structures – narrow yet deep – lend themselves perfectly to romantic dining. Ornate plaster facades and wooden window shutters. Pastel hues with white primary trim. Teak floors and wooden stairways. High-beamed ceilings and red-tiled roofs.

One of the more interesting outlets is Emmerson's Tiffin Rooms at 51 Neil Road, a resurrection of the place immortalized in a Joseph Conrad story called *The Rescue*. Mr. Emmerson and his sea dog tales passed away in 1883, but the original Tiffin Rooms survived

The art of tea, at Tang Dynasty Village.

until 1905. Conrad is said to have taken some of his stories from tales heard there. Nowadays the place is a cool haven from the tropical heat, with "crossroads cuisine" offering a blend of East and West.

Also at 51 Neil Road are a permanent exhibition showing the history of Tanjong Pagar and its renovation through old black and white photos, an arts and crafts bazaar selling everything from leather and silk to cane furniture, and the **Fountain Food Court** with Asian-style fast-food including *satay*, chicken rice, fish porridge and noodles.

Tanjong Pagar also has its own luxury "boutique" hotel, the **Duxton**, which rambles through eight Victorian shophouses. The design blends traditional Singaporean and European decor, a harmony of hardwoods, stained glass, wrought iron and marble. And the view from nearly every window presents a panorama of how Singapore looked a hundred years ago.

Tea houses: The sudden appearance of traditional tea houses in Chinatown and Tanjong Pagar goes along with a recent quest by local Chinese to discover their roots. Chinese films, literature and music have become more popular in recent years, Mandarin is being stressed more in local schools, and Confucian values are enjoying something of a renaissance. But the fad is most evident at the new-wave tea houses.

The **Tea Chapter** at 9A Neil Road offers a variety of Chinese teas that may be tasted and savoured in tiny teacups in the traditional way. The top floor features low wooden tables and delicate screens. Brush paintings and calligraphy adorn the walls. Customers rest on soft cushions spread out across the polished wooden floor, reading books or magazines, or playing backgammon. Customers are encouraged to linger for as long as they like. More than a dozen Chinese varieties are offered – including top-quality *bu zhichun* leaves.

Each of the tea houses have something slightly different to offer. **Cha Xiang Tea House** at 8A Sago Street tenders a special table with paper, ink

As pretty as a picture, house facade in Tanjong Pagar, Chinatown.

and brushes for patrons to try their hand at the ancient Chinese art of calligraphy. **Yixing Xuan Tea House** at 23 Neil Road pampers its regular customers by keeping unused tea leaves in containers with the patron's name written on the sides.

Financial District: The core of "Singapore Inc" runs along the waterfront from the Singapore River to Keppel Road and the great Tanjong Pagar Container Terminal. The commercial area once centred on **Raffles Place** which has been transformed into an open-air plaza with a subway station below.

The two main thoroughfares are Shenton Way and Robinson Road, but Cecil Street and Battery Road also brim with skyscrapers. The tallest are **OUB Centre** (Overseas Union Bank) and **UOB Plaza** (United Overseas Bank), both of which reach a height of 280 metres (919ft) – the maximum allowed by civil aviation rules. But there are a number of other distinctive structures. The round **Treasury Building** was designed to resemble a stack of coins. The old **Fullerton Building** (1928) – which houses the General Post Office – is a wonderful example of the Art Deco style that once dominated the district.

But the most distinctive structure of all is **Lau Pa Sat**, the old Telok Ayer Market, which has become Singapore's equivalent of Covent Garden in London, a place where people come together to eat and shop in bygone surroundings. This glorious Victorian structure was built from caste iron, in Glasgow and shipped in 1894 to Singapore where it was reassembled on the waterfront. The market was dismantled in 1986 because of the vibrations from MRT construction and then restored to its former splendour.

Lau Pa Sat now buzzes with activity from early morning to late at night. The food stalls prepare different types of Asian and Western dishes. Buskers and entertainers work the weekend and evening crowds. And trolley carts dispense goods ranging from locally made jewellery to T-shirts.

The waterfront along **Collyer Quay** once bustled with the comings and goings

Festival Market Telok Ayer.

of clipper ships, bumboats and junks. But most of the hustle and bustle has moved to Keppel Harbour and the container terminals. **Change Alley** with its money dealers was once an Asian institution, but it's now a shadow of its former self. However, there is still a good view from the end of **Clifford Pier**, bumboats bobbing in Marina Bay and sleek modern craft heading in from the Southern Islands. At the tip of the headland is the **Merlion**, the half-lion, half-fish fountain sculpture that has become an endearing symbol of Singapore.

Boat Quay: The southern bank of the Singapore River is demarcated by Boat Quay, an area of historic renovation in the same vein as Tanjong Pagar. Dozens of Victorian-era shophouses have been restored in recent years, transformed into trendy bars and restaurants with outdoor seating. The area is especially lively at night, as live music drifts through the doorways and open windows, and as the crowds spill out onto the promenade. Pub crawlers tired of the usual Orchard haunts may find the

Bumboat and buildings at Collyer Quay.

ones here a breathe of fresh air.

Boat Quay has lots to offer if action is what you are looking for entertainment-wise. Neon lights, jukeboxes, karaoke and live bands – you name it and they've got it, and more. When you discovered that you had enough of cigarette smoke and need a breather, head for the outdoor seats for some fresh air and nighttime riverside scenery – something that is not available at other city pubs.

A large expatriate crowd gathers at **Harry's** – relaxing – after putting in a hard 8-hour of work in one of the offices in nearby Shenton Way. A live band plays soothing jazz music after 9pm nightly. Pop down to the **River Bank Restaurant and Pub** where the locals mingle and croon. There are three levels of fun to choose from – easy listening oldies on the ground floor (recorded music), catchy karaoke on the second level, and breezy open-air verandah with karaoke and MTV right at the top. The pub also has an extensive snacks menu which includes *sushi*, oysters, and fried chicken Japanese style. It will be a pleas-

ant surprise to be greeted by colourful flight of stairs which takes you to the different levels.

Another pub with the similar concept is **Hyper Entertainment** where you can listen to jukebox music on the ground level and karaoke on the second. There are four KTV rooms on the third level where you can sing to your heart's content in complete privacy. For a more homely atmosphere, check out **Taps Pub and Entertainment** where a live band Roger and Silvers plays country and western favourites nightly. Acoustic music buffs can visit the **Off Quay Bar**, at 36-A Boat Quay, where live acoustic music is dished out nightly. It's a welcome alternative for those wishing to take a break from the karaoke craze.

Having enough of drinks, it's time to look for something more substantial. Feast on old art while you dine – at **Kinara North Indian Shore Cuisine**, art aprreciation is as important as serving Indian cuisine. The walls of the restaurant are decorated with the traditional art of *phad* painting. *Phad* paint-

ing is a large painted scroll made of cloth depicting the folk epics of heroes and deities.

The **River Place Restaurant** serves Chinese and Indonesian dishes under one roof; or rather one sky, as most of the patrons here prefer to dine under the stars at the tables placed outside. One Indonesian dish to try is *tauhu telor* which comes with a generous amount of bean sprouts, carrots and lettuce strips covered with black sauce. The mixed seafood grill is also recommended – especially the grilled squid.

Some wholesome dishes prepared without MSG or sugar can be found in the **Good Life Healthfood Restaurant**. Even the beverages are sugar-free as only natural sweetners like fruit juice, barley and rice malt are used. For a complete macrobiotic (diet intended to prolong life) lunch or dinner, try the set meal which includes a soup, rice dish and a cup of *kukicha* tea.

Chinese delicacies never go out of style – at least for one shop at Boat Quay. It still believes in good old Chi-

Picturesque Boat Quay is lined with food and entertainment outlets.

nese medicinal foodstuffs. **Guan Sang Co**, an old kid on the block for over half a century, specialises in products such as bird's nest, dried seafoods and Chinese herbs. Bird's nest or swallow's spittle, one of the shop's most saleable products, is hot item because of the belief that it is good for health. It is said to contain minerals and calcium, and nourishes the lungs and throat. Regular consumption is supposed to help maintain a healthy complexion and improve blood circulation.

Boat Quay affords good views of Empress Place and Parliament on the far side of the river, as well a keen angle on the wall of skyscrapers right behind the waterfront.

Along the Singapore River, **Clarke Quay** – bounded by River Valley Road, Tan Tye Place and North Boat Quay – features Singapore's first riverside festival village combining dining, shopping and a heritage inspired adventure ride. On the site are five buildings housing 60 godowns and shophouses, restored to their original 19th century style.

The Merlion overlooks the mouth of the Singapore River.

River cruise: Singapore River Cruise & Leisure Pte Ltd. Tel: 3366119. Departure time from 9am to 6.30pm on the hour. Adult: S$6 and Child: S$3. One of the best ways to appreciate the dramatic skyline, is from bumboat rides up the historic Singapore River.

Bumboats are the traditional workhorses of the river. Before the days of containerised shipping, these hardy vessels piled cargo back and forth between ships moored in the busy port and the many warehouses along the riverbank. These hardy vessels are still the best away to see the Singapore River, where the city's history as a vital centre of trade began. A succession of bridges dating as far as 1869, gives an indication of the age of some of the quarters you pass through.

Other points of interest include the landing site of Singapore's founder, Sir Stamford, Parliament House, the Merlion statue which stands guard over the harbour entrance. The tours also pass the newly restored Empress Place Building which is Singapore's finest neo-classical building.

SENTOSA AND THE WEST COAST

Sometimes, buried in the city and its shopping centres, it's easy to forget that Singapore is in the tropics, so take the opportunity to get offshore and enjoy a little island hopping. The most popular of the outlying islands is Sentosa, which has become a major resort and recreation area over the last few years after its previous life as a military base. Several other islands can be easily reached, ranging from tiny specks like the Sisters Islands to larger places like St John's and Lazarus.

Sentosa: This lush island opposite the World Trade Centre guards much of Singapore harbour from the open sea. **Sentosa** was once called Blakang Mati, which means "Back of the Dead" in Malay, a name that is said to derive from the fact that the island was a burial place for victims of the local pirates. But when the government decided to de-velop the island into a leisure spot for tourists and locals alike, it was decided that a less offensive name was in order.

A whole day should be set aside for Sentosa; in fact, there is probably enough to keep you busy for several days. You can reach the island by air, sea or land. Perhaps the most famous way is by **cable car** shuttling 65 metres (213ft) above the water, from **stations at Mount Faber** and WTC, and offering a bird's-eye view of and the busiest container port in the world, where a ship arrives or departs every 7 minutes. Cable cars run from 8.30am to 9pm daily.

The island is also served by **ferries** from WTC (every 20 minutes from 7.30am to 11pm daily) or you can take a taxi, bus or walk across a new **causeway** that connects Sentosa to mainland Singapore. Sentosa buses run every 10–15 minutes, from 7am to 11pm. Bus service "A" runs from WTC; services "B" and "C" run from Tiong Bahru MRT station; service "E" from Orchard Road.

Once you're on the island, buses and a monorail make getting around quite

Preceding pages, fine-feathered friends at the Bird Park.

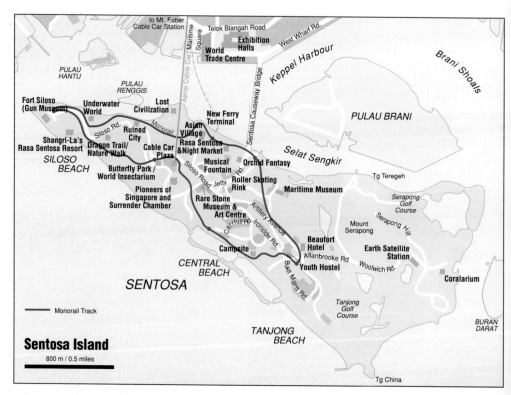

Sentosa Island

800 m / 0.5 miles

easy. The energetic can walk, or cycle a bike hired from a kiosk near the ferry terminal. Cost depends on how you get to Sentosa and how much you want to see. The cheapest way is to walk or bike: basic admission is just S$4 for adults and S$2.50 for children. Buses cost S$5 for adults and S$3 for children including admission. Ferry transfers are S$5.70 for adults and S$3.70 for children including admission. Return cable car fares are S$5 for adults and S$2.50 for children, plus admission. Basic admission includes access to the park areas and beaches, plus unlimited monorail rides, but not any of the major attractions.

Nearly all the attractions have separate admission fees. However, you can purchase package tickets. The Sentosa Saver includes all major sights except Underwater World and the Asian Village at S$9.50 for adults and S$5 for children. The Sentosa Discovery ticket includes hotel transfer and entrance all attractions at S$34 for adults and S$18 for children. For information on at Sentosa call 7438668.

The island's newest temptation is **Asian Village**, which opened in early 1993. Three separate villages cluster around the shores of a small lagoon, with architectural motifs borrowed from China, India, Thailand, Indonesia and the Philippines. The emphasis is on food, shopping and entertainment. You can sift souvenirs from a dozen different lands including hand-carved masks from Sri Lanka, exquisite Vietnamese lacquer ware, hilltribe embroidery from northern Thailand and Balinese *batik*. There are street performances by Asian cultural troupes, and once the hunger pangs start, you can dig into fresh Chinese seafood or various Malay delights.

The kids will head straight for **Adventure Asia**, a fun fair that features thrill rides like a roller coaster, bumper cars (dubbed "Tuk Tuk Jam" in a poke at Bangkok traffic) and a spinning octopus ride called "Sotong Balls" after one of Singapore's more famous seafood dishes. Admission to Asian Village is S$4 for adults and S$2 for children; rides are extra. Just down the monorail

A causeway now links Sentosa to the main island.

line is something completely different. **Underwater World** has to rate as one of Asia's best aquariums and one of Singapore's most outstanding attractions. A film shown in the Marine Theatre gives an introduction into marine life. Tanks display beautiful corals and exotic invertebrates. Nasty stone fish, sea urchins and moray eels lurk behind the rocks with other dangerous species.

Then step onto a moving walkway for a crystal clear close-up of tropical sea creatures. An acrylic tunnel leads through huge tanks containing about 3 million litres of water and 2,300 tropical sea creatures from bright, luminous reef dwellers to sinister stingrays and sharks. Entrance is S$9 for adults, S$6 for teenagers and S$3.50 for children.

The next stop on the monorail is **Fort Siloso**, its guns and tunnels built for the defence of Singapore but never fired in anger. Exhibits and displays explain the history of the fort and life as a POW during the years of Japanese occupation. Admission is S$1 for adults and S$0.50 for children.

History also comes alive at the **Pioneers of Singapore** exhibit where wax figures tell the story of Singapore from its days as a powerful Malay sultanate through British colonial times. Chinese coolies and Indian convict workers share space with Mad Ridley with his rubber tree and Miss Joaquim and her orchid, now the national flower. The adjoining **Surrender Chamber** takes you through the years of World War II with photographs, films, various wartime mementoes and wax displays depicting surrender by the British in 1942, then by the Japanese in 1945. Admission is S$3 for adults and S$1 for children.

Nearby is the enchanting **Butterfly Park** with more 3,000 live butterflies that flit and flutter about between lush tropical plants in a large enclosed garden. The adjacent **Insect Kingdom Museum** has more than 4,000 mounted bugs including some of the world's largest and rarest creepy crawlies. Entrance is S$4 for adults and S$2 for children.

Further along is the interesting **Maritime Museum** where the history of the

A ride on the monorail covers all the main attractions.

Port of Singapore is documented. Life-sized boats and precise models of old sailing vessels and steamships explain the history of trade, while the fishing industry is illustrated with traps, harpoons and all the necessary equipment. Admission is S$1 for adults and S$0.50 for children. Other features include the **Coralarium** with tide pools containing live sea creatures you can actually touch, **Orchid Fantasy** with its collection of orchids from all over the world, the **Rare Stone Museum** and the fascinating world of myths and legends in the **Enchanted Grove of Tembusu**.

More attractions are on the drawing board, features that will continue to enhance the overall appeal of Sentosa. A S$50-million water park is scheduled to open in 1994 including white-water river rides, a snorkelling lagoon with live sea creatures and a submarine simulator with high-tech video projection, animation and robotics that can emulate any number of sub-aquatic escapades. An adventure golf course – a glitzy version of miniature golf – and a new gourmet food centre are also planned. The monorail continues back to the Ferry Terminal where there are restaurants, outdoor food stalls and souvenir shops, as well as a bicycle hire depot and rollerskating rink. A short walk from the Ferry Terminal is the glorious **Musical Fountain** which comes to life each evening with coloured jets of water dancing to music. After that it's time to browse among the little stalls of the **night market** before returning to the main island on the last ferry.

Sentosa's other great appeal is recreation, especially water sports and golf. Golden sand stretches along the southern shore, framed by saltwater lagoons and coconut groves. Windsurfers, canoes, pedal boats and aquabikes can be hired and those who want an extended beach holiday can check into the new **Rasa Sentosa** resort hotel. **Golf courses** dominate the eastern end of Sentosa. On the fringe of the greens is the **Beaufort Singapore hotel** which caters to anyone interested in escaping from the hustle and bustle of city life.

The fountain at Sentosa makes sweet water music.

Southern Islands: Beyond Sentosa is an archipelago of tiny islands that lie within Singapore's territorial waters, ranging from unihabited coral outcrops to popular weekend retreats like Kusu and St John's. Because thousands of ships ply the Straits of Malacca and Singapore Harbour each year, the government has been vigilant in preventing water pollution and protecting the natural beauty of these islands.

Many of them are still enveloped in coral reefs, and the Nature Society of Singapore has started a coral conservation project to transplant reefs that are threatened by land reclamation and industry. Two entire reefs have been moved thus far, from the endangered waters around Pulau Ayer Chawan and Buran Darat to new homes off the south coast of Sentosa. Meanwhile, the government is drawing up plans to establish marine conservation areas to protect the reefs near Sudong, Hantu, Semakau and St John's Island. Two of the offshore islands can be reached by regular ferry service from mainland Singapore; to reach the others you must join a tour or hire your own boat.

Kusu Island is a place of both rest and worship. Also called Turtle Island, legend has it that two shipwrecked sailors – one Chinese, one Malay – were saved when a giant turtle transformed itself into an island. Each man gave thanks according to his own beliefs, and so today the Taoist temple of **Tua Pek Kong** with its turtle pool and the Muslim *keramat* or shrine on the hill are popular places of pilgrimage.

In the ninth month of the lunar calendar, both Malays and Chinese flock to the island. The Chinese arrive in brightly coloured boats with candles and joss sticks and then trek to the temple where they pray for prosperity, good luck and fertility. Offerings of flowers, fruit, eggs and chickens are left before golden gods in the shrine. The Malay pilgrims climb 122 steps to the *keramat* to offer their prayers to Allah. Supposedly haunted by the ghost of a Malay warrior, **Pulau Hantu**, which means Ghost Island, attracts those who love to snorkel or fish

Temple grounds on Kusu Island.

in the clear water there. Also haunted according to some is **St John's Island**. It was here that Raffles anchored before meeting the Temenggong on the Singapore River in 1819. Nowadays the lagoons, shady paths and picnic spots make the island a popular weekend venue. The two lovely **Sisters Islands** are also favourites for relaxation, as is **Lazarus Island**, soon to be developed into a tropical beach resort.

Pulau Seking lies to the west, wedged between the great refinery islands, almost lost amid the supertankers and smokestacks. But for some reason Seking has been able to ignore the march of progress, its Malay village or kampong peacefully balanced on stilts over the water. You can walk around Seking in half an hour. Duck into the Teok Brothers store, which is like something out of Conrad or Kipling. Watch the island women hang their colourful sarongs out to dry. And get one of the old men to show you his hand-carved *jong* boats, tiny wooden craft with bright canvas sails. Regular ferries ply from the World

Quiet Kusu beach.

Trade Centre wharf to Kusu and St John's, departing on weekdays at 10am. and 1.30pm and on Sunday and public holidays at 90-minute intervals between 9.10am and 7.40pm. Return fair is S$6 for adults and S$3 for children. The journey to Kusu takes about 30 minutes; with another half hour until you reach the dock at St John's.

Lazarus, the Sisters, Hantu and Seking are not served by regular ferries, so to reach them it's best to hire your own boat. Bumboats can be hired at Clifford Pier on Marina Bay. Prices start at about S$30 an hour, but you can usually negotiate a half day rate of S$100 to S$150 or a full-day rate in the region of S$250.

Boat Tours: An alternative (but more expensive) way to see the harbour and the outdoor islands is to go on a private cruise. A number of companies offer water tours that range in duration from one to three hours. All harbour cruises depart from **Clifford Pier** at Collyer Quay in downtown Singapore. You can also charter boats. For more information consult Travel Tips at the back of

this book. The section on harbour cruises and charters is on Travel Tips page 284.

West Coast: The shores of western Singapore have a dual function: hard-working industrial areas with docks, factories and refineries, and a major recreation zone that embraces some of Singapore's top green spaces and theme parks. The **Ayer Rajah Expressway** leads into the heart of the west, linking downtown Singapore with a bustling industrial suburb called Jurong. But a more pleasant way to explore the coast is by way of Telok Blangah and Pasir Panjang roads, which hug tight to the shore. Another alternative is jumping on a harbour cruise or chartering your own boat for a seafaring exploration of Singapore's western shore.

Start your exploration of the west coast atop **Mount Faber** which affords a panoramic view of downtown and the massive port area – and a **cable car** link to the Sentosa Island that gives you a bird's-eye view of action in Keppel Harbour. The cable car operates 8.30am to 9pm daily. The return trip is S$5 for adults and S$2.50 for children.

The **Port of Singapore Authority** (PSA) has several major wharf areas. **Pasir Panjang** is where cargo from ocean-going vessels as well as lighters and barges is handled. **Keppel**, the oldest terminal, deals in non-containerized cargo. The high-tech **Tanjong Pagar Terminal** pulls containers right off the decks of the world's biggest cargo ships, moving the boxes to computer-assigned storage locations from where they will eventually be placed on the back of trucks. A new terminal is nearing completion on **Pulau Brani**, a small island wedged between Sentosa and the mainland.

On average, ships are turned around in about nine hours, with the massive cranes working as many as 63 containers per hour. In the year 1992, the port handled 238 million metric tons – second in the world to Rotterdam (293 million tons). However, Singapore is the world's biggest container port (7.56 million container units in 1992) and most active in terms of ship movements (81,334 in 1992).

The overhead route to Sentosa.

At the base of Mount Faber is the **World Trade Centre** (WTC) with its waterfront exhibition halls, ferry terminal and lofty cable car tower. Major trade shows and commercial fairs are staged here, and one portion of the **Harbour Pavilion** is reserved for concerts, plays and other cultural performances. The complex also houses a shopping mall that specializes in sports clothing and equipment, as well as ticket booths for boats to Sentosa and the Indonesian islands of Batam and Bintan. Adjoining the WTC is the Singapore Cruise Centre, where passenger ships from all around the world dock.

Guinness World of Records Exhibition: 1 Maritime Square, #02-70 World Trade Centre. Tel: 2718344. Hours: 9.30am to 7.30pm daily. Admission: Adult: S$5; Child and senior citizen: S$3. This exhibition has a permanent display of life-size models, videos and computerized touchpad data banks of the smallest, tallest and other superlatives in Asia and the world.

The next landmark along the waterfront is **Telok Blangah Hill**, off Henderson Road, which sits in the middle of luxuriant tropical gardens with walkways, picnic areas and an exercise course. The opulent house near the crest of the hill is **Alkaff Mansion**, recently restored to 1920s splendour and transformed into a romantic bar and restaurant. Built by the wealthy Alkaff family of Arab trades, the mansion offers superb Asian and European cuisines for lunch and dinner.

The western end of Keppel Harbour is marked by a small cape called **Tanjong Berlayar**. British Army engineers built a powerful bastion here in 1892. They installed six-inch guns and christened their citadel the Labrador Battery, believing that it would forever protect imperial shipping. The builders could never have guessed that within a century, their sturdy ramparts would become a park.

There are actually two parks. **Labrador Park**, where the old batteries and bunkers are overwhelmed by thick tropical vegetation. Along the shore is **Tan-**

Looking south from the container port.

jong **Berlayar Park** with its rolling lawns, flower beds and a waterfront promenade. Further west, off South Buona Vista Road, is **Kent Ridge Park**. From the bluff you can see dozens of ships anchored in the western harbour and a myriad of Indonesian isles. The workout course here is popular with joggers from the nearby university and science park. Kent Ridge has its own slice of history, the notorious Battle of Opium Hill took place here in February 1942, as Japanese troops overwhelmed an Allied garrison comprised largely of Malay troops.

Haw Par Villa Dragon World: 262 Pasir Panjang Road. Tel: 7740300. Hours: 9am to 6pm daily. Admission: Adult: S$16; Child: S$10. In days gone by this property was called Tiger Balm Gardens, a collection of grotesque statues that illustrated various Chinese mythological themes, as well as notorious crimes and vices from Singapore history. But in 1990 the gardens were transformed into Haw Par Villa Dragon World, billed as the world's first high-tech Chinese mythological theme park.

That's about the best way to describe it, because there is nothing else quite like Haw Par anywhere else on the planet.

There are all kinds of animated attractions, most of them based on ancient Chinese legends. Its 2,000-seat open-air **South China Sea** amphitheatre conducts daily live performances, while the second amphitheatre, the **Four Seasons**, dominates the highest point in the gardens and stage dramatic shows. The 500-seat **Spirits of the Orient** theatre features a multi-media presentation of "Creation of the World". No theme park is complete without rides. Board the **"Wrath of the Gods"** flume ride, or enjoy a more relaxed boat ride in an ancient Chinese vessel, and meet up with Chinese mythological spirits. More than a thousand of the original statues remain, including the Laughing Buddha, which has become something of a symbol of Singapore. Hours can be spent in this wonder world surrounded by the fascinating mythology of the Chinese.

Anchoring the west coast is **Jurong**, the pleasantly green industrial area,

Chinese mythology is relived at the Haw Par Villa.

where about 270,000 or 10 percent of Singaporeans are employed. There are over 5,000 factories in this part of the island. Nevertheless, it's not all work and no play, for Jurong has a number of parks, gardens and wildlife collections.

Singapore Science Centre: Science Centre Road, off Jurong Town Hall Road. Tel: 5603316. Hours: 10am to 6pm daily (closed Monday). Admission: Adult: S$2; Child: S$0.50. The principles of flight, the animal kingdom and the complex world of electronics are just some of the subjects embraced by the 60 exhibits at the Singapore Science Centre. There is a special hands-on gallery for children called the **Discovery Centre** where various scientific principles are explained.

The adjacent **Omni-Theatre** presents three planetarium shows each day (10am, 11am and 5pm) as well as wide-screen omnimax movies with images on a hemispheric screen and sound from 72 amplifiers (seven screenings each day between noon and 8pm). Planetarium shows are S$6 for adults and S$3 for children; omnimax films are S$8 for adults and S$4 for children.

The Chinese Garden and Japanese Garden: Jurong Park, Yuan Ching Road. Tel: 2643455. Hours: 9am to 7pm. Monday to Saturday; 8.30am to 7pm Sunday and public holidays. Admission to both gardens: Adult: S$4, Child: S$2.

Two distinctly different yet equally beautiful gardens lie side by side. The Chinese Garden, known as Yu-Hua Yuen in Chinese, is actually a collection of theme gardens, in the style of the Summer Palace in Beijing. The architecture, reflecting the designs of the Sung Dynasty, harmonizes with nature. The lovely pagoda affords a glorious view of the gardens and you can take a boat out on the lake. Learn all about the medicinal value of plants in the Herb Garden, inhale the balmy scent of the Garden of Fragrance and marvel at the classic Lotus Pond. The latest attraction of the Chinese Garden is the S$6-million Yun Xiu Yuan ("Garden of Beauty") which is a Suzhou-style "penjing" garden with more than 3,000 bonsai trees.

Harmony with nature at the Chinese Garden.

This is the largest penjing collection outside China and includes many valuable plants, like a pair of 200-year-old plants shaped like lions.

Then simply cross the lovely long bridge to the **Japanese Garden**, also called the Garden of Tranquillity. Here the emphasis is on simplicity, with small shrubs, stone lanterns, a miniature waterfall, hillocks and a teahouse to induce a feeling of serenity. Feed the brilliantly-coloured carp or wander through the shady groves of the Forest of the Sages and amid the rocks and streams of the Garden of Zen. The gardens demonstrate two entirely different – but Oriental – approaches to horticulture, giving an insight into two cultures that are both closely related and surprisingly distinct.

Not far away is **Ming Village** (32 Pandan Road; 9am to 5.30pm daily; admission free) where potters and painters painstakingly recreate old porcelain masterpieces. Watch the process of making moulds, throwing and glazing and see how intricate designs are carefully painted by hand. Then enjoy the magnificent display of porcelain and take home a beautiful souvenir.

Tang Dynasty City: 2 Yuan Ching Road. Tel: 2611116. Hours: 9.30am to 6.30pm daily. Admission: Adults: S$15; Child: S$10. Take a trip back in time Tang Dynasty City, a replica of an ancient Chinese imperial city. The 12-hectare (30-acre) complex is billed as a combination movie studio and historical theme park, but with Singapore's film industry still in its infancy, the emphasis is definitely on history.

Tang City is fashioned along the lines of 7th-century Chang-An, the capital of Tang Dynasty China and the place where an army of terracotta soldiers was buried with one of the dead emperors. Chang-An was a vibrant centre of trade and cultural, and Tang City tries to replicate that tradition with activities like a Chinese wedding procession, Henan dance troupe, kungfu show, and handicraft workshops.

High walls with guard towers surround the complex, built with bricks that are smaller replicas of those of the

Aerial stunts are crowd pleasers at Tang Dynasty Village.

228

Great Wall of China. From the ramparts you can look out over the Imperial Palace, Hua Chang Pool and the seven-storey Pagoda of the Monkey God.

Jurong Bird Park: Jalan Ahmad Ibrahim. Tel: 2650022. Hours: 9am to 6pm daily. Admission: Adult: S$7; Child (under 12): S$2.50. Scarlet ibis welcome visitors at the entrance of this 20-hectare (49-acre) park which is home to 6,000 birds of 500 different species from all over the world. Acknowledged as the leading bird park in the region and committed to avian conservation, the park attracts more than a million visitors each year. Start the day by taking "Breakfast With the Birds" on Songbird Terrace, a delightful experience that takes place each day between 9 and 11am. Then move on to various shows and exhibits.

Penguin Parade recreates an Antarctic habitat for humboldt, rockhopper, fairy and macaroni penguins as well as four species of flying seabirds. Outside, brightly coloured parrots enjoy the sunshine and delicate pink flamingos wander in and out of the lake. More than a hundred species of Southeast Asian birds fly almost free in an enormous walk-in aviary that reproduces the atmosphere of the rain forest.

The Hornbill and Toucan Exhibit, one of the world's largest collections of Asian hornbills and South American toucans, comprises huge, lofty enclosures that house these extraordinary creatures – all except one, that is. A hornbill born in the park roams free, often gliding gracefully down to make an appearance at the Hornbill Chit-Chat show. The world renowned Waterfall Aviary opened again at the end of 1993 after extensive renovations. With an extremely high roof and spacious walkways, the aviary is perfect for observing birds as they fly, feed and nest in their landscaped habitat.

A relaxing way to explore the Bird Park is by the custom-designed, electric monorail system called the **Panorail**, so named because of the panoramic vistas it affords. Built at a cost of S$20 million, the elevated Panorail covers a route of 1.7km (1 mile). Tickets for the ride costs S$2 (adult) and S$1 (child).

Big-beaked hornbill greets visitors to the Bird Park.

TO THE EAST

Most Asian cities grew in ramshackle fashion, but Singapore was planned from the very start. Raffles, on his second visit to the island, sketched a masterplan for his trading entrepot that divided urban Singapore into various ethnic districts including Kampong Glam. Little India was a later addition, a suburb that grew up around a camp for Indian convict workers, who were free to farm their own land along Serangoon Road.

Little India: Over by Serangoon Road the visitor is plunged into the subcontinent, with undulating music punctuated by car horns and bicycle bells, women drifting gracefully along in vivid *saris* and the pungent aromas of spices.

Kandang Kerbau Market (KK Market) – officially called Zhu Jiao Centre – sells all kinds of colourful Asian produce as well as being an excellent venue for a local breakfast. Stalls selling Malay, Chinese and Indian food draw crowds in the morning. Light dough is slapped onto a hot griddle to make *roti prata*, served with curry sauce, a firm local favourite. Later in the day, the upstairs stalls offer the browser a chance to pick up bargains and exotic knickknacks.

Serangoon Road is lined with brightly lit shops spilling over with spices, fabrics, brass ware and glittering jewellery. Watch a garland maker entwine brilliant blooms of orchid, jasmine and ixora, the pan maker wrapping areca nut, gambier, tobacco and lime in *serai* (betel nut leaf) and a green parakeet named Mani choosing tarot cards based on Hindu mythology for a dollar.

In the jewellery shops, silver sheets embossed with parts of the body may be seen. A representation of the ailing limb or organ will be bought and taken to the temple by relatives of the sick person, entreating healing from the gods. Wander around the small side streets and look up at the lovely old facades and pretty bat windows. Watch out for mirrors above the doors, said to deflect evil which travels in a straight line.

232

Little India is chockablock with interesting religious sights, not just Hindu temples, but shrines representing the entire spectrum of Singapore faith. Tucked away on Dunlop Street is the lovely old **Abdul Ghafor Mosque** with its courtyard and small houses for Malay and Indian worshippers.

Hindus congregate at the **Sri Veeramakaliamman Temple**, dedicated to Kali, Shiva's consort, who epitomizes the struggle against evil. She is shown ripping a hapless victim apart. Kali's sons – Ganesh, the elephant god, and Murugan, the child god – are depicted with her at the side of the temple.

Further up Serangoon Road, the great *gopuram* of **Sri Sreenivasa Perumal Temple** (a gazetted national monument) is visible, showing the different incarnations of Vishnu. The annual Thaipusam procession sets off from here. Devotees, their tongues and cheeks pierced by great metal skewers supporting *kavadis* (cage-like constructions decorated with wire and peacock feathers) make their way to the **Chettiar Temple** in Tank Road. This is done in gratitude or supplication to Lord Murugan.

Race Course Road may have lost its horses, but the street is now renowned for its "banana leaf" curry restaurants. Down the street are three very different Chinese temples. The small **Beo San Hood Chor** is dedicated to Kuan Yin, the ever popular Goddess of Mercy. **Liong San See Temple** is richly carved and ornately decorated. At the back is a spacious courtyard and numerous ancestral tablets.

Over the road is the stunning **Temple of 1,000 Lights** where a 15-metre-high (49-ft) Buddha sits in a halo of light, atop a base depicting scenes from the life of Prince Siddharta Gautama. Worshippers may illuminate the lights around the statue for a small donation. What distinguishes this temple also called the Sakya Muni Buddha Gaya Temple, is its personal touch. The entire complex – including the Buddha statue and the wire-whiskered tigers guarding the gate – was built years ago by a Thai monk named Vutthisasara.

The Temple of 1,000 Lights has the aura of a Thai wat.

Sikhism: There are also several Sikh temples in the Little India area. Easily recognizable by their turbans, Sikhs believe in one God and follow the teachings of 10 gurus, from Guru Nanak to Guru Gobindh Singh. Their religion is a synthesis of Hinduism and Islam, their holy book being the *Adi Granth*. **Khalsa Jiwan Sudhar Sabha** on Kerbau Road in Little India is a small Sikh temple. For a most substantial example, try **Khalsa Dharmak Sabha** on Niven Road (behind Selegie Complex). Shoes must be removed and head-coverings are provided for visitors.

Kampong Glam: Raffles allocated this area to Sultan Hussein Shah the Malay ruler of Singapore, who built a palace and homes for his royal retainers. Today the neighbourhood is landlocked, but in former times it ran along the shore (hence the name **Beach Road**) with many of the houses built on stilts above the tidal mudflats. The name means "Village of the Glam Tree" (*Melaleuca Leucadendron*) in Malay. The bark of these trees had medicinal value and was used by the Malays to caulk their ships, although it would be difficult to find a glam tree in the area today.

At the very heart of the district is **Istana Kampong Glam**, the old royal palace, built in the early 1840s by Sultan Ali Iskandar Shah. It was probably designed by Coleman, who combined traditional Malay motifs with the Palladian style then popular in England. About 80 descendants of Sultan Ali still live in the palace, although the government has proposed turning the mansion into a Malay heritage centre.

Arab traders – together with Bugis, Javanese, Sumatrans, Malays and people from the Riau islands – eventually settled in the area, transforming Kampong Glam into a commercial hub, especially the stretch along **Arab Street** which still draws those looking for bargains. Settle on a mutually agreed price for *batik* cloth, either in *sarong* lengths as worn by the Malays, or fashioned into delightful clothes, table linen and paintings. Baskets of every shape, size and colour are piled on the pavement and

Quiet morning in Kampong Glam.

234

hanging from the eves. There's leatherware and ethnic jewellery too, as well as gold and silver, *songket* fabric, prayer mats and alcohol-free perfumes.

Dominating the *kampong* skyline is the great golden bulk of **Sultan Mosque** (the largest mosque in Singapore) where the *muezzin* calls the faithful to prayer five times a day, the women to their enclave upstairs, the men to the main prayer hall. With its glorious golden domes and soaring minaret, this is one of the loveliest and the most important place of Muslim worship in Singapore.

Kampong Glam has several other beautiful mosques. At the corner of Jalan Sultan and Victoria Street is the **Malabar Muslim Jama-Ath Mosque**, a quiet place of worship with a bygone ambience that harkens back to the era when the *kampong* was founded. The nation's oldest **Muslim cemetery** lies in tranquillity beneath fragrant frangipani trees a little further along Victoria Street.

Hajjah Fatimah Mosque is just off Beach Road. The structure is named after a faithful Muslim woman who, after her husband's death, ran his shipping business so well that the proceeds enabled her to build the mosque on the site of their home.

Bugis Street: Arguably Singapore's most famous (or infamous) attraction until it was demolished some years back to make way for an underground station, Bugis Street is back in its new guise as **Bugis Junction**. Known for its delicious street food, spontaneous entertainment and uninhibited transvestites in the days gone by, the resurrected Bugis lies on the western edge of Kampong Glam, at the corner of Rocher Road and Victoria Street.

The old shophouses have been restored to pristine beauty and many of the original hawkers have returned to peddle Chinese and Malay food again. The government has banned transvestite shows, but there are provocative musical reviews each night at the **Boom Boom Room** on Albert Street. However, it remains to be seen whether the atmosphere of the old Bugis Street can be recreated.

The Sultan Mosque is Singapore's largest.

Geylang Serai: Although it's not one of the original districts established by Raffles, Geylang has a strong ethnic flavour. More than Kampong Glam, this is the heart of Malay society and culture in Singapore, and home to much of the island's best Malay shops and food. Geylang is 3km (2 miles) east of Kampong Glam by way of Victoria Street and Kallang Road. You can also reach it by alighting at Paya Lebar MRT and walking two blocks south along Paya Lebar Road.

Originally covered in coconut or rubber plantations and lemon grass fields, by the early 20th century Geylang had become thoroughly urbanized with rows of two-and-three-story Victorian shophouses similar to those found in Chinatown and Kampong Glam. Today the heart of Geylang is the section of **Geylang Road** between Jalan Eunos and Aljunied Road, lined with numerous restaurants and shops that are often open until late at night.

New on the scene is the **Malay Village** opposite Paya Lebar MRT station.

The complex draws together various aspects of Malay art, music, history and food into a setting comprised of traditional *bambung panjang* **architecture** – wooden and thatched-roof buildings with high-pitched roofs and steep, slightly flared sides. The village is open daily 10am to 10pm. Admission is free.

East Coast

Millions of visitors have their first interface with Singapore while travelling into town from Changi Airport along the lush east coast. The area could be aptly described as Singapore's "riviera" with coconut groves and white-sand beaches on one side of the coastal highway, and expensive condominium blocks on the other. The east coast is packed on weekends as Singaporeans escape for a day at the beach, but during the week the beaches and picnic areas are virtually deserted.

The part of the east coast closest to

Many of Geylang's casual eateries open till the wee hours.

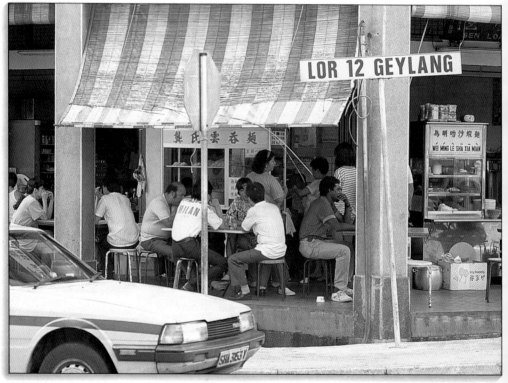

downtown is dominated by the **Kallang** sports and entertainment complex. Major sporting events and National Day celebrations are staged in the massive National Stadium, while the wedge-shaped Singapore Indoor Stadium plays host to both sports and concerts. Kallang Theatre is the island's main venue for large stage productions, with visiting shows from London and Broadway.

East Coast Park stretches for more than 10km (6 miles) along the coast between Marina Bay and Changi Airport. Fringed with casuarinas, coconut palms and flowering trees, the park affords superb views of ships anchored in the Singapore Strait and the nearby Indonesia islands. The sea breeze blows gently and it's peaceful enough for birds to flock to special high-grass sanctuaries. The waves are inviting and the fresh sea air is an invigorating contrast to the still city heat and humidity.

Picnic tables and barbecue pits are set up under the trees, and as always in Singapore, there plenty of eating places, from burgers and pizza to mouth-watering local seafood. The beach does tend to be crowded on weekends, but there's always plenty of space for your beach blanket in the coconut groves and wooded areas behind the shore.

Like Sentosa, there is plenty to keep you occupied. The **East Coast Sailing Centre** (Tel: 4495118) offers windsurfers (S$10 per hour) and small sailboats (S$20 per hour) for hire. Two-day and four-day sailing courses and scuba diving trips are available.

Cycles can be hired from several kiosks in the park, including mountain bikes, children's and tandem models. There is a well-marked bike path along the coast, or you can go "off road" along the dirt and gravel trails of the reclaimed land beyond the western terminus of the bike path. Other recreational diversions include the tennis courts, golf driving range, fitness course and ten-pin bowling alley.

A lot of people come to the East Coast just to eat, especially at the famous UDMC Seafood Centre near the swimming lagoon. The specialities range from

Shady spot in East Coast Park.

steamed garupa fish in ginger and soya sauce, to chili crab and grilled prawns.

Big Splash: 902 East Coast Parkway. Tel: 3451211. Hours: Noon to 5.45pm on weekdays; 9am to 5.45pm on weekendsand public holidays; 10am to 5.45pm on school holidays. Admission: Adult: S$3; Child: S$2.

The largest water slides in Southeast Asia are featured at Big Splash, an aquatic fun park in East Coast Park. There is also a Wave Pool with counterfeit whitecaps and a Flow Pool that mimics the pull of a strong current. Another pool and slide area is set aside for small children.

Singapore Crocodilarium: 730 East Coast Parkway. Tel: 4473722. Hours: 9am. to 5.30pm. Admission: Adult: S$2; Child: S$1.

The Crocodilarium is also in the western part of the park, near the Fort Road exit. Great indolent beasts with gaping jaws and gnarled backs slumber in the murky water. The two-foot babies are almost cute, especially when they're lying on top of each other. There are more than a thousand live, a skeleton to study and eggs too. Of course, the souvenir shop is crammed with crocodile accessories. Feeding times are Tuesday and Thursday at 11am.

Changi: Before the international airport was opened in the early 1980s, Changi village was the only reason to venture to the far eastern shore of Singapore. This far corner of the island is full of memories and has retained some of the calmer atmosphere of Singapore's earlier years.

The Japanese Imperial Army developed a **POW camp** at Changi after they captured Singapore in early 1942 after a 70-day march down the Malay Peninsula. The camp became a notorious place where both military and civilian prisoners were interned by the thousands. Many of the POWs were sent to work on the infamous bridge over the River Kwai in Thailand, but those who remained at Changi weren't much better off. They had to endure horrible conditions, described in a number of poignant books including *King Rat* by James Clavell.

The historic prison chapel at Changi.

Changi Prison Chapel and Museum: Main entrance, Changi Prison. Hours: 9.30am to 4.30pm. Monday to Saturday; closed Sunday and public holidays. Services: 5.30pm and 6.30pm Sunday.

There is still a Changi Prison, but it's now a place for modern hard-core criminals. All that remains of the POW camp is the Changi Prison Chapel and the adjacent museum where drawings by W.R.M. Haxworth, photographs by George Aspinall and other wartime memorabilia are on display. Life as a POW is depicted in searing clarity. The courage and undaunted spirit of those who suffered and died under occupation is remembered. Fresh flowers from the garden and small messages of appreciation are left in the chapel, a replica of those built and used for worship in wartime.

The famous **Changi Murals**, painted and recently restored by Stanley Warren, are to be found in St. Luke's Chapel at the Selarang Barracks off Martlesham Road, another peaceful place for reflection upon the effect of the war in the Far

East. Yet another POW tribute is housed at the **Meridien Changi Hotel** where there is a permanent exhibition of Aspinall's photos, taken and developed in great danger while he was interned by the Japanese.

Changi Beach is a short but pleasant stretch of sand with views across the water to Malaysia and Pulau Tekong island, which is a Singapore military training area. The beach is peaceful and fairly deserted during the week, but full of joyful activity at weekends. The nearby wharf offers ferry service to Pulau Ubin (Singapore's second largest island) and Tanjung Belungkor on the Malaysian mainland.

Around the northeast coast is Pasir Ris, end of the eastern MRT line and home to an excellent nature reserve called **Pasir Ris Park**. The reserve protects an area of mangrove swamp, where many migrating shore birds feed and build their nests. A wooden boardwalk leads across the mudflats and brackish ponds, with information boards that give descriptions of the flora and fauna.

Changi Beach bench with a view of Pulau Ubin.

Singapore Changi Airport was opened in July 1981. Today, it is linked directly to 109 cities in 53 countries. With its capacity at 24 million passengers a year, and over 1,900 flights a week, Singapore Changi Airport is the only Asia/Pacific airport with handling capacity for international passengers. Its two terminals (called T1 and T2) can each handle 5,000 passengers per hour during peak hours. With passenger traffic escalating to such heights, this airport has been conceived for travellers' maximum comfort and convenience. So much so that it has been acclaimed as "a city within a city". Arrival and departure routes are clearly marked and processing facilities easily located. The airport's baggage handling system is capable of sorting 10,700 bags per hour.

For passengers travelling between T1 and T2, there is the high-speed automated "Changi Skytrain". This system, the first of its kind in the East, transport passengers between both terminals in the space of just one minute, compared to a walking distance of 15 minutes.

The Home Country Direct Service telephones links the traveller to an operator in his own country. Or dial directly to 180 overseas destinations through the credit card payphones. For business travellers, the Business Centre, the first in Asian airport, provides a comprehensive range of business communications and secretarial services.

Singapore's reputation as a shoppers' paradise begins here. With 95 shops selling everything from cosemetics to candies, tobacco to toys, liquors to lingerie, the traveller can easily fill up her shopping bags here. With prices closely monitored by Civil Aviation Authority of Singapore (CAAS), there is the assurance of quality at competitive prices.

For hungry traveller, cuisines that cater to different palates are dished up in the nine restaurants. Other facilities include money changing, banking and postal services, photo-developing, hairdressing outlets, even a supermarket. There are also specially designed telephones, toilets, ramps and elevators for the disabled visitors.

Departure terminal at Changi Airport.

The new master plan for the airport will call for a third passenger terminal to meet with the increase in air traffic. Currently, reclamation of land for another terminal complex and the third runway has began.

Punggol village on the northeast coast is a good place for seafood, with outdoor cafes arranged along the main street and waterfront. This is also the place to head if you want to water ski. William Water Sports (tel: 282 6879) offers boats, drivers and water skiing gear at about S$60 an hour. Boats can also be hired to explore the offshore islands and Johor Strait.

Pulau Ubin: Opposite the eastern tip of Singapore is Pulau Ubin, which basks in the Johor Strait within a stone's throw of the Malaysian coast. A 15-minute boat ride from **Changi Jetty** ($1) is all it takes to reach Ubin. Alternatively, private arrangements with boat-owners can be made from Punggol Point.

Left behind by rapid developments on the main island, Ubin has become the last stronghold of old Singapore. De-spite scars caused by heavy quarrying in some parts of the island, its pastoral charm remains intact, a tapestry of sandy roads, prawn farms, abandoned rubber plantations and coconut groves.

The island is also one of Singapore's last great nature areas, with vast tracts of secondary jungle and mangrove swamp that sustain a wide variety of animals such as the flying fox, monitor lizard, crested goshawk, ruby-cheeked sunbird, buffy fish owls and various types of egrets and herons. Most visitors walk around Ubin, but you can hire bikes or taxis from near the ferry pier.

Fish farming from floating plastic platforms close to the shore and prawn farming in ponds are burgeoning industries and a new source of income for the inhabitants of Ubin. Simple accommodation and delicious seafood are available, and the best spot for both is the **Pulau Ubin Seafood House**, located on stilts over the Straits of Johor at the northwestern corner of the island. Sit back and relax while you wash down tasty garlic prawns with a cold Tiger beer.

Ubin's rural facade.

JOHOR AND THE RIAU ISLANDS

Singapore shares many cultural and historical links with its neighbours, the Malaysian state of Johor to the north and the Indonesian islands of the Riau archipelago in the south. In fact, for thousands of years before the arrival of Raffles and the British, the three areas were part of a single socio-political entity that encompassed most of Peninsular Malaysia and the islands in the Straits of Malacca. As in other parts of the developing world, it was European intervention that broke the areas into separate political spheres, a factor that was reinforced by the independence of Singapore, Malaysia and Indonesia after the World War II.

But in the wake of Southeast Asia's economic boom and the smoothing of diplomatic relations over the last decade, Singapore once again finds itself moving closer to its neighbours in terms of business and culture. There was always some cross-border trade and travel, but the movement of goods and people has accelerated rapidly in recent years behind a comprehensive plan called the "growth triangle" concept that is being actively endorsed by the governments of Singapore, Johor and Riau.

The concept is based on a mutual exchange of natural and human resources. Singapore has limited space, an acute labour shortage and finite energy and water, but the island-state can offer a bounty of technological expertise and investment capital. Johor and Riau, on the other hand, have abundant land, large and economical work forces, and ample natural resources. The idea is to combine these scattered virtues into a stronger whole.

But the growth triangle concept reaches beyond trade and industry into the realm of tourism, for another important goal is the development of the more scenic parts of the Riau islands and mainland Johor into tropical beach and golf resorts using Changi Airport in Singapore as an international gateway.

Singapore's most important interface with Malaysia is the city of Johor Bahru, just across the causeway from Woodlands. Affectionately called "JB" by residents and visitors alike, the city isn't anything like the drowsy, poverty stricken "border towns" you find in other parts of the developing world. What you find instead is a bustling city of half a million souls with a fierce tradition of self-reliance, the capital of a state that is now well on its way to becoming Malaysia's third most important industrial centre (after the Klang Valley and Penang) with a thriving economy based on the assembly of electronics and computers.

Johor Bahru also stands apart from its frontier counterparts in other parts of the world because its heritage is so astoundingly different. It was a sleepy waterfront village called Tanjung Puteri until Sultan Abu Bakar, the great Rajah of Temenggong, moved his

---

Preceding pages, cruising the islands in a chartered yacht is the *only* way to travel. **Left**, net checking is an important task.

royal capital from Singapore to the mainland in 1866 as part of a strategy to avoid increasing British hegemony on the island.

By the 1890s, the entire royal family and all government offices had moved to the re-christened Johor Bahru. In keeping with Abu Bakar's fascination with European civilization, his new capital became a thoroughly modern town with impressive public buildings and state-of-the-art technology. The sultan also kept his own army, separate from British forces or the local police. In fact, Johor Bahru didn't even become a border town until 1965, when Singapore broke away from the newly independent Federation of Malaysia.

The **Riau Archipelago** of Indonesia was severed from Singapore and Malaya in the early 19th century when the British and Dutch carved the area into separate colonial domains. The islands are now part of Riau Province, which also includes the Lingga Archipelago further south, a large slice of southeastern Sumatra and secluded island groups in the South China Sea like the Natunas with their vast natural gas deposits. The province has more than 3,200 islands – roughly a quarter of all the islands in Indonesia – but many of them are small and uninhabited. Total province population is approximately 2.5 million, however that figure could reach 3 million by the turn of the century.

Riau is considered one of the heartlands of Malay culture. The islands were once part of a vast Malay empire founded by Sultan Parameswara at Malacca in 1402. With the arrival of the Portuguese in the early 16th century, the sultan fled south, establishing new capitals at Johor and then Penyengat island in Riau. Although the region later evolved into separate sultanates, it was essentially one cultural and economic zone until the British and Dutch divided the area amongst themselves.

Batam and **Bintan**, the most important islands, are only a short distance from Singapore by boat. In fact, you can often see the dark green outline of the two islands from Singapore's southern shore. Other important islands include Karimun (which can also be seen from Singapore), Lingga and Singkep.

While most of the Riau islands remain quaint tropical backwaters, change has come swiftly to Batam and Bintan behind a rush of billions of dollars in investment funds and hundreds of thousands of immigrants from other parts of Indonesia who have come to Riau in search of work and a better life. Batam is being transformed into the industrial heartland of Riau and a weekend retreat from Singapore with luxury condos set around golf courses. Bintan, on the other hand, has been earmarked for development into a major beach resort along the lines of Nusa Dua in Bali.

Container ship off Singapore.

ACROSS THE CAUSEWAY: JOHOR

Lying just across the causeway from Singapore, Johor Bahru is the first interface with Malaysia for millions of visitors each year. Singaporeans flock to "JB" for the various recreational opportunities in the Johor area (including golf and beaches) as well as the tasty seafood and bargain shopping. Restaurants, supermarkets, department stores and service stations tend to be leagues cheaper than back home. Meanwhile, many Johor residents work in Singapore. Which means the causeway is often strained to capacity, with waits of two or three hours on holiday weekends.

The transport infrastructure is being upgraded to deal with the increased flow. The Malaysian government has given M$93 million for improvements at Senai International Airport in JB, while a second crossing between Singapore and Johor (this time a bridge) is expected to

be finished by the late 1990s. There's already talk of a third crossing and an underwater link with the Singapore's Mass Rapid Transit (MRT) system that would put JB within a smooth half-hour ride from Orchard Road.

The stark white facade of the **Istana Besar** (or Grand Palace) looks out over the wide Straits of Johor, no more than a five-minute drive from the Malaysian side of the causeway. The rambling structure was commissioned by Abu Bakar in 1864 as the primary royal residence. Over the last century it has hosted royalty from around the globe, including the Duke of Edinburgh (Queen Victoria's son), Archduke Franz Ferdinand of Austria (on whose behalf World War I was started) and the future King Edward VIII of England (who abdicated to marry Wallis Simpson).

While the Istana Besar remains in royal hands, it no longer a residence as such. Instead, its doors were thrown open to the general public in 1991 as a dazzling museum dedicated to the golden age of Johor.

Dotted route on map is only a suggested itinerary to follow.

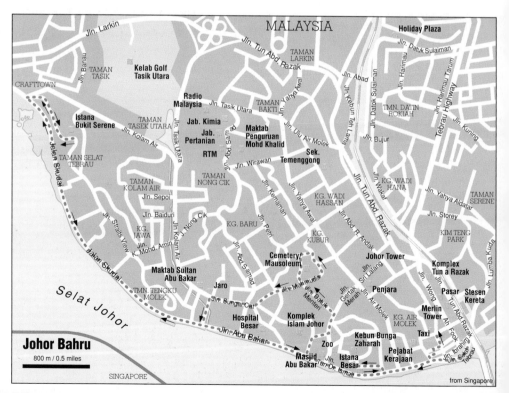

It's no exaggeration to say that there is no other collection in Southeast Asia quite like this one. The experience is reminiscent of visiting the aristocratic homes of rural England and presents a very rare opportunity to study the everyday life of a typical Asian royal family (not something you can do in, say, Thailand or Japan).

The first stop on the palace tour is the **Dewan** (audience hall) which has been transformed into a gallery detailing the history of the Johor sultans. One of the displays says that Abu Bakar "worked energetically for the advancement of Johor during his lifetime" and that he visited Europe on several occasions "to study developments and advancements in knowledge" and to establish good relations with the royal houses of Europe. In fact, the sultan died in London in 1895 during one such visit. Many of the sultan's prized possessions are on display – a medal from King Kalakaua of the Hawaiian Islands received in 1874 and the Order of the Rising Sun from the Meiji Emperor of Japan.

Nightlife in JB is surprisingly good.

But the highlight of the tour is undoubtedly a stroll through the **Grand Palace** itself. It takes a good hour to inspect everything and read all the plaques. The four-poster beds in the **State Bedrooms** are made from teak with Corinthian-style columns fashioned by a master craftsman in England during the 1860s. They are still used for the lying-in-state of deceased members of the royal family. Further down the hall is the opulent **Reception Room**, with a Baccarat crystal table and matching crystal chairs. The nearby **Throne Room**, with its matching guilt thrones, is used each year for investiture ceremonies on the sultan's birthday. Yet the crowning glory of the palace is the **Banqueting Room**, which can match the opulence almost anything found in Europe.

The last part of the tour takes you through numerous **royal collections** – although it's said that only 80 percent of the hoard is on display. Of particular interest are the traditional Malay hand arms (*keris, badiks* and *sundangs*) and the splendid assembly of state regalia

and gold. In a separate wing is an exihibition of royal hunting trophies, which show the amazing wealth of wildlife that once prowled the jungles and plantation lands of rural Johor – including a rare Sumatran rhino shot at Mersing in 1928 and a tiger dispatched just outside Johor Bahru in 1921.

Surrounding the palace are the **Istana Gardens**, with rolling parkland, immaculate lawns and several flower gardens. Just uphill from the Dewan is a Japanese garden and tea house presented by Crown Prince Hirohito on the occasion of his state visit to Malaysia in 1936. The western part of the gardens is taken up by the small but interesting **Johor Zoo**, with many native Malaysian species.

The next landmark along the waterfront is **Sultan Abu Bakar Mosque**, one of the most impressive places of worship in all Malaysia. Abu Bakar laid the foundation stone in 1892, yet died before the mosque was finished eight years later. The architecture is a bizarre blend of Italian rococo, classical Greek and traditional Muslim styles, painted a faint yellow with white trim, yet the overall effect is surprisingly fluid.

Non-Muslims are barred from entering the mosque, but you may be able to sneak a peak through one of the doorways. Be sure to remove your shoes if you invited to venture inside. The interior is endowed with Corinthian columns, crystal chandeliers and wall-to-wall carpets. At the front of the main hall are a fabulously ornate gilt *minbar* (pulpit) with a clock set in the face, and an ancient grandfather clock. Hawkers frequent the mosque grounds selling prayer rugs, velour wall hangings, postcards, knock-off watches and other souvenirs.

At the northwestern end of the waterfront is **Istana Bukit Serene**, home of the present ruler, His Majesty Sultan Iskandar. The huge complex is off-limits to the general public, but you can get a good view of the palace from Jalan Skudai (which runs along the waterfront) or Straits View Road.

Bukit Serene's design is something of a cross between a Japanese railway sta-

The distinctive Sultan Abu Bakar Mosque.

tion and a national park lodge in the Rocky Mountains: thick stone walls surmounted by a green-tiled roof and a 350-metre-high (1,148ft) stone tower. The building is a good example of the rustic Art Deco popular in the late 1930s when the palace was built. The massive grounds contain a private air strip, huge satellite dish, orchid garden and menagerie.

The skyline of **downtown** JB changes by the day as new high-rise buildings take shape. With so much construction, the place has a real boom-town feel – muddy streets, platoons of sweaty workers and a constant cacophony of jackhammers and pile drivers. At the hub of all the activity are Johor's newest landmarks: the luxury Puteri Pan Pacific Hotel and adjacent shopping malls like Plaza Kotaraya which features the same modern air-conditioned ambience and eclectic shopping you find along Singapore's Orchard Road.

Yet the skyline is still dominated by a structure more than half a century old. **Bangunan Sultan Ibrahim** rests on the crest of Bukit Timbalan hill, a 64-me-

tre-high (210-ft) hulk of a building that contains the State Council Chamber and Secretariat as well as numerous other government offices. The overall design is called "Saracen" – great arches and columns and enclosed stone balconies – similar to the public buildings built in Cairo during the 1930s and faintly reminiscent of the Moorish architecture of southern Spain. A silver crescent and star crowns the central tower, while a gold seal of the State of Johor marks the massive front doors. The ceiling of the foyer is covered in mosaic tiles.

Unfortunately, the open-air gallery at the top of the tower is no longer open to the public. With a little cajoling, you can usually persuade one of the security guards to ask permission for a trek to the top. The view is magnificent, looking out over downtown Johor and across the strait to Singapore. The local office of the Malaysian Tourist Promotion Board (MTPB) is located on the fourth floor.

Amid the hustle and bustle of the downtown district are a remnants of old Johor. The waterfront area behind **Jalan**

Unrestricted view of JB from Bukit Serene.

Ibrahim and much of **Jalan Wong Ah Fook** are clusters of old shophouses, where Chinese and Indian traders flog everything from spices and joss sticks to tailored suits and the latest colour TVs. Mixed in among the shops are cheap Chinese restaurants and Indian cafes where "banana leaf" curry and *roti* are the specialties.

In the shadow of the new skyscrapers are an elaborate Hindu temple called **Rajamariamman Kovil** ("Tokong Hindu" in Malay) and an old and venerable Chinese **Taoist shrine** ("Tokong Cina"), both along Jalan Terus. Crowning the crest of the nearby hill is the gleaming white spire of **St Joseph's Catholic Church**. The **Pasar Besar** (central market) and the old colonial train station are in this same neighbourhood.

Residents tend to browse the modern shopping malls around the Pan-Pacific, but there are several good **handicraft centres** which cater to the tourist trade. One of the better known outlets is **JARO** (Johor Area Rehabilitation Organization) with a showroom and workshop on Jalan Sungai Chat (Tel: 230739) where handicapped people make cane furniture, soft toys, rattan baskets and smocking. One of their other specialties is customized binding: they rebind old books or create personalized diaries, photo albums and address books.

In recent years Johor Bahru has earned a reputation as the place where many Singaporeans come to let their hair down. The **nightlife** attractions are cheaper drinks and less censorship, although it must be said that the town council has started a clean-up campaign to get rid of the more sinister side of JB nightlife. Johor has numerous nightclubs, discos, hostess clubs and lounges which come alive after dark. The larger clubs have started to attract well-known singing and cabaret stars from Hong Kong.

The many **golf clubs** in the Johor region are another enticement. At least a dozen new courses have taken shape over the last few years and more are on the way. Among the best are the 18-hole Royal Johor Golf Club (Tel: 07-242098), Desaru Golf Club (Tel: 07-821187) and

Kampong living recalls life's simple pleasures.

252

the 36-hole Palm Resort (Tel: 07-596205) not far from Senai Airport. Those interested in a day of golf are strongly advised to book at least three days in advance.

The rural parts of Johor State are best explored by private car or as part of a small guided tour from Singapore. Much of the state is covered in rubber, palm oil and pineapple plantations, but there are still large tracts of jungle and splendid beaches on both the east and west coasts.

Mount Pulai: To visit the forest around Mount Pulai (654 metres/2,146ft), follow the tract at the **Ladang Midlands** signboard on the left of the Kuala Lumpur trunk road, 3km (2 miles) north of Kulai, and after 14km (9 miles), turn left onto the road leading uphill to the carpark. It is the most accessible, largely unspoilt, and serves as the water-catchment for Pulai Reservoir. Camping is permitted, but it is crowded on Sundays. Watch out for the Pig-tailed Macaque – so named because of its cute little tail that is usually arched over its hindquarter. A large troop with many young has

Pig-tailed Macaque finds food for thought.

been regularly seen foraging at the fringe of the jungle. Named "berok" by the Malays by virtue of its "brok" grunts, these monkeys can be trained to pluck coconuts and even botanic specimens from high up in the forest.

The two-hour walk to the summit of Pulai is an exhilarating exercise. White-handed Gibbons can be seen swinging along the high branches and groups of Dusky Leaf Monkeys and Long-tail Macaques run along tree branches and crash away into the deeper jungle as the visitor passes. The Cream-coloured and the Black Giant Squirrel may be seen foraging in the higher branches.

The rich birdlife of the jungle here can be conveniently sampled from the road. Bulbuls and flowerpeckers of many species abound, busy flitting along the roadside vegetation. The incessant "tock-tock-tock" rattling of the Yellow-crowned Barbet and the mighty vomitive cough of the Rhinocerous Hornbill reverberates across the canopy.

Those who wish to sample a rougher but not too arduous uphill excursion,

will make for Mount Panti (481 metres/ 1,578ft) whose attraction is swamp forest which is botanically interesting. To reach there, turn right into the junction at the Police Station of Kampung Batu Empat along the Kota Tinggi Waterfall Road, and head for Kampung Bukit Melintang, about 3km (2 miles) away, where you can park your car and walk in. The climb to the summit, which has a small camping site, takes several hours. Water is not available and has to be fetched further back along the trail.

The jungle around **Panti** is heavily logged but enough vegetation has been left to harbour a small population of large mammals. Small herds of the Asiatic Elephant still roam the jungle. Tigers are very much in evidence, judging by their many pug-marks on the muddy grounds.

To cool down after Panti visit the **Kota Tingi Waterfall**, about 15 minutes up the road from Kampung Batu Empat and is 40km (25 miles) northeast of Johor Bahru at the junction of the Johor River and the East Coast Highway – an area renowned for its natural beauty. At the foot of the falls is a deep pool where bathing and swimming in the cold water can be fun. Chalets for rent are available. Try to plan your visit on a weekday, when it is not crowded.

Desaru snuggles in the southeastern corner of the state, facing out onto the turquoise waters of the South China Sea. Famous for its long, unspoilt and frequently deserted beach, **Desaru** can be reached by way of Kota Tinggi (a total distance of 94km (59 miles) from downtown JB) or via a new ferry service from Singapore's Changi Point to **Tanjung Belungkor** on the Malaysian side, which is only 32km (20 miles) from Desaru. With a capacity of 70 cars and 450 passengers, the catamaran ferry makes the 45-minute crossing three times each day. The return journey costs S$32 for vehicles, S$24 for adults, S$21 for students and S$15 for children.

The sea at Desaru can sometimes be treacherous, but there are plenty of watersports, golf and miles of sand for walks, picnics or just lazing about. The air is bracing after the languid heat of **Long distance travel is the norm.**

Singapore. Chalets can be rented or rooms facing the sea and overlooking the lovely pool at the **Desaru View Hotel** for those who prefer to stay overnight (Singapore office; Tel: 2232157/2065).

Further up the east coast is **Mersing** (131km/81 miles), jumping off point to a number of offshore islands framed in coconut palms, bleached white sand and coral reefs. Among the better known islands are **Pulau Besar**, **Pulau Rawa** and **Pulau Tioman**. Diving and snorkelling are excellent around all the islands, while accommodation varies from modest beach huts to the luxury Berjaya Imperial **Beach Resort** with its golf course and tennis courts (Singapore office: Tel. 7335488). Tioman can also be reached from Singapore by direct air and high-speed ferry.

The west coast of Johor State offers an opportunity to see rural Asian life, little kampongs or villages where families live life at a gentle pace surrounded by fruit trees and chickens. Bright-eyed children play happily while the women, clad in bright, floral sarongs cope with the chores

Tioman is on everyone's "world's best islands" list.

and the men work, in the vast plantations. The quickest way to reach the west coast is driving north along Route One, then west along Route Five passing through **Pekan Nenas** with its vast pineapple fields. The road hits the coast at **Pontian Kecil** (59km/37 miles) from JB, a sleepy fishing village known for its seafood restaurants and spectacular sunsets.

South of Pontian is an even smaller village called **Kukup**, which has become something of a hub for daytrippers from Singapore. Boats can be hired for a short exploration of the seafaring community, built over the water on stilts, and several outlets offer typical Malaysian seafood. Even further south is **Tanjung Piai**, the southernmost tip of the Asian mainland.

Beyond Johor are numerous other scenic parts of Malaysia. Further up the east coast are the beautiful beaches of Pahang and Trengganu states. Further along the west coast is venerable old Malacca, once the capital of a vast Malay empire and a trading entrepot under the Portuguese, Dutch and British.

RIAU ISLANDS

About 20km (13 miles) south of Singapore, Batam is the fastest growing part of the Riau and the easiest to reach from Singapore. In recent years, the island has become popular with daytrippers and weekend visitors who flock to Batam for its fairways, beaches, duty-free shopping, delicious seafood – and the satellite TV that's banned in Singapore. In 1992, more than 670,000 tourists landed on Batam, more than any other place in Indonesia except Jakarta and Bali. Ferries ply every 30 minutes during daylight hours between the World Trade Centre in Singapore and either Sekupang or Batu Ampar on the north coast of Bintan.

Sekupang is just 30 minutes by high-speed ferry from the WTC dock. The ferry terminal at Sekupang has about half a dozen duty-free shops selling everything from European cognac to Balinese handicrafts and Sumatran woodcarvings. Prices are about half to one-third of that in Singapore for the same items. There is a taxi stand in front of the ferry terminal (the cross-island journey takes about 40 minutes and should not cost more than Rp 15,000) and a bus terminal next door.

Indah Puri Golf Club is just outside Sekupang – the closest place for Singaporeans to tee off (nine holes at present). Jalan Marta Dinata leads southwest from Sekupang into the heart of the island. The road branches off at the first big junction, with Jalan Kartini heading south to future development areas like **Sagulung** and **Tanjung Uncang** on the southwest coast of Batam. The main road (Jalan Gajah Mada) continues east towards the island's main population centres and industrial areas, spanning **Ladi Reservoir** by means of a long causeway. The intersection with the little white clock tower is Batam's major crossroads, with routes leading north to Nagoya, east to Batam Centre and southeast to the airport and Kabil.

Nagoya, the island's largest town, was built by Japanese soldiers during World War II, although it bears little resemblance to its namesake in Japan.

Just a short ferry ride away from Singapore, a different world awaits.

Perhaps the Japanese changed the name because the place was originally called Lubuk Baja or "Pirate's Waterhole." Nagoya's central business district has numerous hotels, restaurants, discos and karaoke bars to cater to visiting businessmen and construction workers. There's a small health and sports complex, and two shopping malls: City Plaza and Lucky Plaza. But there isn't really of much interest to regular tourists except a small Chinese temple. Just north of Nagoya is Batam's second port, **Batu Ampar**, with more duty-free shops and a ferry connection to Singapore.

Although there isn't much in place at the present time, **Batam Centre** will be the island's capital someday, a purpose-built city that is currently rising from the mangrove swamps and secondary jungle around **Teluk Tering** bay. Look out over the whole island from **Bukit Senyum** or Smiling Hill and have lunch at the seaside *kampong* of **Batu Besar** before relaxing on the beach at **Nongsa**. The beach at Nongsa is one of the best on Batam, with fine white sand, rocky outcrops and tiny offshore isles. If you can't bear to leave, stay at one of the new places along the beach, the cosy Balinese-style **Turi Beach Hotel** or the highrise **Batam View Hotel** with its views across the straits to Singapore.

Hang Nadim Airport – named after a 15th-century admiral who is buried on Bintan island – dominates the eastern end of Batam, along with a huge industrial park being developed with Taiwanese money. Down in the southeast corner is the small port of **Kabil** where you can catch speedboats to Tanjung Pinang, the largest town on Bintan (Rp 10,000). The journey takes about 45 minutes. The rickety docks in Kabil offer at least one modest restaurant and drinks stalls where you can stalk up for the voyage to Bintan.

Bintan: Nearly three times the size of Singapore (1,030sq km/398sq miles), Pulau Bintan or "Star Island" is the largest of all the Riau islands. It remains largely undisturbed, a massive expanse of jungle, swamp and mountains (the highest is **Gunung Bintan** at 335 metres/1,099ft) with isolated *kampongs* that

Peace and tranquility on Turi Beach.

betray little 20th century influence. But like neighbouring Batam, the island is changing fast. Several industrial zones have been mapped out and the entire northern shore is slated to become a "mega-resort" with dozens of hotels and other tourist facilities.

The north coast of Bintan is just 45km (28 miles) from Singapore, but the island's major port and tourist area is Tanjung Pinang, on the southwest coast, which is about two hours from Singapore by high-speed ferry. The boat passes along the north shore of Batam island and its new resort hotels, then past **Tanjung Uban** with its silver tank farm at the western tip of Bintan. From there the ferry hugs close to the coast, past fishing villages built on stilts over the water and tiny desert islands framed in coconut palms. Look out for wooden "fences" in the shallows – those are traditional Malay *kelongs* or fish traps, which have virtually disappeared from Singapore waters. Fish are carried into the traps by the rising tide, and then trapped in areas where the stakes converge.

Tanjung Pinang: the capital of Riau province is a bustling city with traces of Malay, Chinese and Dutch influence. Accommodation is available for those wishing to stay overnight and small boats may be hired to explore other tiny islands in the immediate area. Tanjung Pinang is also a jumping off spot for trips to the smaller Riau islands and the Lingga Archipelago. In addition, there are two weekly ferry connections to Jakarta.

You can change money at a kiosk in the main ferry terminal, next to a small tourist office with a computer guide to Bintan's hotels, restaurants and attractions. Taxis are available at the top of the pier, although you won't find two that are exactly the same. Many of the cabs are old Chevys and Holdens from the 1960s. The *bemo* **terminal** and post office are both on Jalan Merdeka.

Much of older part of Tanjung Pinang is built on stilts over the harbour, with myriad piers and rickety wooden walkways in place of streets. **Jalan Merdeka** is the main street, east-west through the heart of the city, a jumble of provision

A fisherman heads towards his *kelong*.

shops, open-air cafes, video and cassette stores, boat agents and money changers. The daily **market** is a block away, on Jalan Pos and Jalan Pasar. Close by is Pelantar Satu (Pier One) with speedboats to Batam (Rp 10,000).

Away from the water, the city's sights tend to be religious in nature. The building with a pale yellow spire overlooking the harbour **Santa Maria Church**, built during the time when the Dutch were still masters of Bintan. Another old Dutch structure is **Bethel Church** on Jalan Yusup Kahar, a spitting image of the canal-side buildings in Amsterdam. Further down the street are the municipal stadium and the **city mosque** with its dark green domes. The small but interesting **Riau Museum** is situated on Jalan B.G. Katamso in the eastern suburbs. The collection includes clothing, weapons, musical instruments and furniture that once belonged to the Riau sultans.

From Pelantar Dua (Pier Two) you can catch a speedboat (Rp 500) across to **Senggarang**, a kampong on the far side of the Riau River from Tanjung Pinang.

Tanjung Pinang's city mosque.

Many of the inhabitants are Chinese who immigrated hundreds of years ago from Fujian province on the east coast of China. The village has four Chinese shrines including the **Banyan Temple**, a 200-year-old clan house suspended in the arms of a giant banyan tree in the same manner as some of the ruins of Angkor Wat.

Penyengat: More than any other place in the Riau archipelago, this tiny island near Tanjung Pinang is considered a cradle of Malay civilization. During the 18th and 19th centuries, this was the home base of the sultans of Riau, with a lavish court and royal city that encompassed nearly 10,000 citizens at one point. Arts and letters flourished on Penyengat. The book called the *Bustanul Katibin*, the first Malay grammar, was published on the island in 1857, laying the foundation for Bahasa Indonesia, the *lingua franca* of the entire Indonesian archipelago. The Riau sultanate prospered until 1910 when the Dutch finally ended its political and military autonomy.

Sampans to Penyengat (Rp 500) leave

from the old wooden pier to the left of the main ferry terminal. The passage takes about 10 minutes. More than 2,000 people live on the island today, spread among five *kampongs*. Most people stay in simple wooden houses, but they are kept in immaculate shape and nearly every home has a tidy garden. People go about their daily chores much as they did a hundred years ago when the sultans reigned, mending fishing nets, fixing boats, harvesting papayas and coconuts, or washing clothes. Penyengat is a fascinating insight into what life must have been like in Singapore before the advent of European rule.

The best way to explore the island is on foot, but trishaws can be hired for a modest price. Motor vehicles are not allowed on the island. An archway with the words "Selamat Datang" welcomes visitors to Penyengat. Just beyond is the **Royal Mosque** (Masjid Raya Sultan Riau) decorated in the same yellow and green motif you see throughout the island. The mosque was built in 1818 and still remain as the most important place of Muslim worship in the Riau islands. Try to visit the mosque during the service on Friday afternoon, when worshippers are dressed in their finest clothes. Remember to dress modestly and remove your shoes before entering the building.

Directly east of the mosque by way of the coastal path is a ruined two-storey mansion where the royal physician once lived and a **royal graveyard** (*komplex makam*) where many of the sultans are buried. The most important tomb is that of Raja Hamidah, (1760–1812), the wife of the Sultan of Johor, who received the Riau islands as part of her wedding dowry. Hamidah (also known as Engku Puteri) is considered a Muslim saint and her tomb is a place of pilgrimage for people from all over Riau. Four other sultans are buried here.

Another path leads across the island – past the **Palace of Raja Ali Marhum** (Istana Ali Marhum) with its faded yellow facade and red-riled roof – and down to the southern shore, where there are several ruined mansions. The most

The Royal Mosque features soothing colours and clean architectural lines.

impressive of these is the **House of Tungku Bilek**, an elegant two-story structure which is nearly engulfed in roots and other vegetation. Notice the wrought-iron gateway, the stout wooden doorframes and the old stone well in the garden. There are several other 19th-century ruins and cemeteries on this "back side" of Penyengat.

On a hill overlooking the town is **Bukit Kursi Fort**, built in the late 18th century as a defense against the Dutch. The fort has been nicely restored in recent years – including the excavation of three old canon – and affords superb views of Penyengat, Tanjung Pinang and smaller islands to the west. Be careful not to fall into the moat.

Bintan beaches: Beyond Tanjung Pinang, vast tracts of Bintan remain untouched by modern development. There is a petroleum facility at Tanjung Uban in the west, and an airport and industrial park at **Kijang** on the southeast coast, but otherwise life moves at a languid tropical pace.

Trikora Beach in eastern Bintan is one of the finest strands in Southeast Asia, an unspoilt stretch of white sand and coconut palms with beautiful turquoise water. There are a few thatched-roof restaurants and several hotels and guest houses for those who want to spend the night.

Stretching for 14km (9 miles) along the north coast is **Pasir Panjang Beach** which is being transformed into the **Bintan Beach International Resort** (BBIR) – a sprawling complex of 20 hotels, 13 golf courses and 40 holiday housing estates that will take shape in the next 15 years. The developers – a consortium of Singapore and Indonesian investors – hope to attract more than one million people a year to a variety of attractions including beaches, shopping malls, theme parks, gardens, nature reserves and various recreation clubs. The total cost is put at US$2 billion. The first two beach hotels were expected to open by the end of 1994 and a ferry terminal is being built at Tanjung Sebung to handle passengers directly from Singapore.

Many Riau sultans are buried in Penyengat.

INSIGHT GUIDES
Travel Tips

INSIGHT GUIDES

COLORSET NUMBERS

INSIGHT *Pocket* GUIDES

• •

United States: **Houghton Mifflin Company, Boston MA 02108
Tel: (800) 2253362 Fax: (800) 4589501**

Canada: **Thomas Allen & Son, 390 Steelcase Road East
Markham, Ontario L3R 1G2
Tel: (416) 4759126 Fax: (416) 4756747**

Great Britain: **GeoCenter UK, Hampshire RG22 4BJ
Tel: (256) 817987 Fax: (256) 817988**

Worldwide: **Höfer Communications Singapore 2262
Tel: (65) 8612755 Fax: (65) 8616438**

❝ I was first drawn to the Insight Guides by the excellent "Nepal" volume. I can think of no book which so effectively captures the essence of a country. Out of these pages leaped the Nepal I know – the captivating charm of a people and their culture. I've since discovered and enjoyed the entire Insight Guide Series. Each volume deals with a country or city in the same sensitive depth, which is nowhere more evident than in the superb photography. ❞

Sir Edmund Hillary

So, you're getting away from it all.

Just make sure you can get back.

AT&T Access Numbers
Dial the number of the country you're in to reach AT&T

AMERICAN SAMOA	633 2-USA	**INDIA**◆	**000-117**	NEW ZEALAND	000-911
AUSTRALIA	**1800-881-011**	**INDONESIA**◆	**001-801-10**	*PHILIPPINES	105-11
CHINA, PRC◆◆◆	**10811**	*JAPAN	0039-111	**SAIPAN**†	**235-2872**
COOK ISLANDS	09-111	**KOREA**	**009-11**	SINGAPORE	800-0111-111
FIJI	004-890-1001	**KOREA**◇◇	**11** ✳	SRI LANKA	430-430
GUAM	**018-872**	MACAO	0800-111	*TAIWAN	**0080-10288-0**
HONG KONG	**800-1111**	*MALAYSIA	**800-0011**	THAILAND◆	0019-991-1111

Countries in bold face permit country-to-country calling in addition to calls to the U.S. **World Connect**℠ prices consist of **USADirect**® rates plus an additional charge based on the country you are calling. Collect calling available to the U.S. only. *Public phones require deposit of coin or phone card. ◇◇From public phones only, push the red button, wait for dial tone and then dial. †May not be available from every phone. ◆Not available from public phones. ◆◆◆Not yet available from all areas. © 1994 AT&T

Here's a travel tip that will make it easy to call back to the States. Dial the access number for the country you're in to get English-speaking AT&T operators or voice prompts. Minimize hotel telephone surcharges too.

If all the countries you're visiting aren't listed above, call **1 800 241-5555** for a free wallet card with all AT&T access numbers. Easy international calling from AT&T. **TrueWorld Connections.**

AT&T

TRAVEL TIPS

GETTING THERE

Voted the world's best airport three times by Britain's *Business Traveller* magazine, even without the new second terminal, Changi Airtropolis now smoothly and efficiently handles 24 million passengers annually. In November 1990, the Airtropolis' second terminal opened for operations. The two terminals are linked by the Sky Train, an automated miniature rapid transit system with a track of 600 metres (2,000ft). It is the first of its kind outside USA and UK.

Terminal 1 has 43 shops, six restaurants, a medical centre, movie theatrette, transit hotel as well as the usual services including car rentals, hotel reservations, money changing facilities, post and telecommunications offices, business centre, hairdressing salon, children's play area etc.

Terminal 2 has a business centre, a health centre, 56 day rooms with en suite facilities, a fully-equipped medical centre, exhibition centres, a 200-seat auditorium, cellular phone rentals, a science discovery corner, nine restaurants and a supermarket. You will, of course, find money changing facilities, car hire desks, hotel reservation and tourist information desks too.

The national carrier, Singapore Airlines (SIA) flies to 67 cities in 40 countries. In all, 52 airlines operate out of Changi, with 310 flights daily to 110 cities in 54 countries. The amount of cargo handled is well in excess of 700,000 tonnes in 1992.

The aim is for passengers to be on their way to their hotels within 20 minutes of landing, and indeed, the formalities are brief, luggage arrival is speedy, and taxis queue up outside.

You are whisked into town along the highway lined with brightly coloured bougainvillea and lush tropical foliage. At sea, ships from all over the globe wait their turn at the world's busiest port. Ahead, silver highrises of the city shimmer in the sunlight.

BY SEA

Arriving slowly by sea, as everyone did in days gone by, is a pleasant experience; sailing in past 600 or so other vessels lying at anchor, watching the skyline clarify into looming skyscrapers. Singapore is the world's busiest port in terms of tonnage, with 238 million tonnes handled in 1992. Most visitors arrive at one of the three terminals of the Singapore Cruise Centre, World Trade Centre, which can accommodate up to 1,000 passengers at a time. When the five planned additional terminals are completed, ships over the present 245 metre (800ft) length, 12½ metre (42ft) depth and 52 metre (172ft) mast height limit will be able to berth at this impressive facility.

BY RAIL

Down the west coast of Peninsular Malaysia by train and then over the Straits of Singapore on the causeway is a leisurely way to arrive. Daily train departures from Bangkok (3.15pm) get you to Kuala Lumpur the following evening (8.15pm) and a later (10.15pm) departure will bring you into Singapore in the early morning (7am), arriving at Keppel Road Station. Other trains leave Kuala Lumpur for Singapore at 7.30am, 8.30am, 3pm and 8.15pm.

First Class fare from Bangkok is S$237.80 and from Kuala Lumpur, S$68. For details call the railway station. Tel: 2225165.

OVERLAND

There are good roads down the west and east coasts of Peninsular Malaysia crossing the causeway into Singapore. It's a fascinating drive, through oil palm and rubber plantations, past *kampongs* (villages) and dusty little towns, rather like Singapore used to be, many years ago. Nowadays the contrast is immediate as you arrive in the clean, green and well regulated republic.

There are private air-conditioned buses running from Malaysia (Butterworth, Kuala Lumpur, Kuantan, Malacca, Mersing and Penang) to Singapore. They ply through Johore Bahru and enter Singapore via the Causeway. The fare ranges from S$11 to S$30, depending on your departing point.

TRAVEL ESSENTIALS

VISAS & PASSPORTS

As long as you have a valid passport, onward travel reservations and adequate finance; only citizens of Afghanistan, Algeria, China, Russia, India, Iraq, Kampuchea, Kuwait, Laos, Lebanon, Libya, Syria, Tunisia, Vietnam and Yemen are required to produce a visa.

Swatch. The others just watch.

seahorse/fall winter 94-95

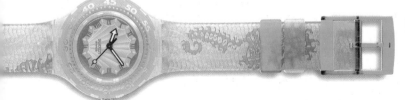

shockproof
splashproof
priceproof
boreproof
swiss made

swatch✛
SCUBA 200

Pack your trunks for a holiday that's smooth as silk.

Few countries can provide such a choice of exotic holiday experiences as Thailand.

Elephants still roam wild in Thai forests and have played an important cultural and working role since the early days of the Kingdom.

Today, you can enjoy the unforgettable thrill of a trek atop your own private elephant, on trails that lead through lush northern forests.

If riding a two-ton elephant isn't the holiday you had in mind, how about sailing aboard a traditional seventeen metre junk in the Andaman Sea?

Or relaxing in a luxury hotel and swimming in crystal blue waters at one of Thailand's famous beach resorts?

ROYAL
ORCHID

Holiday

Then there's the shopping - but that's another story.

The first thing you need is our Royal Orchid Holidays brochure. In it you'll find every holiday imaginable in this exotic and mystical land.

Pick up a free copy from your travel agent or nearest Thai office and discover the treasures of the Kingdom.

And, of course, the best way to fly to Thailand is on Thai International, where you'll enjoy our world renowned Royal Orchid Service while you fly there smooth as silk.

American Express offers Travelers Cheques built for two.

Cheques *for Two*™ from American Express are the Travelers Cheques that allow either of you to use them because both of you have signed them. And only one of you needs to be present to purchase them.

Cheques *for Two* are accepted anywhere regular American Express Travelers Cheques are, which is just about everywhere. So stop by your bank, AAA* or any American Express Travel Service Office and ask for Cheques *for Two*.

MONEY MATTERS

At time of press, the Singapore Dollar is about 1.50 to the US$ and 2.35 to the Pound Sterling. The Brunei dollar is equal in value to the Singapore dollar and is valid currency here. The Malaysian dollar is valued slightly lower. However, there are no restrictions on the amount of currency you can bring into the country.

Banks and licensed money changers offer better rates than hotels and you are never far from one or the other. Major credit cards are widely accepted.

If you wish to deal with banks for your traveller's checks and other foreign currency transactions, it is advisable to do so on weekdays. Some banks do not handle such transactions on Saturdays while others conduct them in small amounts only, based on Friday's rate.

HEALTH

Singapore is as clean and green as billed. Safe drinking water and strict government control of all food outlets make this a hygienic place to visit, but should the need arise, medical facilities are excellent.

A vaccination against smallpox is necessary if you are arriving from an infected country; and against yellow fever if arriving from a country where the disease is endemic.

WHAT TO WEAR

The daytime trend is pure casual comfort. Light summer fashions, easy to move in, are the right choice for a full day out in town. Wear a white shirt and tie for office calls.

In the evening, only a few plush nightclubs and exclusive restaurants favour the traditional jacket and tie. Most hotels, restaurants, coffee houses and discos accept casually elegant attire. However, jeans, tee-shirts and sneakers are taboo at some restaurants and discos. To avoid embarrassment, it is best to call in advance to check an establishment's dress code.

QUARANTINE

The minimum quarantine period for animals from countries other than Australia, New Zealand and UK is 30 days. A compulsory anti-rabies vaccination is given.

CUSTOMS

There is no restriction on the amount of currency allowed. Unless arriving from Malaysia, duty-free goods as indicated at the arrival points may be brought into Singapore. For adults the allowance is 1 litre of spirits, 1 litre of wine, 1 litre of beer, stout or ale. No duty-free cigarettes are allowed.

Prohibited items include drugs (the penalty can be death), firecrackers, obscene or seditious publica-tions, endangered wildlife or their by-products and reproductions of copyright publications, videos, discs, records or cassettes.

ON ARRIVAL

Porters are available and rows of trolleys await passengers at Changi Airport. There are hotel reservations and tour booking counters at the airport.

VISA EXTENSIONS

You will normally be given a two-week tourist visa, so remember to check the date and renew if necessary at the Immigration Office, Pidemco Centre. Tel: 5322877.

ON DEPARTURE

There is a S$15 airport tax charge for all departing passengers. Airport tax coupons can be prepaid at most hotels, travel agents and airline offices.

GETTING ACQUAINTED

GOVERNMENT & ECONOMY

Singapore enjoys a unicameral parliamentary gov-ernment, with elections held every four years. The People's Action Party (PAP), in power since full independence in 1965, is now led by Prime Minister Goh Chok Tong. President Ong Teng Cheong is Head of State.

Singapore is the world's busiest container port. Lacking in natural resources, oil refining, shipbuild-ing and repair and high tech manufacturing are the basis of Singapore's thriving economy. An industri-ous populace has led to BERI (Business Environment Risk Information) rating the Singaporean as the world's top three worker for the past 10 years.

The aim is to improve the already efficient infra-structure and become the business hub of the Asia Pacific, offering first class products and services.

GEOGRAPHY & POPULATION

Lying between latitudes 1.09°N and 1.29°N and longitudes 103.38°E and 104.06°E, the Republic City State of Singapore consists of the main island, about 616sq km (246sq miles) in area, and 58 other islets, making a total land area of 626.4sq km (250sq miles). Located at the southern tip of Peninsular Malaysia, it is joined to the latter by a causeway carrying road and rail traffic.

The population is now about 2.8 million, including foreign workers. Of these, 77.6 percent are Chinese, 14.2 percent Malays, and 7.1 percent Indians with just 1.1 percent "others".

TIME ZONES

Singapore is 8 hours ahead of Greenwich Mean Time (GMT). Aside from time variations made in certain countries during specific seasons, international time differences are staggered as follows:

Singapore	12pm today
Hong Kong	12pm today
Bangkok	11am today
New Delhi	9.30am today
Bonn	5am today
Paris	5am today
London	4am today
New York	11pm yesterday
San Francisco	8pm yesterday
Hawaii	6pm yesterday
Sydney	2pm today
Tokyo	1pm today

CLIMATE

The average daily temperature is 27°C, often rising to around 32°C in the heat of the day, and cooling only to around 23°C at night. Humidity is high, and varies between 64 and 96 percent.

The north-east monsoon blows from December to March, and the south-west from June to September, and wind speeds are light, all year round.

Spectacular thunderstorms occur frequently between the monsoons, in April–May and October–November; and the average rainfall is 2,369mm.

LOCAL LAWS & CUSTOMS

The customs, religions and languages of nearly every nation in the world have converged in Singapore at some time in history. Adjectives beginning with "multi" are common sounds on the Singapore scene, and a cosmopolitan tolerance is part of the city's character. With everyday etiquette relaxed and straightforward, visitors behaving courteously stand little chance of unintentionally giving offence. Some ceremonies and special occasions, however, recall inherited traditions and a familiarity with certain customs will set everyone at ease.

TEMPLES & MOSQUES

Removing one's shoes before entering a mosque or an Indian temple has been an unspoken tradition for centuries. Within, devotees do not smoke, though neither of these customs generally applies to Chinese temples where more informal styles prevail. Visitors are most welcome to look around at their leisure and are invited to stay for religious rituals. While people pray, it is understood that those not participating in the service will stand aside. A polite gesture would be to ask permission before taking photographs: the request is seldom, if ever, refused. Modest clothing is appropriate for a visit.

Most temples and mosques have a donation box for funds to help maintain the building. It is customary for visitors to contribute a few coins before leaving.

PRIVATE HOMES

It is pleasant to enjoy the hospitality of a Singaporean friend. In private homes, visitors are received as honoured guests.

If you are invited to a Singaporean's home, it is customary to bring a small gift – whether some pastries, a cake, exotic fruit, chocolates or flowers. As many locals do not drink alcohol, wine or beer may not be appreciated.

You can almost guarantee that you will be offered refreshments during your visit. Naturally, nothing will please your hosts more than knowing you enjoy what they offer.

Most Singaporeans remove their shoes at the door so as not to bring dirt into the house. No host would insist his visitors do so, but it is only polite to follow "house rules".

SHARING A MEAL

Chinese and Japanese food is mainly eaten with chopsticks. Most Malay and Indian food is eaten with the right hand (never the left), Indonesian and Thai food with a large spoon and fork.

Asian meals are usually served in large bowls placed in the centre of the table, with each diner helping himself (or herself) to a little from each bowl. Piling up your plate with food is not only impolite but unwise. With more dishes to follow, by taking a little, you can always help yourself to more. Local people are inwardly pleased if you join them in their styles of dining, for a simple reason: they know it tastes better that way.

WEDDINGS

A gift of money – $40 each is an acceptable sum – is customary at all weddings. The gift is generally used as a contribution to the cost of the wedding banquet, often a lavish affair with many guests invited. The money should be placed inside an envelope with your name written on the back, and given to the bride or groom. Chinese present gifts of money in an *hong bao*, a small red envelope obtainable from most stationers. Traditionally, an even number of notes or coins is considered lucky.

TIPPING

Hotels and larger restaurants usually levy a 10 percent service charge which is added to your bill. Adding more to this amount is not necessary. Bellboys and porters receive from $1 upwards, depending upon the complexity of the errand.

Beyond these international thoroughfares, tipping is exceptional. In small local restaurants, food stalls and taxis, there is no service charge and no tipping – a smile with a simple thank you (*terima kasih* in Malay), is sufficient.

ON THE ROAD

When driving, be sure to put on the seat belt unless you want to enrich the Singapore economy by $150. This seat belt ruling, implemented to reduce risks of fatal car accidents, also applies to both front and backseat passengers of private cars and taxis. If there are no seatbelts installed in the backseat, the rule does not apply.

Police patrols never hesitate to issue tickets when warranted, and they always have a good reason for doing so – exceeding speed limits, failing to give way, failing to obey road signs, etc.

Pedestrians must use a designated crossing if one is available within 50 metres (165ft), or else risk a fine of $50. Designated crossings are zebra crossings, overhead bridges, underpasses, and traffic light junctions fitted with green man and red man lights.

LITERING

Singapore *is* clean and green. Much pain has been taken by the Government not only to keep it that way but also to inculcate civic-conscious habits in its citizens. Litter bins dotting the island at short distance intervals make it inexcusable to litter (be it a bus ticket, a cigarette butt or a sweet wrapper). First offenders are subject to a $1,000 fine and $2,000 for repeat offenders. Repeat offenders are also sentenced to participate in the corrective work order programme whereby they have to collect trash in a public place for a pre-determined period of time.

TOILETS

Failure to flush urinals and water closets after use in public toilets (hotels, shopping complexes, etc.) will result in a $500 fine.

SMOKING

Smoking is banned in air-conditioned restaurants and shopping centres as well as cinemas, theatres, libraries, lifts, buses and government offices. There is a fine of up to $1,000 for the first offence. Signboards that serve as reminders are on display in such places. Youths under 18 years are prohibited to buy cigarettes and smoke in public.

QUEUEING

Singapore follows the first-come-first-served concept. So whether you need a postage stamp, a take-away hamburger, a taxi or help from an information counter, the key word is "queue".

WEIGHTS & MEASURES

Most transactions in Singapore are metric, although the old imperial system is still occasionally used and the local *kati* (about 1⅓lbs) may be used at the market. In Chinatown, the wooden beam scale, the *daching*, is still in use, and the abacus for totting up the price.

ELECTRICITY

Electrical supply is on a 220–240 volt, 50 Hz system. Most hotels have transformers for 110–120 volt, 60 Hz appliances.

BUSINESS HOURS

Business hours are from 9am until 5pm and banks are open from 10am until 3pm on weekdays, and from 9.30am to 11.00am on Saturdays. Some also open on Sundays from 11am until 4pm.

Shops open at about 10am until about 7pm and many department stores are open until 9pm. Most shops open on Sundays too.

PUBLIC HOLIDAYS

New Year's Day	January 1
Chinese New Year	January 31 & February 1*
Hari Raya Puasa	March 3*
Good Friday	April 14*
Labour Day	May 1
Hari Raya Haji	May 5*
Vesak Day	May 14*
National Day	August 9
Deepavali	October 23*
Christmas Day	December 25

* Dates are variable depending on the relevant Chinese, Muslim or Hindu calendars. Check with the Singapore Tourist Promotion Board for exact dates.

FESTIVALS

From the western New Year on January 1st to the Chinese New Year in February, Hari Raya Puasa at the end of Ramadan and Deepavali, Singapore celebrates festivals of all kinds all year round. See chapter on *Events and Festivals* or the official Singapore Tourist Promotion Board publications for details.

CONVENTIONS

Singapore's full-fledged career as a leading convention centre in the East began modestly at the top with the Commonwealth Prime Ministers Conference in January 1971, held for the first time ever in Asia.

The reasons for Singapore's popularity are simple. The airport is modern and efficient, telecommunication is among the best in the world and top-class accommodation is plentiful.

By 1995 Singapore's convention capabilities will be dramatically increased with the opening of the Singapore International Convention and Exhibition Centre at Suntec City. Suntec's column-free plenary and exhibition halls will have an area of 12,000sq metres (130,000sq ft) each, allowing for a capacity of 12,000 participants.

More than 60 trade and consumer exhibitions are held each year at the World Trade Centre. There are 48,000sq metres (512,000sq ft) of exhibition space available, as well as a convention centre with a 1,000-seat auditorium and a 400-seat conference hall.

The Tourist Promotion Board will gladly furnish details of where and how to convene.

RELIGIOUS SERVICES

In multi-racial, multi-religious Singapore, most major religions have their adherents and hours of worship may be ascertained from the various temples, mosques etc. The Sunday services in English at **St. Andrew's Cathedral** are at 7am, 8am, 11am and 5pm. There is a special service at **Changi Prison Chapel** at 5.30pm on Sundays.

COMMUNICATIONS

MEDIA

NEWSPAPERS

The *Straits Times* and *Business Times* are good English language dailies, with the tabloid *New Paper* appearing in the afternoons. The *International Herald Tribune* is available on the day of publication, arriving by fax from Paris and printed here, and from Britain *The International Express* is faxed from London and also printed here. American, British and European newspapers and magazines are widely available here at newsstands, hotel kiosks and bookstores.

RADIO

Radio 1 (90.5 FM), Radio 10 (98.7 FM) and Heart (91.3 FM) are the popular English entertainment channels. Symphony (92.4 FM) airs classical music while Class (95 FM) has contemporary music. There is also the BBC World Service (88.9 mMHz) to keep you up to date on the international scene.

TELEVISION

In one evening, one can enjoy a Malay variety show, Mandarin drama serial, wrestling, a feature from the largest film industry in the world (India), Disney cartoons and American soap operas. These, spiced with sales pitches for Burger King or Pepsi Cola make an evening with the "telly" and friends, good company. Programmes are transmitted on channels 5 (from 6am to 1am) and 8 (from 3pm to 1am). Channel 12 telecasts documentaries, sports, opera and ballet from 7.30pm (some evenings earlier) to 12.15am. Most sets also receive RTM 1 and 2 and TV3 from Malaysia. Check the newspapers or *8 Days* (a weekly entertainment magazine) for programme schedules.

POSTAL SERVICES

Singapore's communication system is advanced and fast. An aerogramme to anywhere but the moon costs 35 cents while an airmail postcard to similar destinations costs 30 cents. Letters weighing not more than 10 grams to the USA, Europe, Africa and Middle East countries cost 75 cents while to Australia, New Zealand, Japan and all countries in Southeast Asia 35 cents. The fee for a registered item is $2.00 (plus postage).

An express mail service called "speedpost" is available to more than 40 countries: any item under 0.5kg sent by this service to the USA costs $40.

Most hotels handle mail service or you may post letters and parcels personally. Post offices offering 24 hour service are at the General Post Office in the Fullerton Building in the city (Tel: 5338899); and in the Comcentre in Exeter Road (Orchard Road area) opposite the Phoenix Hotel. The post office at Changi Airport, Terminal 2 is open 8am to 10pm.

Most other branches are open from 8.30am to 5pm on weekdays (Wednesdays 8am to 8pm) and from 8am to 1pm on Saturdays.

Call 165 for general postal enquiries.

TELECOMMUNICATIONS

Singapore is completely up to date and efficient in all kinds of telecommunications. The public telephone book has a wealth of information on what services are available. Most hotels and offices have fax machines, and almost every hotel room has an IDD phone, with 005 being the international code. For international directory assistance and operator assisted, collect or person to person calls dial 104.

Don't be overcharged for overseas calls.

Save up to 70% on calls back to the U.S. with WorldPhone.®*

While traveling abroad, the last thing you need to worry about is being overcharged for international phone calls. Plan ahead and look into WorldPhone – the easy and affordable way for you to call the U.S. and country to country from a growing list of international locations.

Just dial 1-800-955-0925 to receive your free, handy, wallet-size WorldPhone Access Guide – your guide to saving as much as 70% on phone calls home.

When calling internationally, your WorldPhone Access Guide will allow you to:
- Avoid hotel surcharges and currency confusion
- Choose from four convenient billing options
- Talk with operators who speak your language
- Call from more than 90 countries
- Just dial and save – regardless of your long distance carrier back home

WorldPhone is easy. And there's nothing to join. So avoid overcharges when you're traveling overseas. Call for your free WorldPhone Access Guide today – before you travel.

Call 1-800-955-0925.

THE TOP 25 WORLDPHONE COUNTRY CODES.			
COUNTRY	**WORLDPHONE TOLL-FREE ACCESS #**	**COUNTRY**	**WORLDPHONE TOLL-FREE ACCESS #**
Australia (CC)◆		**Japan (cont'd.)**	
To call using OPTUS■	008-5511-11	To call anywhere other than the U.S.	0055
To call using TELSTRA■	1-800-881-100	**Korea** (CC)	
Belgium (CC)◆	0800-10012	To call using KT■	009-14
China (CC)	108-12	To call using DACOM■	0039-12
(Available from most major cities)		Phone Booths+	Red button 03, then press*
For a Mandarin-speaking Operator	108-17	Military Bases	550-2255
Dominican Republic	1-800-751-6624	**Mexico** ▲	95-800-674-7000
		Netherlands (CC)◆	06-022-91-22
El Salvador◆	195	**Panama**	108
France (CC)◆	19▼-00-19	Military Bases	2810-108
Germany (CC)	0130-0012	**Philippines** (CC)◆	
(Limited availability in eastern Germany.)		To call using PLDT■	105-14
Greece (CC)◆	00-800-1211	To call PHILCOM■	1026-12
Guatemala◆	189	For a Tagalog-speaking Operator	108-15
Haiti (CC)+	001-800-444-1234	**Saudi Arabia** (CC)+	1-800-11
Hong Kong (CC)	800-1121	**Singapore**	8000-112-112
India (CC)	000-127	**Spain** (CC)	900-99-0014
(Available from most major cities)		**Switzerland** (CC)◆	155-0222
Israel (CC)◆	177-150-2727	**United Kingdom** (CC)	
Italy (CC)◆	172-1022	To call using BT■	0800-89-0222
Japan◆		To call using MERCURY■	0500-89-0222
To call to the U.S. using KDD■	0039-121		
To call to the U.S. using IDC■	0066-55-121		

(CC) Country-to-country calling available. May not be available to/from all international locations. Certain restrictions apply.

+ Limited availability.

▼ Wait for second dial tone.

▲ Rate depends on call origin in Mexico.

■ International communications carrier.

◆ Public phones may require deposit of coin or phone card for dial tone.

WORLDPHONE^{SM} From MCI

Let it take you around the world.

FOR THOSE
WITH MORE THAN
A PASSING INTEREST
IN TIME...

Before you put your name down for a Patek Philippe watch *fig. 1*, there are a few basic things you might like to know, without knowing exactly whom to ask. In addressing such issues as accuracy, reliability and value for money, we would like to demonstrate why the watch we will make for you will be quite unlike any other watch currently produced.

"Punctuality", Louis XVIII was fond of saying, "is the politeness of kings."

We believe that in the matter of punctuality, we can rise to the occasion by making you a mechanical timepiece that will keep its rendezvous with the Gregorian calendar at the end of every century, omitting the leap-years in 2100, 2200 and 2300 and recording them in 2000 and 2400 *fig. 2*. Nevertheless, such a watch does need the occasional adjustment. Every 3333 years and 122 days you should remember to set it forward one day to the true time of the celestial clock. We suspect, however, that you are simply content to observe the politeness of kings. Be assured, therefore, that when you order your watch, we will be exploring for you the physical—if not the metaphysical—limits of precision.

Does everything have to depend on how much?

Consider, if you will, the motives of collectors who set record prices at auction to acquire a Patek Philippe. They may be paying for rarity, for looks or for micromechanical ingenuity. But we believe that behind each $500,000-plus

bid is the conviction that a Patek Philippe, even if 50 years old or older, can be expected to work perfectly for future generations.

In case your ambitions to own a Patek Philippe are somewhat discouraged by the scale of the sacrifice involved, may we hasten to point out that the watch we will make for you today will certainly be a technical improvement on the Pateks bought at auction? In keeping with our tradition of inventing new mechanical solutions for greater reliability and better time-keeping, we will bring to your watch innovations *fig. 3* inconceivable to our watchmakers who created the supreme wristwatches of 50 years ago *fig. 4*. At the same time, we will of course do our utmost to avoid placing undue strain on your financial resources.

Can it really be mine?

May we turn your thoughts to the day you take delivery of your watch? Sealed within its case is your watchmaker's tribute to the mysterious process of time. He has decorated each wheel with a chamfer carved into its hub and polished into a shining circle. Delicate ribbing flows over the plates and bridges of gold and rare alloys. Millimetric surfaces are bevelled and burnished to exactitudes measured in microns. Rubies are transformed into jewels that triumph over friction. And after many months—or even years—of work, your watchmaker stamps a small badge into the mainbridge of your watch. The Geneva Seal—the highest possible attestation of fine watchmaking *fig. 5*.

Looks that speak of inner grace *fig. 6*.

When you order your watch, you will no doubt like its outward appearance to reflect the harmony and elegance of the movement within. You may therefore find it helpful to know that we are uniquely able to cater for any special decorative needs you might like to express. For example, our engravers will delight in conjuring a subtle play of light and shadow on the gold case-back of one of our rare pocket-watches *fig. 7*. If you bring us your favourite picture, our enamellers will reproduce it in a brilliant miniature of hair-breadth detail *fig. 8*. The perfect execution of a double hob-nail pattern on the bezel of a wristwatch is the pride of our casemakers and the satisfaction of our designers, while our chainsmiths will weave for you a rich brocade in gold *figs. 9 & 10*. May we also recommend the artistry of our goldsmiths and the experience of our lapidaries in the selection and setting of the finest gemstones? *figs. 11 & 12*.

How to enjoy your watch before you own it.

As you will appreciate, the very nature of our watches imposes a limit on the number we can make available. (The four Calibre 89 time-pieces we are now making will take up to nine years to complete). We cannot therefore promise instant gratification, but while you look forward to the day on which you take delivery of your Patek Philippe *fig. 13*, you will have the pleasure of reflecting that time is a universal and everlasting commodity, freely available to be enjoyed by all.

Should you require information on any particular Patek Philippe watch, or even on watchmaking in general, we would be delighted to reply to your letter of enquiry. And if you send us

fig. 1: The classic face of Patek Philippe.

fig. 4: Complicated wristwatches circa 1930 (left) and 1990. The golden age of watchmaking will always be with us.

fig. 2: One of the 33 complications of the Calibre 89 astronomical clock-watch is a satellite wheel that completes one revolution every 400 years.

fig. 5: The Geneva Seal is awarded only to watches which achieve the standards of horological purity laid down in the laws of Geneva. These rules define the supreme quality of watchmaking.

fig. 3: Recognized as the most advanced mechanical regulating device to date, Patek Philippe's Gyromax balance wheel demonstrates the equivalence of simplicity and precision.

fig. 6: Your pleasure in owning a Patek Philippe is the purpose of those who made it for you.

fig. 7: Arabesques come to life on a gold case-back.

fig. 8: An artist working six hours a day takes about four months to complete a miniature in enamel on the case of a pocket-watch.

fig. 9: Harmony of design is executed in a work of simplicity and perfection in a lady's Calatrava wristwatch.

fig. 10: The chainsmith's hands impart strength and delicacy to a tracery of gold.

fig. 11: Circles in gold: symbols of perfection in the making.

fig. 12: The test of a master lapidary is his ability to express the splendour of precious gemstones.

PATEK PHILIPPE
GENEVE
fig. 13: The discreet sign of those who value their time.

A Wise Man Never Thinks How Far He's Come. He Thinks How Far He Can Still Travel.

REMY XO BECAUSE LIFE IS WHAT YOU MAKE IT

For IDD country codes, dial 161. Local directory assistance is 100.

There are four types of public payphones. Coin-operated phones for local calls, phonecard and credit card operated phones for local, STD and IDD calls, as well as dedicated, country direct phones which allow you to make collect or charged calls through your home country operator. This latter Country Direct Service is also possible through using a special telephone number from any telephone in Singapore.

Phone cards are available in $2, $5, $10, $20 and $50 denominations and can be used for both local and overseas calls. Local calls cost 10 cents for the first 3 minutes and 10 cents for every subsequent 3 minutes, for a maximum of 9 minutes.

You may call a ship in port by dialing 2747111 for the Port of Singapore Authority. If a ship is at sea, less than 80km (50 miles) away, dial 105. To contact a ship which is further than 80km away, the number is 1800-4813668. Call 163 with enquiries.

All forms of Telecoms can be filed at the General Post Office (GPO), Fullerton Building, Collyer Quay as well as at Singapore Telecoms Comcentre branch, 31 Exeter Road; and Hill Street Branch at 15 Hill Street. There are Telecoms outlets in the transit lounges of both terminals at Changi airport which offer extensive services 24 hours. Some services at Comcentre and the GPO are available 24-hours; the rest between 8am to 6pm, Mon–Fri and 8am to 2pm, Sat. Telecoms Hill Street branch is open 8am to 9pm daily.

Emergencies

KEY TELEPHONE NUMBERS

In an emergency dial 999 for the police, and 995 for the fire brigade or the ambulance service.

LOSS

Call the police in cases of loss, or ROV (Registry of Vehicles), for items left in taxis at 4505349.

PHARMACIES

In Singapore, most doctors dispense their prescribed medication but there are also numerous registered pharmacies. You'll always be able to find one nearby with a qualified pharmacist on duty.

The largest ones include Medical Hall which has outlets in Straits Trading Building, Wellington Building and Scotts Shopping Centre; Guardian Pharmacy at The Promenade, Lucky Plaza, Cold Storage Centrepoint, Plaza Singapura, Raffles City Shopping Centre, World Trade Centre, Tangs, United Square, Marina Square, Wisma Atria, Peninsula Plaza; and Watson's at Funan Centre, Marina Square, International Plaza, Wisma Atria, Holland Village, OUB Building and Meridien Shopping Complex. Check the Yellow Pages for additional listings or ask at your hotel.

Most pharmacies also stock personal care, baby products, hair care products, toiletries, cosmetics and even unrelated articles like gift cards and sweets.

DOCTORS

There is no shortage of these in Singapore, all speak at least English and one other language. They are professionally trained either here or abroad and an average cost per visit varies between $10 to $35 for a practitioner and $35 to $70 for first consultation by a specialist. Ask your embassy to recommend a private practitioner or specialist.

GOVERNMENT HOSPITALS

Government hospitals are numerous all over the island. They compare favourably with those in the West. The hospitals here are advanced and well-equipped to cope with the most complicated and difficult operations. Most of their services are made available to non-citizens who pay a slightly higher rate than the citizens. The Singapore General Hospital is at 7 Outram Road. Tel: 2223322.

There are also several good private hospitals including Mount Elizabeth Hospital, 3 Mount Elizabeth Road, Tel: 7372666 and Gleneagles, 4/6 Napier Road, Tel: 4737222.

Most have 24-hour emergency services.

LEFT LUGGAGE

There are left luggage facilities at both terminals at Changi Airtropolis.

GETTING AROUND

ORIENTATION

Singapore is small and generally clearly signed. Public transport is efficient and reasonably priced. For a good look at all corners of the island, walk around the **Observation Lounge** at the **Mandarin Hotel**, or the **Compass Rose** at the **Westin Stamford** or the top of **High Street Centre** at the corner of High Street and North Bridge Road. The centre is open 10am until 7pm.

MAPS

There are several excellent free maps, which give more detailed sections of parts of the city which would be of interest to the visitor. Most bookshops also stock larger maps of Singapore and Malaysia.

Then there's the *Secret Map of Singapore* which gives a fascinating insight into the lifestyles and traditions of Singapore and points out all kinds of places that might interest visitors.

SINGAPORE TOURIST PROMOTION BOARD

In the inner circles of the travel trade, Singapore's Tourist Promotion Board is highly esteemed for the crisp efficiency characteristic of the place it represents. Through its steady campaigns to add extra sheen to the Republic's facilities, the Board convinces taxi drivers that it pays to have tidy upholstery. It rewards service stations if they look nice. It encourages shops through every incentive, including the award of a metal plaque, to keep their premises clean, display their items attractively, and serve their customers with honesty and courtesy.

Tour operators and travel agents are gleaned with a fine comb to make sure their services rank high by international standards. And to see that Singapore's new arrivals are well received, the Board goes down to the grass-roots level by organizing "Courtesy Courses" for employees stationed at the island's principal points of entry. "So they will know the meaning of PR and how to exercise it," a Board member explains.

Since the Board's numerous services command such diligent attention, they are bound to be professionally tailored to a visitor's needs. And the traveller who appreciates smooth organization and

quick answers will find they work well as a cushion for feeling at home.

The Singapore Tourist Promotion Board's (STPB) main office is situated on the 36th floor of Raffles City Towers, 250 North Bridge Road. Tel: 3396622. There are also two visitor information offices where wide range of brochures, maps etc. are available as well as friendly personal advise. One is in Scotts Shopping Centre, 6 Scotts Road, Unit 02-02/03. Tel: 7383778. The other is on the ground floor of Raffles City Shopping Complex, (#01-19), 252 North Bridge Road. Tel: 3341335. There are also information booths at the airport.

FREE PUBLICATIONS

It is safe to say that just about every practical tip a traveller needs to get around in Singapore is available in free publications. The STPB's *Official Guide to Singapore* has the advantage of clear, condensed information in the form of one small booklet. You may follow the numbers in the *Secret Map of Singapore* for orientation to the city plan. Visitors can be kept informed daily with a calendar of current affairs and religious ceremonies, Chinese operas, art exhibits and other happenings with *Singapore This Week* and *The Singapore Visitor*. These publications are distributed to all leading hotels and shopping centre information counters.

Publicity writers, journalists, photographers, or editors, whether on assignment to feature Singapore in travel publications or seriously considering the idea, are welcome to take a short cut through the Tourist Promotion Board. By writing in advance, complimentary tours, suggested itineraries, a bundle of literature and 9,000 slides, conveniently filed in special subjects for articles, is at your disposal. And if research demands more depth, the Board refers writers to specific publications and library references, or to officers heading its departments who personally handle the subject.

FROM THE AIRPORT

The Airport is linked to the city centre by the East Coast Parkway (20 minutes travelling time) and to the rest of Singapore by the Pan-Island Expressway.

There are three types of transport from the airport – private car, taxi or public bus. At both Terminal 1 and 2, the taxi rank is situated on the same level as the Arrival Hall. A surcharge, $3 more than the fare shown on the taxi meter, is charged if you board a taxi at the Airport. In Terminal 1, inclined travellators in the Arrival Hall descend to a short tunnel that leads to the Passenger Crescent, where a private car pick-up point is located. In Terminal 2 the car pick-up point is on the same level as the Arrival Hall. In the basement of both Terminals there are bus depots. Bus #16 leaves regularly between 6am and 11.45pm for a 40–50 minute ride downtown. The trip costs $1.30.

MASS RAPID TRANSIT (MRT)

The $5 billion, 67-km (42-mile) Mass Rapid Transit (MRT) system was officially opened in early 1988. It has 66 air-conditioned trains running over a north–south and east–west line. The six-car trains, each of which can accommodate 1,800 persons, travel at 45 kph (30 mph) and stop at each of the 42 stations for 20–30 seconds. About one-third of the stations are underground and rate as among the most handsome underground stations in the world. A journey aboard the MRT, especially on the underground section, which runs through the heart of tourist and business Singapore, is a must for all visitors.

Fare collection is automatic: magnetically coded plastic cards costs between 60 cents for 3½km (2 miles) and $1.50 for single-trips. You can purchase these tickets at the stations.

If you are going to be moving around a lot by public transport, it is wise to buy a TransitLink Farecard which is a stored-value card usable on the MRT and buses. The Farecard is available from MRT stations and bus interchanges for S$12 and S$22, which includes a S$2 deposit. An MRT Tourist Souvenir Ticket is also available for $6.

Depending on the station, the first train rolls out at about 5.30am and 6am, Mondays to Saturdays, and between 6.45am and 7.25am on Sundays and holidays. Last trains are between 11pm and mid-night; 15 minutes earlier on Sundays and public holidays.

BUSES

Nearly 250 bus services ply the paved roads of Singapore and connect every corner of the island.

Buses (single and double-deckers) run from 6.15am to 11.30pm on the average, with an extension of about a half hour for both starting and ending times on weekends and public holidays. Fares are cheap (minimum S$0.60 to a maximum of S$1.30 on air-conditioned buses) and the amount payable is structured according to fare stages. There is an extensive sample list of fares in the *Official Guide to Singapore*, but bus drivers are generally very helpful and will tell you the fare on boarding.

An especially helpful source for all information pertaining to this mode of transportation is the *Bus Guide* which is available at most bookstores and newsstands. For S$0.70 this booklet gives complete details of all bus routes and contains a section on bus services to major tourist spots. Or call Singapore Bus Service, Tel: 2848866.

The TransitLink Farecard (a common stored-value ticket) enables you to travel on buses fitted with validator machines. The Farecard can be purchased at bus interchages and MRT stations.

For good value, purchase the **Singapore Explorer** ticket and get the special Explorer Route Map: $5 for a one-day ticket, or $12 for a three-day ticket. Holders can hop on and off, as frequently as they

wish, the buses run by the Singapore Bus Services and the Trans-Island Bus Service. Tour the island by following the colour-coded and clearly indicated major routes and visit points of interest on the map. Tickets are available from travel agents and major hotels. Contact the SBS PR Office, Tel: 1-800-2872727 (8am to 4.30pm weekdays, 8am to 12.30pm Saturdays) for further information.

TAXIS

One of the rarest sights in Singapore is a main street without a taxi. More than 10,000 taxis are on the roads and everyone uses them. It is the fastest and easiest way to move around in comfort. The vehicles are clean and kept in tip-top condition (the cleanest taxis get a prize in Singapore). Black, yellow, light blue, green and white or red and white – all with "SH" or "SHA" on their license plates – taxis run by meter. Each taxi may carry a maximum of four passengers. The fare is $2.40 for the first mile (1½km) and 10 cents for each 250 meters thereafter.

Most taxi stands are found just outside shopping centres and other public buildings. You may join the queue at these or you may hail one on the road (except those marked with double yellow lines).

Designed to alleviate traffic congestion, the Central Business District is a restricted zone for cars and taxis without an area license from 7.30am to 6.30pm on weekdays and 7.30am to 3pm on Saturdays and Eve of Public holidays. Daily area licenses ($3 per vehicle) are payable by the passenger unless the taxi already displays a valid license.

Other surcharges payable, above the metered fare, at different times and for different reasons, include $3 per taxi for trips originating from the Changi Airport; $2.20 for a radio cab and $3 for a taxi-booking made in advance.

Most drivers speak or understand English. Still, it is better to be sure the driver knows exactly where you want to go before starting. Tipping is purely optional and is discouraged by the government.

Taxis on radio call are available 24 hours at 4686188, 7624040, 2653049, 2614774, 4668386, 4747707, 4815151 and 2827700.

TRISHAWS

A direct descendant of the historical rickshaw – covered carriage pulled by man on foot – is the trishaw, a bicycle with a sidecar. This is a vanishing mode of transport among locals due to its slow speed, its lack of sophistication and the unending hassle over the fare with the rider – often a stubborn, grumpy man in his 60s.

However, it is fast becoming a hot favourite among visitors. Its selling point lies in the fact that it goes at a speed slow enough for its passenger to absorb what goes on around, but fast enough to cover most of the picturesque sights of downtown within an hour. For full information of itinerarised trishaw tours at standard prices, call 8283133 or ask at your hotel's tour desk.

A word of caution: for a ride by a freelance rider, be sure you agree upon a fare before getting on. Licensed riders are distinguished from these by coloured badges.

CAR RENTALS

Rent-A-Car: Singapore has great roads and driving here is relatively painless, except you should keep a keen eye out for tail gaters and lane drifters. Rent-a-car services provide the wheels if you provide a valid international driver's licence. Self-drive cars cost from $65 to $255 a day plus mileage, depending on the size and comfort of your limousine. A chauffeur-driven Mercedes costs S$40 per hour.

Before you head out, be sure to stock up on parking coupons and ask the rental companies to explain about Central Business District stickers (required between 7.30–6.30pm on weekdays and 7.30am–3pm on Saturdays and Eve of Public holidays.)

Avis, Tel: 7371668
Budget, Tel:4690111
Hertz, Tel: 4473388
Elpin Tours and Limousines, Tel: 2353111
Presidential Pacific Limousines, Tel: 2233668
Avis Limousines, Tel: 5428833

For other companies, look in the Yellow Pages under *Motorcar Renting and Leasing*.

BOAT CHARTER

Boats may be hired at Collyer Quay and at the World Trade Centre for trips out to the islands. Arrange the length of time and cost before you set out, and expect to pay about S$30 to S$40 per hour.

Chartering luxury yachts has become more popular recently, and if you can make up a party, you can choose your own itinerary and sail in style, enquiries to Amaril Cruises, Tel: 2216969; Club Travel International, Tel: 7333788; Fantasy Cruises, Tel: 2840424; Pacific Seacraft, Tel: 2706665.

The *Rising Tide*, a 70-ft, twin-masted, ocean-going schooner, is available for charter (see photo on pages 242/243). For bookings, call Daphne at 8612755 or Fax: 8616438.

ON FOOT

Singapore's streets are safe, and although it's hot and humid, the covered ways lining older streets make walking pleasant. And walking enables you to see much more. For a walking tour of the city, follow the itineraries suggested in *The Insight Pocket Guide to Singapore*.

COMPLAINTS

The Singapore Tourist Promotion Board and the Consumers Association of Singapore (CASE) has full authority to protect the interest of visitors whether they are here to shop, trade or to see.

Stringent measures, including imposition of heavy fines and suspension of licences, have been taken against shopkeepers, taxi drivers or trishaw riders who tried to fleece a visitor. Since then, shams are rare. But, if you have a legitimate complaint, or fall victim to unethical practices, bring it to the attention of the board which will assist you promptly and efficiently.

Note: The Singapore Tourist Promotion Board (STPB) has a telephone number with assistance on the receiving end: 3300431/22.

WHERE TO STAY

HOTELS

Unless stated otherwise all hotels have colour television and IDD in bedrooms and a swimming pool. The hotels are listed in alphabetical order.

Allson Hotel, 101 Victoria Street, Singapore 0718. Tel: 65- 3360811; Telefax: 65-3397019. 412 rooms plus serviced apartments; restaurants serving local, continental, Chinese and Thai food; ballroom. Other facilities: conference room; banquet room; business centre; health centre; doctor.

Amara Hotel, 165 Tanjong Pagar Road, Singapore 0208. Tel: 65-2244488; Telefax: 65-2243910. 350 rooms; restaurants serving Chinese, Thai and Western food; pub; karaoke room and lounge. Other facilities: conference room; banquet room; business centre; massage centre; tennis and squash courts.

ANA Hotel Singapore, 16 Nassim Hill, Singapore 1025. Tel: 65-7321222; Telefax: 65-2351516. 456 rooms (no smoking floor), restaurants serving local, continental and Japanese food; disco/bar/bistro. Other facilities: function room; business centre; fitness centre; gift shop.

Apollo, 33 Havelock Road, Singapore 0316. Tel: 65-7332081; Telefax 65-7331588. 317 rooms (no smoking floors); restaurants serving local, Indonesian, Japanese and Chinese food; disco; club. Other facilities: conference room; banquet room; business centre; health centre; shops.

Asia, 37 Scotts Road, Singapore 0922. Tel 65-7378388; Telefax: 65-7333563. 146 rooms; restaurants serving Chinese, local and continental food; lounge. Other facilities: function rooms. (No swimming pool. Rooms do not have IDD.)

Bayview Inn, 30 Bencoolen Street, Singapore 0718. Tel: 65-3372882; Telefax: 65-3382880. 117 rooms; cafe serving Asian food; lounge. Other facilities: conference room.

Beaufort Sentosa, 2 Bukit Manis Road, Sentosa, Singapore 0409. Tel: 65-2750331; Telefax: 65-2750228. 214 rooms and 4 villas with private pools, restaurants serving seafood, Japanese, local and continental cuisine; lounge; bar. Other facilities: conference and banquet rooms; ballroom; business centre; tennis and squash courts.

Boulevard, 200 Orchard Blvd, Singapore 1024. Tel: 65-7372911; Telefax: 65-7378449. 500 rooms; restaurants serving local, continental, Chinese and Japanese food; lounge. Other facilities: conference room; business centre; fitness centre; hairdresser.

Cairnhill, 19 Cairnhill Circle, Singapore 0922. Tel: 65-7346622; Telefax: 65-2355598. 217 rooms; Western and Chinese restaurants; lounge. Other facilities: conference room; health centre; shops.

Carlton, 76 Bras Basah Road, Singapore 0718. Tel: 65-3388333; Telefax: 65-3396866. 420 rooms (no smoking floors); restaurants serving local, Western and Chinese food; lounge. Other facilities: conference and banquet rooms; boardroom; business centre; health centre; shops.

Cockpit, 6/7 Oxley Rise, Singapore 0923. Tel: 65-7379111; Telefax: 65-7373105. 176 rooms; restaurants serving Chinese and Western food; bar. Other facilities: conference room. (No swimming pool.)

Concorde, 317 Outram Road, Singapore 0316. Tel: 65-7330188; Telefax: 65-7330989. 497 rooms; Chinese and Japanese restaurants; lounge. Other facilities: conference and banquet rooms; ballroom; business centre; tennis courts; shops.

Crown Prince, 270 Orchard Road, Singapore 0923. Tel: 65-7321111; Telefax: 65-7327018. 288 rooms (no smoking floors); restaurants serving local, continental, Japanese and Chinese food; 24-hour coffee shop. Other facilities: conference and banquet rooms; business centre.

Duxton Hotel, 83 Duxton Road, Singapore 0208. Tel: 65-2277678; Telefax: 65-221232. 49 rooms, French restaurant. Other facilities: meeting room, business equipment available; fitness room. Situated in the heart of the Tanjong Pagar conservation area. (No swimming pool.)

Equatorial, 429 Bukit Timah Road, Singapore 1025. Tel: 65-7320431; Telefax: 65-73794226. 195 rooms; restaurants serving local, Chinese, Japanese and Swiss food; lobby bar. Other facilities: conference and banquet rooms; business centre; shops.

Excelsior, 5 Coleman Street, Singapore 0617. Tel: 65-3387733; Telefax: 65-3393847. 274 rooms; restaurants serving local, continental, Indian, Japanese and Chinese food. Other facilities: conference and banquet rooms; business counter; health centre.

Furama, 60 Eu Tong Sen Street, Singapore 0105. Tel: 65-5333888; Telefax: 65-5341489. 355 rooms; restaurants serving local, continental and Chinese food; bar. Other facilities: conference and banquet rooms; business centre; shops; fitness centre.

Garden, 14 Balmoral Road, Singapore 1025. Tel: 65-2353344; Telefax: 2359730. 209 rooms; restaurant serving local and continental food; bar. Other facilities: conference and banquet rooms.

Golden Landmark, 390 Victoria Street, Singapore 0718. Tel: 65-2972828; Telefax: 65-2982038. 397 rooms; local, Western and Chinese restaurants; lounge. Other facilities: conference and banquet rooms; business centre; shops.

Goodwood Park, 22 Scotts Road, Singapore 0922. Tel: 65-7377411, Telefax: 65-7328558. 192 rooms; Chinese, Japanese and continental, seafood restaurants; bar. Other facilities: conference and banquet rooms; business centre; shops.

Grand Central, 22 Cavenagh Road, Singapore 0922. Tel: 65-7379944; Telefax: 65-7333175. 344 rooms; local, continental, Japanese and Chinese restaurants; karaoke lounge. Other facilities: conference and banquet rooms; health centre; shops.

Harbour View Dai-Ichi, 81 Anson Road, Singapore 0207. Tel: 65-2241133; Telefax: 65-2220749. 420 rooms; restaurants serving local, Western, Japanese and Chinese food. Other facilities: conference and banquet rooms; fitness centre; shops.

Hilton International, 581 Orchard Road, Singapore 0923. Tel: 65-7372233; Telefax: 65-7322917. 406 rooms (no smoking floors); restaurants serving local, continental and Chinese food; disco; lounge; ballroom. Other facilities: conference and banquet rooms; business centre; health club; shops.

Holiday Inn Park View, 11 Cavenagh Road, Singapore 0922. Tel: 65-7338333; Telefax: 65-7344593. 320 rooms; restaurants serving continental, Asian, Chinese and Indian food; bar; ballroom. Other facilities: conference and banquet rooms; business centre; shops.

Hyatt Regency, 10 Scotts Road, Singapore 0922. Tel: 65-7331188; Telefax: 65-7321696. 748 rooms (no smoking floors); restaurants serving local, Chinese and continental food; 24-hour coffee house; pub; disco; lounge; bar. Other facilities: conference and banquet rooms; 24-hour business centre; health club; tennis, squash and badminton court.

Imperial, 1 Jln Rumbia, Singapore 0923. Tel: 65-7371666; Telefax: 65-7374761. 560 rooms; restaurants serving local, continental, Chinese and Indian food; 24-hour coffee shop; lounge; disco; ballroom. Other facilities: conference and banquet rooms; business centre; shops; health centre.

Inn of the Sixth Happiness, No 9–35 Erskine Road, Singapore 0106. Tel: 65-233266; Telefax: 65-2237951. Antique Chinese inn with 48 rooms; restaurants serving Italian, Chinese and other Asian dishes; Chinese style club; function room. (No swimming pool.)

Katong Park, 42 Meyer Road, Singapore 1543. Tel: 65-3453311. 170 rooms; restaurant serving Chinese food. Other facilities: conference room; banquet room. (No IDD.)

King's Clarion, 403 Havelock Road, Singapore 0316. Tel: 65-7330011. 319 rooms: Japanese, Chinese, continental and local restaurants; lounge; pub/karaoke lounge.

Ladyhill, 1 Ladyhill Road, Singapore 1025. Tel: 65-7372111; Telefax: 65-7374606. 170 rooms; restaurants serving local and continental food. Other facilities: seminar and banquet rooms.

Le Meridien Changi, 1 Netheravon Road, Singapore 1750. Tel: 65-5427700; Telefax: 65-5425295. 272 rooms; restaurants serving local and continental food; lounge. Other facilities: conference and banquet rooms; ballroom; health centre; shops.

Le Meridien Singapore, 100 Orchard Road, Singapore 0923. Tel: 65-7338855; Telefax: 65-7327886. 398 rooms (no smoking floors); restaurants serving local, continental and Indonesian food; bar. Other facilities: conference and banquet rooms; ballroom; business centre; shops.

Mandarin Singapore, 333 Orchard Road, Singapore 0923. Tel: 65-7374411; Telefax: 65-7322361. 1,200 rooms (no smoking floors); restaurants serving local, continental, Chinese and Japanese food; disco; lounge. Other facilities: conference and banquet room; ballroom; business centre; fitness centre; tennis and squash courts; putting green; shops.

Marina Mandarin, Marina Square, 6 Raffles Boulevard, Singapore 0103. Tel: 65-3383388; Telefax: 65-33949777. 575 rooms (no smoking floors); restaurants serving local, continental, Chinese and Japanese food; disco; lounge; pub. Other facilities: conference and banquet rooms; ballroom; business centre; fitness centre; tennis and squash courts; attached to Singapore's largest shopping mall.

Melia at Scotts, 45 Scotts Road, Singapore 0922. Tel: 65-7325885; Telefax: 65-7321332. 245 rooms; restaurants serving continental food; 24-hour coffee house; bar; music and dance lounge. Other facilities: conference and banquet rooms; business centre; health club; shops.

Metropole, 41 Seah Street, Singapore 0718. Tel: 65-3363611; Telefax: 65-3393610. 54 rooms; restaurants serving Western and Chinese herbal food; business facilities.

YMCA Metropolitan , 60 Stevens Road, Singapore 1025. Tel: 65-7377755; Telefax: 65-2355528. 87 rooms; restaurant serving Western and local food. Other facilities: function rooms; fitness centre; squash courts; gift shop.

Miramar, 401 Havelock Road, Singapore 0316. Tel: 65-7330222; Telefax: 65-7334027. 333 rooms; restaurants serving local, continental and Chinese food; lounge. Other facilities; conference and banquet rooms; business services; health club.

New Otani, 177A River Valley Road, Singapore 0617. Tel: 65-3383333; Telefax: 65-3392854. 386 rooms (no smoking floors); Japanese, Chinese and continental restaurants; bar; lounge. Other facilities: conference and banquet rooms; fitness centre; business centre; adjoining shopping complex.

New Park, 181 Kitchener Road, Singapore 0820. Tel: 65-295533; Telefax: 65-2972827. 508 rooms (Japanese floor); restaurants serving local, Western and Chinese/Thai dishes; lounges; function and banquet rooms; shops.

Novotel Orchid Inn, 214 Dunearn Road, Singapore 1129. Tel: 65-2503322; Telefax: 65-2509292. 412 rooms; restaurants serving local and Chinese food; music pub; lounge. Other facilities: conference and banquet rooms; business centre; health club; putting green; shops.

Omni Marco Polo, 247 Tanglin Road, Singapore 1024. Tel: 65-4747141; Telefax: 65-4710521. 603 rooms (no smoking floors); restaurants serving local and continental food; disco; coffee house. Other facilities: conference and banquet rooms; business centre; fitness centre.

Orchard, 442 Orchard Road, Singapore 0923. Tel: 65-7347766; Telefax: 65-7335482. 350 rooms; restaurant serving continental food; 24-hour coffee shop; bar. Other facilities: conference and banquet rooms; ballroom; squash and tennis courts; shops.

Orchard Parade, 1 Tanglin Road, Singapore 1024. Tel: 65-7371133; Telefax: 65-7330242. 270 rooms (no smoking floors); restaurants serving local, continental, Chinese and Japanese food; lounge; bar. Other facilities: conference and banquet rooms; business centre; fitness centre.

The Oriental Singapore, 5 Raffles Boulevard, Singapore 0923. Tel: 65-3380066; Telefax: 65-3399537. 518 rooms (no smoking floors); restaurants serving Asian and continental cuisines; lounge. Other facilities: conference and banquet rooms; business centre; fitness centre; tennis and squash courts; shops.

Pan Pacific Singapore, Marina Square, 7 Raffles Boulevard, Singapore 0103. Tel: 65-3368111; Telefax: 65-3391861. 800 rooms (no smoking floor); restaurants serving local, continental, Japanese and Chinese food; bar; lounge. Other facilities: conference and banquet rooms; ballroom, business centre; fitness centre; tennis courts; mini putting green.

Paramount, 25 Marine Parade Road, Singapore 1544. Tel: 65-3445577. 250 rooms; restaurant serving local, continental and Chinese food; bar. Other facilities: conference room; banquet room; shops; hairdresser; massage centre.

Peninsula, 3 Coleman Street, Singapore 0617. Tel: 65-3378091; Telefax: 65-3393580. 306 rooms; 24-hour restaurant serving local and continental food; Chinese nightclub; lounge. Other facilities: conference and banquet rooms; health centre.

Phoenix, 277 Orchard Road, Singapore 0923. Tel: 65-7378666; Telefax: 65-7322024. 300 rooms; coffee house; bar. Other facilities: conference and banquet rooms. (No swimming pool.)

Plaza, 7500A, Beach Road, Singapore 0719. Tel: 65-2980011; Telefax: 65-2963600. 350 rooms and service apartments; restaurants serving local, Chinese, Thai seafood and continental food; disco; karaoke club and lounge. Other facilities: conference and banquet rooms; business centre; fitness centre; badminton and squash courts; shops.

Premier, 22 Nassim Road, Singapore 1025. Tel: 65-7339811, Telefax: 65-7335595. Operated by the Singapore Hotel Association Training and Educational Centre. 28 rooms; restaurants serving local and continental food at budget prices; function room.

Raffles, 1 Beach Road, Singapore 0718. Tel: 65-3378041; Telefax: 65-3397650. 104 suites; 12 restaurants and bars offering continental, American, Asian and local cuisine along with your favourite refreshments. Other facilities: Function and boardrooms; ballroom; health club; shopping arcade.

Rasa Sentosa, 101 Siloso Road, Sentosa Island. Tel: 65-2750100; Telefax: 65-2750355. 459 rooms; Chinese restaurant; coffee shop; lounge; pub; bar; soda fountain. Other facilities: conference and banquet rooms; ballroom; business centre; health club; sea sports centre; children's playroom; shops.

RELC International House, 30 Orange Grove Road, Singapore 1025. Tel: 65-7379044; Telefax: 65-7339976. 128 rooms (no smoking floor); restaurant serving Chinese food. Other facilities: conference room; business centre. (No swimming pool.)

Regent, 1 Cuscaden Road, Singapore 1024. Tel: 65-7338888; Telefax: 65-7328838. 441 rooms; restaurants serving local, continental, and Chinese food; bar. Other facilities: conference and banquet rooms; ballroom; business centre; shops; fitness centre.

River View, 382 Havelock Road, Singapore 0316. Tel: 65-7329922; Telefax: 65-7321034. 472 rooms (no smoking floors); restaurants serving local, continental, Japanese and Chinese food; coffee shop; lounge; disco. Other facilities: conference and banquet rooms; business centre, fitness centre.

Royal, 36 Newton Road, Singapore 1130. Tel: 65-2534411; Telefax: 65-2538668. 299 rooms; Chinese, Japanese, Western and local food restaurants; lounge. Other facilities; conference and banquet rooms; health club; gift shop.

Royal Holiday Inn Crowne Plaza, 25 Scotts Road, Singapore 0922. Tel: 65-7377966; Telefax: 65-7376646. 493 rooms; restaurants serving local, Asian and Western food; bars. Other facilities: conference and banquet room; ballroom; business centre; health centre; gift shop.

Sea View, 26 Amber Close, Singapore 1543. Tel: 65-3452222; Telefax: 65-34843355. 435 rooms; restaurant serving local and continental food; bar. Other facilities: conference and banquet rooms; business centre; shops.

Shangri-La, 22 Orange Grove Road, Singapore 1025. Tel: 65-7373644; Telefax: 65-7337220. 750 rooms divided into three wings (no smoking floors); restaurants serving local, continental, Japanese and Chinese food; 24-hour coffee shop; disco; bar; lounge. Other facilities: conference and banquet rooms; ballroom; 24-hour business centre; fitness

centre; tennis and squash courts; golf pitch and putt; garden; shopping arcade.

Sheraton Towers, 39 Scotts Road, Singapore 0922. Tel: 65-7326000; Telefax: 65-7371072. 404 rooms, all with butler service (no smoking floors); 3 restaurants serving Chinese, Italian and other Western food; ballroom. Other facilities: conference and banquet rooms; ballroom; business centre; fitness centre. A businessmen's hotel.

Sloane Court, 17 Balmoral Road, Singapore 1025. Tel: 65-2353311; Telefax: 65-7339041. 32 rooms; English-style pub; restaurant serving international dishes. (No IDD in rooms, no swimming pool.)

Strand, 25 Bencoolen Street, Singapore 0718. Tel: 65-3381866; Telefax: 65-3363147. 130 rooms; coffee house; bar. (No swimming pool.)

Supreme, 115 Kramat Road, Singapore 0922. Tel: 65-7378333; Telefax: 65-7337404. 86 rooms; restaurant; karaoke lounge. (No swimming pool.)

Westin Plaza, 2 Stamford Road, Singapore 0617. Tel: 65-3388585; Telefax: 65-3382862. 796 rooms; 16 restaurants serving local, continental, Japanese and Chinese food; disco; jazz bar. Other facilities: large conference and banquet rooms; ballroom; executive centre; fitness centre; tennis and squash courts; surrounded by a shopping complex; MRT station within complex.

Westin Stamford, 2 Stamford Road, Singapore 0617. Tel: 65-3388585; Telefax: 65-3371554. 1,253 rooms; same facilities as the Westin Plaza.

YMCA Orchard, 1 Orchard Road, Singapore 0923. Tel: 65-3366000; Telefax: 65-3373140. 111 rooms; fast food outlets within premises. Other facilities: conference and banquet rooms; business centre; fitness centre; sports facilities. (No IDD in rooms.)

York, 21 Mt. Elizabeth, Singapore 0922. Tel: 65-7370511; Telefax 65-7321217. 324 rooms; restaurants serving local, continental and Chinese/Thai food; bar. Other facilities: conference and banquet rooms; business centre.

SERVICE APARTMENTS

The Ascott Executive Residences, 6 Scotts Road #01-21, Singapore 0922. Tel: 7320033. 177 units; short and long term leases.

Palm Court Service Apartments, 15 Cairnhill Road, Singapore 0922. Tel: 2350088; Telefax: 7843161. 144 fully furnished studio, one- and two-bedroom apartments with kitchen. Other facilities: business centre; gym; laundromat; tennis and squash courts.

FOOD DIGEST

WHAT AND WHERE TO EAT

Singaporeans live to eat, their pre-occupation with culinary matters means that finding food here presents no problem. Whether you fancy cuisine nouvelle or spicy local dishes, the choice is yours, for it's all here.

Most hotels have several restaurants including coffee shops that often open round the clock. International style restaurants abound and you can find most cuisines of the world on offer. Food centres with stalls selling all kinds of local favourites are hygienic (the government maintains strict controls) and are fun to try. There are also local coffee houses on most street corners, where Singaporeans enjoy a chat over a bowl of noodles or a cup of coffee, at any hour of the day.

The list below gives restaurant recommendations with an indication of the price for a meal for one person, without drinks.

$$$$	Very Expensive	S$50 and above
$$$	Expensive	S$30–S$50
$$	Moderate	S$15–S$30
$	Reasonable	S$15 and below

CHINESE CUISINE

BEIJING

Jade Room, Hotel Royal. Tel: 2548603. $$
Pine Court, Mandarin Singapore. Tel: 7374411. $$$
Prima Tower Revolving Restaurant, 201 Keppel Road. Tel: 2728822. It takes almost two hours for a complete revolution; so enjoy a spectacular view of the port as you eat. $$$
Taikan-En, Hotel New Otani, 177A River Valley Road. Tel: 3383333. Great boneless crispy duck and braised "monkeyhead" mushrooms with Chinese ham. $$

CANTONESE

126 Eating House, 126 Sims Avenue. Tel: 7464757. A wide selection of Hong Kong *dim sum* dishes. $$
Canton Garden, The Westin Plaza. Tel: 3388585. $$$
China Palace, Wellington Building, 20 Bideford Road. Tel: 2351378. $$$
Fatty's, 60 Albert Street. Tel: 3381087. Good home-cooked food in modest surroundings at a reasonable price. The locals and savvy backpackers swarm here. $
Garden Seafood, Goodwood Park Hotel. Tel: 7344806. $$$
Grand City, Cathay Building. Tel: 3383622. $$$
Grand Pavilion, Chinese Swimming Club. Tel: 4402222. $$$
Hai Tien Lo, Pan Pacific Hotel. Tel: 3368111. Classic Cantonese dishes are on offer here, including *Buddha Jumps Over The Wall*. Magnificent view. $$$
House of Blossoms, Marina Mandarin Hotel. Tel: 3383388. $$$
Huan Long Court, Apollo Hotel. Tel: 7339677. $$$
Inn of Happiness, Hilton International Hotel. Tel: 7372233. $$$$
Kirin Court, Devonshire Building, 20 Devonshire Road. Tel: 7321188. $$$$
Lei Garden, Boulevard Hotel. Tel: 2358122. Peking duck and lobster are recommended here. $$$
Li Bai, Sheraton Towers Hotel. Tel: 7376888. Named after the famous Tang Dynasty poet, house specialties include suckling pig, grilled boneless duck breast and seafood dishes. $$$$
Long Jiang, Crown Prince Hotel. Tel: 7349056. $$$$
Loy Sum Juan, Blk 31, Outram Park. Tel: 2206809. $$
Mitzi Cantonese Restaurant, 24/26 Murray Street. Tel: 2228281. A local favourite. $$
Noble House, UIC Building, 5 Shenton Way. Tel: 2270933. $$$
Ru Yi, Hyatt Hotel. Tel: 7331188. One of the best Cantonese restaurants in Singapore. $$$$
Shang Palace Restaurant, Shangri-La Hotel. Tel: 7373644. Chinese courtyard setting for *dim sum* at lunchtime and a wide range of *a la carte* choices of ancient Chinese recipes in the evening. Peking duck is good here, served in style. $$$
Sim Lam Tong, New Nam Thong, 8–10A Smith St. Tel: 2232817. $$
Spice Garden, Hotel Meridien Shopping Centre. Tel: 7324122. $$$
Summer Palace, The Regent Singapore. Tel: 7338888. $$$
Top of the Plaza, UOB Building. Tel: 5383232. Located on the 60th floor of a bank tower. There is *dim sum* at lunch and the dinner menu includes delicacies such as abalone and shark's fin. $$$$

Tung Lok, Liang Court Complex, #04-07. Tel: 3366022. Shark's fin dishes, abalone and bird's nest are offered at this elegant restaurant. Exotic *dim sum* at lunchtime. $$$
Union Farm Eating House, 435A Clementi Road. Tel: 4662776. $$
Wah Lok Restaurant, Carlton Hotel. Tel: 3388333. *Dim sum* is very popular here, combined with extensive *a la carte* dishes. $$$
Xin, Concorde Hotel. Tel; 7330188. $$$

HOKKIEN

Beng Hiang, 20 Murray Street, Food Alley, off Maxwell Road. Tel: 2216684. $$
Beng Thin Hoon Kee, OCBC Centre, 65 Chulia St. Tel: 5337708. $$

HUNAN

Charming Garden, Novotel Orchid Inn, 214 Dunearn Road. Tel: 2518149. Popular restaurant overlooking a little pool and garden. Try steamed red talipia fish with crispy soya bean crumb topping. $$$
Cherry Garden, The Oriental Singapore. Tel: 3380066. Imaginative dishes served in a Chinese style courtyard. They often hold special food promotions here. $$$
Spice Garden, Hotel Meridien Shopping Centre. Tel: 7324122. $$$

MIXED

Danial Dessert Specialists, 61 Duxton Rd. Tel: 2240776. Hong Kong style dessert and noodle house. $
Her Sea Palace, Forum The Shopping Mall. Tel: 7325688. $$$
L'Express, Westin Stamford. Tel: 3388585. Local buffet. $$
Paramount, Paramount Hotel. Tel: 4403233. $$$
Swee Kee Chicken Rice, 51/53 Middle Road. Tel: 3370314. $$
Westlake Eating House, Blk 4 #02-139 Queen's Road. Tel: 4747283. Located in a housing estate, it is popular with locals and expatriates alike, and you can choose dishes from all over China. $$

SHANGHAINESE

Chang Jiang, Goodwood Park Hotel. Tel: 7377411. $$$$
China Palace, Wellington Building, 20 Bideford Road. Tel: 2351378. $$$
Esquire Kitchen, Blk 231 Bras Basah Shopping Complex. Tel: 3361802. Good value for money. $$
House of Blossoms, Marina Mandarin Hotel. Tel: 3383388. $$$

SZECHUAN

Cherry Garden, The Oriental Singapore. Tel: 3380066. $$$
China Palace, Wellington Building, 20 Bideford Road. Tel: 2351378. $$$
Chinatown, Hotel Imperial. Tel: 7371666. $$$
Dragon City, Novotel Orchid Inn, 214 Dunearn Road. Tel: 2547070. One of the most popular restaurants in Singapore, don't forget to book. $$$
Golden Phoenix, Equatorial Hotel. Tel: 7320431. $$$
Liu Hsiang Lou, Allson Hotel. Tel: 3360811. $$$
Long Jiang, Crown Prince Hotel. Tel; 7349056. $$$$
Mei San, Royal Holiday Inn Crowne Plaza. Tel: 7377966. You can select your seafood live from the aquariums at this restaurant which has Ming Dynasty decor. $$$
Min Jiang, Goodwood Park Hotel. Tel: 7377411 Spicy cuisine in romantic setting. $$$
Szechuan Court, The Westin Plaza. Tel: 3388585. $$$
Tien Court, King's Clarion Hotel. Tel: 7393193. $$$

TEOCHEW

Ban Seng, 79 New Bridge Road. Tel: 5331471. The original Teochew restaurant in Singapore, which has changed little. $$
East Ocean, #02-18 Shaw Centre, 1 Scotts Road. Tel: 2359088. Teochew dishes at their best. $$
House of Blossoms, Marina Mandarin Hotel, 6 Raffles Blvd. Tel: 3383388. Rich decor and beautifully presented dishes. $$$
Peng Catering, 30 Lorong 1, Realty Park. Tel: 2896975. $$
Swatow, DBS Building #B1-15, 6 Shenton Way. Tel: 2235473. $$$
Tye Kheng Teo Chew, Blk 19 Outram Park. Tel: 2217414. $$

VEGETARIAN AND HERBAL

Buddhist Banquet, 760 Upper Serangoon Road. Tel: 2867559. Modest restaurant with good food. $
Fo You Yuan, Lorong 11, 20 Geylang Rd. Tel: 7448009. Taiwanese style vegetarian food. $$
Fut Sai Kai, 147 Kitchener Rd. Tel: 2912350. $$
Happy Realm, #03-16 Pearl Centre, Eu Tong Sen Street. Tel: 2226141. $
Hong Kong Bodhi Restaurant, Marina Square. Tel: 3370703. $
Hong Zhu, 2 Craig Rd. Tel: 2277156. $$
Hua Tuo Guan, 22–24 Tanjong Pagar Rd, Tel: 2224854; 222 East Coast Rd, Tel: 3440798; 360 Geylang Rd, Tel: 7447560; Thomson Yaohan Food Street, Tel: 4590618; Katong Yaohan Food Street, Tel: 3448639; Orchard Yoahan Food Street, Tel: 3390887; Blk 716 Ang Mo Kio Central, Tel:

4599444; 1357 Serangoon Rd, Tel: 2933768. Delicious food and very popular. $

Imperial Herbal Restaurant, Metropole Hotel. Tel: 3370491. Dishes boasting nutritional and medicinal benefits are served. Egg whites and scallops and shark's fin soup are among the specialties but if you are feeling adventurous you can try black ants on shredded potato or drunken scorpions. $$

Lingzhi, Orchard Towers. Tel: 7343788. $$

Miao Yi Vegetarian Restaurant, #03-01/02 Coronation Shopping Plaza. Tel: 4671331. Perfect for the vegetarian who loves local flavours. $

Soup Restaurant, 25 Smith St. Tel: 2229923. $

Woh Mee, 117–119 Kallang Rd. Tel: 2993927. $$

INDIAN CUISINE

NORTHERN

Hazara, 24 Lorong Mambong, Holland Village. Tel: 4674101. Good North Indian food in this intimate restaurant. $$$

Kinara, 57 Boat Quay. Tel: 5330412. $$$

Maharani, #05-36 Far East Plaza. Tel: 2358840. $$

Mayarani, #01-09 Amara Hotel. Tel: 2256244. $$

Moghul Mahal, #01-11, 1 Colombo Court. Tel: 3387794. $$$

Moti Mahal, 18 Murray Street, off Maxwell Road. Tel: 2214338. Considered by many to be the best Indian restaurant in South East Asia. $$

Mumtaz Mahal, #05-22/23 Far East Plaza. Tel: 7322754. $$$

Nur Jehan, 66 Race Course Road. Tel: 2928033. $$

Orchard Maharajah, 25 Cuppage Road, Cuppage Terrace. Tel: 7326331. Great *tandoori* dishes. *Al fresco* or air-conditioned dining choices. $$

Rang Mahal, Hotel Imperial. Tel: 7371666. $$

Royal Bengal, 72 Boat Quay. Tel: 5384329. A shophouse by the Singapore river that has been restored to feel like an aristocratic Indian home. $$$

The Tandoor, Holiday Inn Park View. Tel: 7338333. Romantic ambience in a golden glow with soft music playing as diners enjoy their meal. $$$

PUNJABI

Ujagar Singh's, 7 St. Gregory's Place, off Hill Street. Tel: 3361586. Totally unpretentious room upstairs serving superb food at such low prices that you can afford a wide selection. $

Shayray's, 25 Lorong Mambong. Tel: 4689126. $$

SOUTH & VEGETARIAN

A One Curry, 17 Birch Rd. Tel: 2948590. $$

Anbu, 158 Serangoon Rd. Tel: 2944800. $

Annalakshmi, Excelsior Hotel, #02-10, 5 Coleman Street. Tel: 3393007. Wonderful setting for exquisite cuisine. Lavish lunch and dinner buffets. $$$

Banana Leaf Apollo, 56 Race Course Road. Tel: 2938682. Informal restaurant where various curries are ladled out of large vats onto a banana leaf placemat. Diners can eat with their hands or ask for cutlery. $

Bombay Woodlands, Basement, Tanglin Shopping Centre. Tel: 2352712. Pleasant, unpretentious restaurant in the middle of the shopping district, serving very good vegetarian food. $$

Komala Vilas, 76–78 Serangoon Road. Tel: 2936980. In the heart of Little India, simple but good food. Especially popular at breakfast for its donut-like *vadai* snack. $

Muthu's, 78 Race Course Road. Tel: 2932389. No frills Indian food at its best. A choice of chicken, mutton, prawn and fish head curry. $

MALAY & INDONESIAN

Abu Hurairah Malay Seafood Restaurant, 259B Changi Road. Tel: 7446411. $

Aziza's, 36 Emerald Hill Road. Tel: 2351130. Friendly service, cosy *kampong* atmosphere and good, mildly spiced food. $$$

Bintang Timur, Far East Plaza. Tel: 2354539. $$

House of Sundanese Food, 218 East Coast Rd. Tel: 3455020. $$

Ikobana, Blk 5 Changi Village. Tel: 5453579. $

Jawa Timur, Chiat Hong Building, 110 Middle Road. Tel: 3375532. $$

Kartini, #02-31 Parkway Parade. Tel: 3482228. $$

Kintamani, Level 3, Apollo Hotel. Tel: 7332081. $$

Manis Manis, 2 Cheong Chin Nam Rd, off Upper Bukit Timah Road. Tel: 4686806. $

Mutiara, #B1-10/11 Liang Court. Tel: 3365653. $$

Nora Islamic Restaurant, 285 Changi Road. Tel: 7493182. $

Ramayana, #07-01 Plaza Singapura. Tel: 3363317. $$

Ria Aneka, 27 Lorong Liput. Tel: 4625062. $$

Sanur, #04-17/18 Centrepoint, Tel: 7342192; #B2-03 Yishun Northpoint Shopping Centre, Tel: 7547541; #03-45 Chinatown Point, Tel: 5345152; #04-16 Central Tower, Ngee Ann City, Tel: 7343434. Good old Indonesian food, highly popular with the local crowd. $$

Sate Inn, 257 Changi Road, Tel: 4400658; Picnic Food Court, Tel: 7330740. $

Sukmaindra Restaurant, Level 3, Royal Holiday Inn Crowne Plaza. Tel: 7324677. Serves a superb selection of Malay and Bruneian dishes. $$

Tambuah Mas, #04-10 Tanglin Shopping Centre. Tel: 7333333. Good food in a friendly atmosphere. Packed at lunchtime. $

JAPANESE

Inagiku, Level 3, Westin Plaza. Tel: 3388585. Popular set meals and *a la carte* choices. Choose to sit in the restaurant or in private *tatami* rooms. $$$$
Kampachi, Equatorial Hotel. Tel: 7320431. $$$$
Keyaki, Pan Pacific Hotel. Tel: 3368111. Superb food in a tranquil setting. *Sushi, sashimi* and all the other delicacies. *Teppanyaki* and *robatuyaki.* $$$$
Kobe, #04-06 Tanglin Shopping Centre. Tel: 7346796. A very popular spot with locals for *shabu-shabu, sukiyaki* and Japanese barbecue. $$
Kurumaya, #09-00 Harbour View Dai-Ichi Hotel. Tel: 2241133. $$$$
Kushi Katsu, 29 Lorong Mambong, Holland Village. Tel: 4623420. $$
Nadaman, Level 24 Shangri-La Hotel. Tel: 7373644. Twenty-four floors up leads you to an excellent Japanese restaurant, where authentic *Kansai* cuisine for southwest Japan is served. $$$$
Nanbantei, #05-132 Far East Plaza. Tel: 7335666. Cozy Japanese restaurant that specialises in *yakitori.* $$
Shima, Goodwood Park Hotel. Tel: 7346281. Good restaurant which sometimes offers all-you-can-eat *sushi* at lunch. $$$
Unkai, ANA Hotel. Tel: 7321222. *Sushi, teppanyaki* and *omakase* banquets. Private *tatami* rooms available. $$$

LOCAL CUISINE

Alkaff Mansion, 10 Telok Blangah Green. Tel: 2359533. $$$
Bar & Billiard Room, Raffles Hotel. Tel: 3311612. $$
Baski's Restaurant, 9–11 Erskine Road. Tel: 2219312. $$
Beaufort Hotel, 2 Sentosa Bukit Manis. Tel: 2750331. $$$
Cafe In the Park, ANA Hotel. Tel: 7321222. $$
Cafe Palm, Oriental Singapore. Tel: 3380066. Luxurious, relaxing atmosphere with excellent cuisine. $$
Emmerson's Tiffin Rooms, 51 Neil Road. Tel: 2277518. $$
Ficus Cafe, Orchard Hotel. Tel: 7347766. $$
Green Bamboo Village, Hotel Equatorial. Tel: 7320431. $$
Kopi Tiam, Westin Stamford Hotel. Tel: 3388585. Relaxed, coffee shop ambience serving Chinese, Malay and Indian food. *Roti prata* prepared in the restaurant 6pm until 9.30pm Fridays to Sundays. $$
Melting Pot Cafe, Concorde Hotel. Tel: 7330188. $$
Our Makan Shop, 74 Race Course Road. Tel: 2929475. Indian and Malay dishes served in a simple setting. $
Parrots, Omni Marco Polo Hotel. Tel: 4747141. A sumptuous buffet spread or excellent beef *kuay teow.* $$

Phoenix Coffee House, Basement Hotel Phoenix. Tel: 7378666. $$
Pinnacle, Level 60, OUB Centre, Raffles Place. Tel: 5322166. $$$$
Rendezvous, #02-19 Raffles City Shopping Centre. Tel: 3397508. *Beef rendang,* fermented soya beans and other *nasi padang* specialties. $$
Spice Express, Forum The Shopping Mall. Tel: 7348835. $$
Tiffin Room, Raffles Hotel. Tel: 3378041. A wide assortment of mild curries with a variety of condiments. Great local deserts. $$$
Tradewinds, Hilton International Singapore. Tel: 7372233. Rooftop stalls serve fresh *prata* and *murtabak.* $$
Waterfall Cafe, Shangri-La Hotel. Tel: 7373644. Garden setting, good range of local food. Duck rice is recommended and the Sunday brunch. $$

Food centres are everywhere and this is where the locals eat. You can try all kinds of food, and watch it being cooked. Just place your order and indicate where you are sitting; and the food will be brought to you. It is the best way to sample a wide range of local delicacies, and the best value for money.

Newton Circus is the most well-known of these, but the ones with the most ambience are probably the **Satay Club** down on Queen Elizabeth Walk, where you can dine out at the waterside or **Cuppage Plaza** off Orchard Road, where you can sit out on the promenade and people watch. A good place to have your first encounter with a food centre may be **Scotts Picnic Food Court** in the basement of Scotts Shopping Centre, 6 Scotts Road. Here you will find Eastern and Western food – from noodles to *sushi* to frozen yogurt. If you are planning a day at the races during your visit, you should not miss getting a bite at **Rasa Singapura** at the Bukit Timah Turf Club on Dunearn Road.

NYONYA

Guan Hoe Soon, 214 Joo Chiat Road. Tel: 3442761. $$
Ivins, No 19/21 Binjai Park, Bukit Timah. Tel: 4683060. A fair distance from Orchard Road but worth the trip. A modest restaurant with the best nonya food plus a few Indonesian dishes. Good local deserts too. $
Nonya and Baba Restaurant, 262–264 River Valley Road. Tel: 7341382. Cosy atmosphere in a *kampong* setting for wonderful authentic Nonya dishes. $$
Oleh Sayang Food, 25B Lorong Liput. Tel: 4689859. Unpretentious Nyonya food. $$
Peranakan Inn, 210 East Coast Road. Tel: 4406195. Nothing fancy, just good Nonya food. $

SEAFOOD

Choon Seng, 892 Punggol Road. Tel: 2883472. $$
Garden Seafood Restaurant, Goodwood Park Hotel. Tel: 7377411. Fresh seafood and *dim sum* are house specialties. $$$
Long Beach, 610 Bedok Road. Tel: 4458833. Evenings only, for some of the best chilli and pepper crabs in town. $$$
Long Jiang, Crown Prince Hotel. Tel: 7349056. $$$
Ng Tiong Choon, Sembawang Fishing Pond and Seafood Village, and 59 Lorong Chuntum (off Lorong Gambas). Tel: 7541991/2577939. Off Mandai Road, take a taxi or the MRT to Yishun, then shuttle bus at 9.05, 10.45, 2.45, 4.30 and 7.15. Bus No. 171 or 137 drops you at the main road, then you walk. Away from it all in the countryside, overlooking the ponds, you sit outdoors to eat good seafood and local fare. $$
Palm Beach Seafood Restaurant, National Stadium, Kallang. Tel: 3443088. A firm favorite with locals who queue up for the chilli and pepper crabs and crispy *yu cha kuay* seafood rolls. $$
Punggol (Hock Kee), 896 Punggol Point, Tel: 4817958; #01-124, Harbour Promenade, World Trade Centre, Tel: 2743500. $$
Seafood International, 902 East Coast Parkway. Tel: 4420988. A reasonably priced seafood restaurant with the motto "If it swims, we have it". $$
Siggi's, The Beaufort Sentosa. Tel: 2750331. $$$
Singa Inn, 920 East Coast Parkway. Tel: 3451111. All the seafood favourites in air-conditioned splendour with the added benefit of a free cultural show nightly. $$
Raffles Courtyard, Raffles Hotel. Tel: 337-8041. Marble and wrought-iron tables are set beneath the stars. Lobster and other seafood dishes. Promotions of other cuisines are occasionally offered. $$$$
Tan Chen Lee, 65C Pioneer Road. Tel: 8615428. Very popular with lunchtime crowd. $$$
Tekong Seafood Restaurant, Blk 6 Changi Village. Tel: 5457044. $$$
UDMC East Coast Seafood Centre, East Coast Parkway. A collection of informal, family-type restaurants. A good place to gorge on seafood prepared Singapore-style. The restaurants here include: **Ocean Park**, Tel: 448-1895; **Red House**, Tel: 4423112; **Jumbo**, Tel: 4423435; **Bedok Sea View**, Tel: 2415173; **Kheng Luck**, Tel: 4422690. $

THAI

Bangkok Garden, Keck Seng Tower. Tel: 2207310. $$$
Cairnhill Thai Seafood Restaurant, Cairnhill Place, 15 Cairnhill Road. Tel: 7380703. $$$
Chao Phaya Seafood Market and Restaurant, #02-4272 Blk 730 Ang Mo Kio Ave. 6. Tel: 4560118 and #04-01, 211 Holland Ave. A wide-ranging menu at lunchtime, in the evening you choose your entree raw and select the way you would like them cooked. $$$

Her Sea Palace, Forum The Shopping Mall. Tel: 7325688. Warm and casual restaurant which serves an enticing array of Thai dishes. $$
Paddy Fields, #03-03 South Buona Vista Centre, South Buona Vista Road. Tel: 7759808. Authentic Thai food served in a cosy ambience. $$
Parkway Thai, Parkway Parade. Tel: 3458811. $$$
Siamese Fins, 45 Craig Road, Tanjong Pagar. Tel: 2279795. Try the Thai shark's fins dishes.$$$
Thanying, Amara Hotel. Tel: 2224688. $$$
Tum Nak Thai, 100 East Coast Parkway, East Coast Recreation Centre. Tel: 4420988. Authentic Thai seafood by the seaside. Open 6pm to midnight weekdays and on weekends and holidays, from noon to midnight. $$
Tunk-ka, Marina Square. Tel: 3371312. $$$
Tuk-Tuk Thai Specialities, Magic Land Food Park, Marina Square. Tel: 3371312.

VIETNAMESE

Mekong, East Coast Parkway, Tel: 2424525. $$
Pare'gu, Orchard Plaza. Tel: 7334211. $$$
Saigon Restaurant, Cairnhill Road, Tel: 2350626. True Vietnamese food in a colonial setting. $$$

EASTERN & WESTERN

Alkaff Mansion, 10 Telok Blangah Green. Tel: 2786979. Upstairs this stately home, once owned by one of Singapore's founding families, there is *a la carte* Indonesian and Continental menu. On the ground floor is a East/West buffet and there are barbecues out on the patio on Friday and Saturday nights. Worth a visit for the ambience alone. $$$
Chatterbox Coffee shop, Mandarin Hotel. Tel: 7374411. Open 24-hours, you can snack on Chinese, regional or continental favourites here. $
Compass Rose Restaurant, The Westin Plaza Hotel. Tel: 3308310. Spectacular views over the island and beyond. Pleasant decor and cuisine blending Asian and Western flavours. $$$$
Emmerson's Tiffin Room, 51 Neil Road, #01-22. Tel: 2277518. The decor is turn of the century and the food is described as "crossroads cuisine" – an eclectic East meets West selection.
Food Alley, off Murray Street, is a road full of restaurants of all kinds, a delightful place to wander along while you decide what to eat and where.
The Pinnacle, Raffles Place, #60-00 OUB Centre. Tel: 5322166. $$$$

CONTINENTAL

Baron's Table, Royal Holiday Inn Crowne Plaza. Tel: 7317934. $$$
Berkeley, Sloan Court Hotel. Tel: 2353311. $$
Chesa, Equatorial Hotel. Tel: 7320431. $$$
Coachman Inn, Parkway Parade. Tel: 3483237. $$$
Compass Rose, The Westin Stamford. Tel: 3388585. $$$$

Fourchettes, The Oriental Singapore. Tel: 3380066. Brass oak and candlelight setting with soft background music. $$$

Harbour Grill, Hilton Hotel, 4th floor.Tel: 7372233. Fresh ingredients, simply prepared to enhance natural flavours. Popular with business executives. $$$$

Hubertus Grill, ANA Hotel. Tel: 7321222. German hunting lodge setting. Wild game is included in the evening menu. $$$

La Brasserie, Omni Marco Polo Hotel. Tel: 4747141. $$$$

Latour, Shangri-La Hotel. Tel: 7373644. Sophisticated setting for souffle specialities, excellent menu, and a luscious lunchtime buffet. $$$$

Le Duc, Omni Marco Polo Hotel. Tel: 4747141. Romantic elegance and superb cuisine. $$$$

Movenpick, Scotts Shopping Centre. Tel: 2358700. $$$

New Orleans, Holiday Inn Park View. Tel: 7338333. $$$

Nutmegs, Hyatt Regency. Tel: 7381234. $$$

Oscar's Brasserie and Wine Bar, 30 Robinson Road. Tel: 2234033. Down under the city, a cool haven serving light brasserie-type fare. $$$

Palm Grill, The Westin Plaza. Tel: 3388585. $$$

Raffles Grill, Raffles Hotel. Tel: 3371886. $$$$

The Stables, Mandarin Hotel. Tel: 7374411. $$$$

FRENCH

Harbour Grill, Hilton International Hotel. Tel: 7372233. $$$$

L'Aigle D'or, Duxton Hotel. Tel: 2277678. Situated in the Tanjong Pagar conservation district, it is fast gaining a reputation of being one of the best French restaurants in town. $$$

La Brasserie, Marco Polo Hotel. Tel: 4747141. One of Singapore's longest-lasting favourites. $$$

La Grande Bouffe, 53–55 Sunset Way. Tel: 4676847. A favorite for French food. Although out of the city centre, it attracts discerning diners with its varied menu and reasonably priced wine list. $$$

Latour, Shangri-La Hotel. Tel: 7373644. $$$$

Le Duc, Omni Marco Polo Hotel. Tel: 4747141. $$$$

Le Restaurant de France, Le Meridien Singapore. Tel: 7338855. Elegant decor, good food and service. $$$

Maxim's de Paris, The Regent Singapore. Tel: 7338888. Art deco gives a Parisian feel as does the superb cuisine and service. $$$$

Palm Grill, The Westin Plaza. Tel: 3388585. $$$

Saxophone, 23 Cuppage Terrace. Tel: 2358385. $$$

ENGLISH

Bob's Tavern, 17A Lorong Liput, Holland Village. Tel: 4672419. Hearty English fare in friendly environment. The extensive menu includes fish and chips, chicken pies, ploughman's lunch. $$

Forsters Olde English Eating House, Specialists Shopping Centre. Tel: 7378939. $$$

Gordon Grill, Goodwood Park Hotel. Tel: 7374111. $$$$

The Stables, Mandarin Hotel. Tel: 7374411. $$$$

Minton, The Paragon. Tel: 7383368. $$

AMERICAN

Dan Ryan's, 91 Tanglin Road, Tanglin Mall. Tel: 738800. Chicago food with baby back pork ribs as their specialty. $$

TGI Fridays, 9 Penang Road. Friendly atmosphere and good food. $$

Hard Rock Cafe, 50 Cuscaden Road. Tel: 2355232. Loud and fun with the best hamburgers west of Honolulu. $$

Nutmegs, Hyatt Regency Hotel. Tel: 7331188. Cool decor, interesting California cuisine and delicious dessert buffet. $$$$

Seah Street Deli, Raffles Hotel. Tel: 3378041. Cheerful and noisy deli serving all the Jewish specialties. $$

Tony Roma's, Orchard Hotel Shopping Arcade. Tel: 7388600. $$

ITALIAN

Al Forno Trattoria, Novena Ville, 275 Thomson Road, #01-07. Tel: 2562848. $$

Da Paolo Ristorante, 66 Tanjong Pagar Road. Tel: 2247081. Fresh pasta is made daily by the Venetian owner/chef. There is an expresso bar on the ground floor and the restaurant is upstairs this converted shop house. $$$$

Domvs, Sheraton Towers. Tel: 7376888. $$$$

Luna Luna, 31 Boat Quay. Tel: 5382030. $$

Pasta Brava, 11 Craig Road. Tel: 2277550. A real taste of Italy in a converted old Singapore shophouse. If you don't find the sauce you want for your pasta on the menu, the chef will prepare anything available ingredients will allow. $$

Pasta Fresca Da Salvatore, 30 Boat Quay, Tel: 5326283; Level 4, Shaw House, Tel: 7350373; Blk 833 Royalville, Bukit Timah Rd, Tel: 4694920. Home-made pasta and 20 sauces plus pizzas are served here. The restaurant at Boat Quay is open 24 hours. $$$

Pete's Place, Basement Hyatt Regency Hotel. Tel: 7381234. Cosy atmosphere with magazines to pass the time as you wait for pasta, pizzas or spaghetti. Wonderful salad bar and home-made bread. $$

Prego, Level 3, The Westin Plaza, 2 Stamford Road. Tel: 3388585. A friendly, informal atmosphere and good food. $$$

Ristorante Bologna, Marina Mandarin Hotel. Tel: 3383388. Pleasant restaurant overlooking a waterfall. *Antipasto* buffet and Italian specialities. $$$

MEXICAN

Cha Cha Cha, 32 Lorong Mambong, Holland Village. Tel: 4621650. You'll find the best south of the border food here. $$
Chico's N Charlie's, Liat Towers. Tel: 7341753. $$
El Filipe's, 34 Lorong Mambong, Holland Village. Tel: 4681520. Mexican favourites and great margaritas. $$
Margarita's, 108 Faber Drive, off Jalan Lempeng. Tel: 7771782. Cosy restaurant out in the suburbs. Good *tacos*, *nachos* and *enchiladas*. $

INTERNATIONAL

Capers, Regent Singapore. Serves international cuisines. Tel: 7338888. $$$
Esmirada, 180 Orchard Road, Peranakan Place. Tel: 7353476. Serves Mediterranean. $$
Koreana, Specialists' Shopping Centre. Tel: 2350018. Serves Korean food. $$
Le Chalet, Ladyhill Hotel. Tel: 7372111. A place for Swiss food. $$$
Mövenpick, #B1-01 Scotts Shopping Centre, Tel: 2358700; #B1-00 Robinson Towers, Tel: 2234031; 39 Boat Quay, Tel: 5388200. A Swiss eatery with fondue to veal steaks and a good salad bar. $$
New Orleans, Holiday Inn Park View. Tel: 7338333. Serves Creole and Cajun food. $$$
Shashlik, Far East Shopping Centre. Tel: 7326401. Serves authentic Russian food. $$
Spice Express, #B1-220/21 Forum The Shopping Mall. Tel: 7348835. A trip around Asia's culinary delights at one restaurant. $$
Trader Vic's, Hotel New Otani. Tel: 3372249. Sip colourful cocktails while nibbling *pupus* (titbits) in the bar before dining on Polynesian food in a romantic South Sea atmosphere. $$$$
Stables, Mandarin Singapore. Tel: 7374411. $$$

HIGH TEA

Or, skip lunch and tuck into high tea instead. Normally served from about 2.30pm to 6pm, popular places to try include:

Compass Rose Lounge, Westin Plaza Hotel. Tel: 3388585. The highest of high teas. $$
Cafe L'Espresso, Goodwood Park Hotel. A selection of sandwiches, pastries and cakes are offered. $$
Forsters Olde English Eating House, #02-38 Specialists Shopping Centre. Tel: 7378939. The place to go in Singapore for English Devonshire cream teas. $$$
Green Bamboo Village, Hotel Equatorial. Tel: 7320431. $
Scotts Lounge, Hyatt Regency. Tel: 7331188.

Sandwiches, scones and cakes are served on three tiered plates. Order as many as you can hold. $$
Tea Room, The Westin Stamford. Tel: 3388585. $$
The Atrium Lounge, The Oriental Hotel. Tel: 3380066. $$
The Mezzanine Lounge, Mandarin Singapore. Tel: 7374411. $$$
The Pearl of Casablanca, Pan Pacific Hotel. Tel: 3368111. $$

SANDWICHES & PASTRIES

Dome Café, 138 Cecil St, #01-02. Tel: 2218804.
Mitsubachi, #02-114 Lucky Plaza. Tel: 7349953.
Mr Cucumber, #02-02 Clifford Centre, 24 Raffles Place, Tel: 5340363; 0#2-03 Forum The Shopping Mall, Tel: 2354232.
Ovenpride, Peranakan Place, Tel: 7345112; 140 Upper Serangoon Road, Tel: 2831642; Tanjong Pagar Rd, Tel: 2262875.
Polar Puffs & Cakes, B1-04 OUB Centre, Raffles Place, Tel: 5323553; #02-58 Lucky Plaza, Tel: 7337997; #02-85A International Plaza, Tel: 2255668.
Red House Katong & Co, 75 East Coast Road. Tel: 3448948, 3440763.
Steeple's Deli, #02-05 Tanglin Shopping Centre. Tel: 7370701.

DRINKING NOTES

Two world famous locally brewed beers, *Tiger* and *Anchor*, revive wilting tourists in the tropical heat and go well with Asian food. At Chinese banquets, cognac or Chinese tea is often drunk with a meal. Wines, spirits and liquors of all kinds are usually available, with longer lists in restaurants serving Western cuisine. Fresh lime juice or freshly squeezed exotic fruit juices and punches are refreshing, healthy and delicious.

But don't leave Singapore without trying a "*Singapore Sling*", a delectable mixture of gin, Peter Heering, Benedictine, Cointreau, Angostura Bitter, pineapple juice and fresh lime, decorated with fresh pineapple and a cherry.

THINGS TO DO

TOURS

It's always a good idea on a visit to a new country to consider taking a few pre-packaged tours to get your bearings – particularly if you have limited time. There are a wide array of tours available in Singapore to help you get the most out of your stay. There are trishaw tours by night that weave through the narrow alleyways of Chinatown, junk cruises at sunset, and visits to traditional ethnic areas.

Or you can hire your own tour guide who will tailor an excursion to your needs, and provide you with snippets of juicy gossip and inside information.

TRANSIT TOUR

The STPB offers a free city tour to all transit passengers and can be arranged by calling at the tour desk at the Changi Airport transit lounges.

CITY TOUR

It's a quick catch-all glimpse of Singapore in air-conditioned comfort. Individual tours vary but sights usually include a drive along Orchard Road, passing the Istana or Presidential Palace, down to the colonial heart of Singapore: the Padang, City Hall, and a stop along the Singapore River.

The tour continues on to the busy port, Singapore's financial district, and then to Chinatown, Mount Faber and its panoramic view, a handful of handicraft centres, and the Botanic Gardens.

EAST COAST TOUR

Explore the city outskirts and rural areas that lead to Singapore's eastern beaches. Points of interest include the Malay Cultural Village in Geylang Serai, the famous Changi Prison where Allied prisoners were incarcerated during WWII, and get the feeling of everyday life in Tampines satellite town and a ride on the MRT.

CONTRASTING CULTURES

A glimpse of Singapore's people and their roots takes you to Little India, Arab Street, Chinatown, and their many places of worship. Back in the centre of Orchard Road, the tour concludes with a visit to Peranakan Place, a preserved area commemorating the culture of mixed Malay and Chinese descent.

TRISHAW TOUR

This tour can take you through Little India or Chinatown, by day or by night – though Chinatown gets most exciting and colourful in the evening, especially around the Trengganu Street area. A fast disappearing means of transportation in Singapore, the trishaw, pedals you in the open air for the best possible means of absorbing local flavors.

NIGHT TOUR

For an evening out to sample Singapore's nightlife, these tours usually include dinner at a hawker centre, a cultural show and a nightcap at a local pub or disco. Some tours also include a visit to a public housing estate.

SPECIAL INTEREST TOUR

A special tour for those interested in the local **Culinary Heritage** lasts for five days. For sporty types, there is a six-day **Singapore Golf Tour**. Those with an interest in history would enjoy the **Battlefield Tour** or the longer **World War II Tour**. Or if the heat keeps you in your hotel, why not explore Singapore at night with the **Singapore By Night Tour**. Call STPB at 3396622 for details.

SINGAPORE TROLLEY

Another option to sightsee Singapore, is on the Singapore Trolley. These trolleys are brown-and-maroon, old-fashion tram buses that ply through Orchard Road, Chinatown, Tanjong Pagar and World Trade Centre. You can purchase the ticket ($9 per adult, $7 per child) which allows you unlimited rides on these buses for the whole day. A point to point ticket cost $3. These buses are on service from 9am to 9pm.

Singapore Trolley allows you to pub crawl in good old British tradition by offering unlimited rides plus happy hour prices all day at selected pubs. If drinking isn't your pleasure, this package still offers you a leisurely and scenic way to get around the city.

HELICOPTER TOUR

The helicopter takes a maximum load of four passengers, including the pilot. The tour costs S$150 per adult, $75 per child and takes you round the island (taking off at the Seletar secondary airport, down to the waterfront, round Sentosa island, up west to Jurong and back to Seletar) in 30 minutes. There are flights at noon and 12.30pm Monday–Friday except public holidays. Call Safe & Mansfield Travel Group at 2240000 for more information.

HARBOUR CRUISES

Since the late 1980s harbour cruises have become very much a part of the everyday Singapore scene. Morning, lunch, afternoon, high-tea, dinner and disco cruises are all on offer and the choice of craft lies between sleek, white, modern catamarans (*Equator Dream*, *Island Jade*) which can accommodate more than 200 passengers and traditional *tongkangs* (junks) which, unfortunately because of the Sheares viaduct, have had their masts decimated and cannot raise their sails. The *tongkangs* (*Fairwind*, *Cheng Ho*) can each accommodate about 100 passengers. Or you can even board the hardy bumboat which used to be the traditional way of plying Singapore River in days gone by.

Bumboat cruises, operated by Singapore River Cruise & Leisure (Tel: 2279678), leave Parliament House landing steps every hour from 9.00am to 6.30pm daily. This is a leisurely way to absorb the history of the once-thriving river. This half hour ride costs $6 ($3 for children under 12). A similar cruise (one hour long, with refreshments on board) run by Eastwind Organisation, costs $15 per adult and $9.50 per child under 12.

Tongkang cruises, lasting about two to three hours, depart from Clifford Pier. They all cover the same route, more or less, with some stopping at Kusu island. *Fairwind*, an authentic Chinese junk, cruises four times daily (10.30am, 3, 4 and 6pm) at $20 for adults and $10 for children. Dinner cruises aboard the *Fairwind* cost $36 for adults and $18 for children. Call Fairwind/Eastwind Organisation at 5333432.

The *Cheng Ho*, a replica of a 15th-century Chinese junk, cruises the southern islands with stopover at Kusu Island daily at $23 for adults and $11 for children. It also has high-tea ($28 adults, $14 children) and dinner cruises ($60 adults, $30 children). They also have daily *tongkang* cruises at 10.30am ($20 adult, $10 child) and Singaporean buffet dinner cruises at 6pm ($33 adult, $17 child). Call Ann Leong, Ann Heng at 5339811.

The catamaran *Equator Dream*, operated by J&N Cruises, departs from the World Trade Centre at 12.30pm daily for the lunch cruise ($35 adult, $28 child), 3pm for the high tea cruise ($30 adult, $17 child), 6pm for dinner cruises ($80 adult, $45 child) and 8.30pm for the supper/disco/karaoke cruise ($20 weekdays, $30 weekends). Tel: 2707100.

Resort Cruises operate a dinner cum Asean show on the *Island Jade* catamaran. This is your chance to sample local food and have a taste of the culture from the region while plying Singapore's waters. The cruise departs from the World Trade Centre daily at 6.30pm $85 per adult, $55 per child. Tel: 2784677.

You can also dine in style onboard an exotic floating Cantonese restaurant, *Sea Palace*, which departs from the World Trade Centre at noon till 1.20pm, at 5.40pm, 7.20pm and 8.40pm. Call 8238363 for reservation.

The large, comfortable Port of Singapore (PSA) ferries at Jardine Steps (World Trade Centre) run a regular service to Kusu and St. John's Island. Daily departures are at 10am and 1.30pm while on Sundays and holidays there are eight trips starting at 9am and with the last departure being at 5pm. Adult fare is $6; children $3.00.

If you're heading for Malaysia and do not want to get caught up in the possible congestion of the causeway link to Johor, you could try the 45-minute ferry ride between Changi Point and Tanjung Belungkor. There are three trips daily, 9am, noon and 4.15pm $24 return for adults, $15 return per child. Call Ferrylink: 3236088.

Chartering luxury yachts has become more popular recently, and if you can make up a party from a dozen to 50, you can choose your own itinerary and sail in style. Fantasy Cruises (Tel: 2832182); Eastwind (Tel: 5333432); Amaril Cruises (Tel: 2216969); Resort Cruises (Tel: 2784677).

J & N Cruises offer package tours on the *Equator Triangle* catamaran to Batam and Desaru with the option of spending one or more nights there, before cruising back.

TOUR OPERATORS

STPB, the Singapore Tourist Promotion Board, Tel: 3396622, has details of tours available at their two offices in Raffles City Tower and Scotts Shopping Centre. Otherwise, information can be obtained direct from the tour operators or through your hotel concierge.

Elpin Tours and Limosine Services, Tel: 2353111
Franco Asian Travel, Tel: 2278722
Gray Line of Singapore, Tel: 3318244
Holiday Tours, Tel: 7347091, 7382622
Malaysia and Singapore Travelcentre, Tel: 7378877
RMG, Tel: 7387776
Siakson Coach Tours, Tel: 3360288
Sin Car Tours (Singapore Cablecar Tours), Tel: 2779633/2708855
Singapore Cable Car Tours, Tel: 2708855
Singapore Sightseeing, Tel: 4736900
Singapore Trolley, Tel: 2278218
Tour East, Tel: 2355703

TOUR GUIDES

Trained guides accompany individuals or groups and carry official identification. Call Registered Tourist Guides Association, Tel: 3383441/3383443. For half a day, English speaking guides charge about S$50, foreign language speaking guides about S$85.

Fascinating tours which visitors can join or personally guided tours to destinations of personal choice are given by Geraldine Lowe-Ismail. Tel: 7375250.

Guides accompany individuals or groups and carry official identification which they will produce upon request.

CULTURE PLUS

MUSEUMS

Changi Prison Chapel and Museum, Main Entrance, Changi Prison. Hours: 9.30am to 4.30pm. Closed on Sundays and public holidays. Admission: Free. Displayed are photographs, sketches, memorabilias of life of Allied prisoners under the Japanese occupation of Singapore. There is a service in the chapel on Sundays at 5.30pm and 6.30pm.
Chinaman Scholar Gallery, 14-B Trengganu Street. Tel: 2229554. Hours: 9am to 4pm. Admission: Adult: S$4; Child: S$2. Typical shophouse of the 1920s and 30s, full of photographs and curios, all explained by collector Vincent Tan.
National Museum, Stamford Road. Tel: 3377355. Hours: 9am to 5.30pm daily, except Wednesday, 10.30am to 7pm. Closed on Mondays. Admission: Adult: S$3; Child: S$1. On display are lively dioramas and recreations of dwelling places as well as special exhibitions giving a good insight into Singapore's history and culture.
Pewter Museum, 32 Pandan Road. Tel: 2689600. Hours: 9am to 7pm on weekdays, 9am to 6.30pm on weekends and public holidays. Admission: Free. A fascinating collection of pewter and live demonstrations by craftsmen.
Sun Yat Sen Villa, Ah Hood Road, Toa Payoh. Hours: 10am to 4pm. Admission: Free. Once the revolutionary's Singapore headquarters, now home to a photographic and documentary tribute to his life.
The Empress Place, 1 Empress Place. Tel: 3367633. Hours: 9am to 7.30pm daily. Admission: Adult: S$6, Child: S$3. Converted from government offices to its original neo-classical beauty, this building houses exhibits of ancient China and other civilisations which are changed periodically. Call to find out what's on.
Raffles Hotel Museum, Raffles Hotel, 1 Beach Road. Tel: 3371886. Hours: 10am to 9pm. Admission: Free. A record of the history of Raffles and other grand hotels of Asia.

ART GALLERIES

Look out for details of exhibitions in small galleries located in the shopping centres and in the *What's On* section of *The Straits Times*.

Della Butcher Gallery, Cuppage Road. Tel: 2357107. Hours: 11am to 6pm. Closed Sundays.
Gallery 21, 03/02 River Walk Galleria, 20 Upper Circular Road. Hours: 11am to 6pm daily.
Goethe Institute Gallery, Singapore Shopping Centre. Tel: 3375111.
Graham Byfield Gallery, Balmoral Park. Tel: 7320152 to make an appointment first.
National Art Gallery, Stamford Road, Tel: 3777355. Hours: 9am to 5.30pm. Closed Mondays.
Shenn's Fine Art Gallery, 8 Bukit Pasoh Road, off Neil Road. Tel: 2231233. Hours: 11am to 5pm.
The Gallery, Hilton International Hotel.
The Substation, Armenian Street. Tel: 3377800. Hours: 11am to 9pm. Call to find out if there is an exhibition.

CONCERTS AND THEATRES

Concert and performance details are available from the booking offices and the *What's On* section of *The Straits Times*.

Victoria Concert Hall, Tel: 3396120 or 3381230. The Singapore Symphony Orchestra, founded in 1979, gives regular concerts and has begun to attract guest conductors and soloists from all over the globe.
Classical and Folk Chinese Music, the Nanyang Academy of Fine Arts' and People's Association Chinese Orchestras hold regular concerts. Call NAFA at 3395753 during office hours for more information.
Victoria Theatre, Tel: 3377490.
The Substation, Armenian Street. Tel: 3377800.
National Theatre Trust, Kallang Theatre. Tel: 3458488
Drama Centre, Canning Rise. Tel: 7349090.
The Black Box, Fort Canning Centre. Tel: 3384077.
Theatreworks, a leading local *avant garde* theatre company, puts on works at the Drama Centre and the Black Box. Call 3384077 for more information. The ticketing office is open during office hours. Tel: 3386735.

Singapore Indoor Stadium, **National Stadium**, **Harbour Pavillion** and **World Trade Centre Auditorium** are venues for Asian and international pop and rock concerts. Details are available from the booking offices and the local newspaper.

SISTIC **Ticket Outlets**: Singapore Indoor Stadium, Specialists' Shopping Centre, Scotts Shopping Centre, Forum The Shopping Mall, Cold Storage Outlets (Promenade, Jelita and World Trade Centre), Lau Pa Sat Festival Market, Raffles City Shopping Centre. Telephone bookings: 3485555. Fax bookings: 4406784.

Ticket Charge Outlets: Metro stores, Centrepoint, Wisma Atria, Tangs. Telephone bookings: 29629229.

SHOPPING

MOVIES

There are over 60 cinemas on the island, and details are published every day in the *Life* section of *The Straits Times*. Censorship has recently been relaxed to allow more sophisticated viewing. R(A) films are for over 21 years old, G are for general viewing and PG indicates that parental guidance is advisable.

OTHER EXHIBITIONS

Guinness World of Records, World Trade Centre, #02-70. Tel: 2718344. Hours: 10am to 9pm. daily. Admission: Adult: S$4, Child: S$3.

Singapore Science Centre, Science Centre Road, off Jurong Town Hall Road. Tel: 5603316. Hours: Tuesday to Sunday and public holidays, closed Monday, 10am to 6pm. Admission: Adult: S$2, Child: S$0.50.

Planetarium and Omnimax Theatre, Science Centre Road, Jurong Town Hall Road. Hours: Tuesday to Sunday and public holidays, closed Monday, shows between 10am and 8.30pm. Admission: Adult: S$8, Child: S$4.

Ming Village, 32 Pandan Road, Jurong. Tel: 2657711. Hours: 9am to 5.30pm. See craftsmen at work making Chinese porcelain by hand (including reproduction Ming vases). Admission: free.

ANTIQUES

Abanico
– #05-011 Centrepoint. Tel: 7329502
– #04-08A Trade Mart, 60B Martin Road. Tel: 7336879

Antiques of the Orient, #02-40 Tanglin Shopping Centre. Tel: 7349351

Babazar, 31–35A Cuppage Terrace. Tel: 2357866

Da-Ching Fine Arts, #03-02 Centrepoint. Tel: 7344888

Good Old Days, #04-104 Lucky Plaza. Tel: 7346362

Kwok Gallery, #03-01 Far East Shopping Centre. Tel: 2352516

Ming Village, 32 Pandan Road. Tel: 2657711

Ming-Ching Antique House, 5 Tank Road. Tel: 2356509

One Price Store, 3 Emerald Hill Road. Tel: 7341680

Swans Gallery, 59 Sunset Way. Tel: 4625781

The Chinese Heritage, #02-55 Lucky Plaza. Tel: 2359714

Three Treasures Fine Arts Centre
– 32 Watten Rise. Tel: 4670087
– #01-07 Bukit Timah Industrial Complex, 230 Upper Bukit Timah Road. Tel: 4687707

ARTS & CRAFTS

Isan Gallery, 42 Jalan Kembangan. Tel: 442478

Jessica Arts and Crafts
– #01-10 Cold Storage Jelita. Tel: 4690689
– #02-14 Holland Village Shopping Centre. Tel: 4682336

Lims Arts and Crafts, #02-01 Holland Road Shopping Centre. Tel: 4671300

Ming Village, (porcelain) 32 Pandan Road. Tel: 2657711

Renee Hoy Fine Arts, #01-44 Tanglin Shopping Centre. Tel: 2351596

Tempo Doeloe Ethnic Arts, #02-33 Raffles Shopping Arcade. Tel: 3381038

Thow Kwang Industry, (pottery) No. 85 Lorong Tawas. Tel: 2655808

BEAUTY

Clinique D'Esthetique
– #04-03 Far East Plaza. Tel: 7337000
– #03-11 Holland Road Shopping Centre.
Tel: 4669443
Essence Hair & Beauty Salon, #03-03/04 Raffles
Hotel. Tel: 3343868
Quest
– #0-34 Raffles City Shopping Centre. Tel: 3388949
– #2-18/21 Scotts Shopping Centre. Tel: 7325201
Salon La Prairie
– #03-18/19 Mandarin Hotel. Tel: 2355893/
7374411 ext. 746
– #03-30 Raffles City. Tel: 3396988/3380598

CAMERA

Albert Photo
– #01-07 Tanglin Shopping Centre. Tel: 2351845
– #B1-15 Orchard Towers. Tel: 2352815
– #B1-10 Orchard Hotel Shopping Arcade.
Tel: 7344689
Minolta Singapore, 10 Teban Gardens Crescent.
Tel: 5635533
Cathay Photo Store
– #01-07/08 Peninsula Plaza. Tel: 3380451
– #02-219 Marina Square. Tel: 3396188
Cost Plus Electronics
– #B1-21 Scotts Shopping Centre. Tel: 2353722
– 275 Holland Avenue. Tel: 4693029

CARPETS

Amir & Sons, #03-01/07 Lucky Plaza. Tel: 7349112
Chinese Carpets, 72 Eunos Avenue 7. Tel: 7477583
Eastern Carpets, #03-28 Raffles City Shopping
Centre. Tel: 3388135
Hassan's Carpet
– #03-01/06 Tanglin Shopping Centre. Tel: 7375626
– #01-24 Raffles Arcade. Tel: 3340511
Mohammad Akhtar Carpets, #02-27 Tanglin Shop-
ping Centre. Tel: 7370027
Niko Carpets, #03-210 Marina Square. Tel: 3394576
Qureshi's Carpets
– #05-12 Centrepoint. Tel: 2351523
– #B1-12 Tanglin Shopping Centre. Tel: 7320587

CHINESE MEDICINE STORES

Eng Seng Tong Hoon Kee Medical Hall, #01-35
Hong Lim Complex, Blk 531 Upper Cross Street.
Tel: 5322116
Eu Yan Sang, 269 South Bridge Road. Tel: 2234363
Jing Tai Hong, #01-20 People's Park Complex.
Tel: 5334617

COMPUTERS

Funan Centre, 109 North Bridge Road; **Sim Lim
Square**, 1 Rochor Canal Road, are two shopping
centres packed with numerous computer stores.
Other shops specialising in computers are:

Abacus Computer Systems, #03-60 Sim Lim Square.
Tel: 3363991
C&G Systems
– #06-39 Funan Centre. Tel: 3393380
– #06-58 Sim Lim Square. Tel: 3362376
Challenger Superstore
– #05-11 Funan Centre. Tel: 3390461
– #05-12 Sim Lim Square. Tel: 3399255
Compaq, 1 Yishun Avenue 7. Tel: 7551188
Epson, #03-17 OUB Centre. Tel: 5330477
Global Automation, 60 Martin Road, #12-04
Trademart. Tel: 7346522
Microhouse
– #05-37 Funan Centre. Tel: 3366840
– #02-30/31 Lucky Plaza. Tel: 7389909
– #06-74 Sim Lim Square. Tel: 3342671
The MacPlace, #13-08 Sim Lim Square.
Tel: 2991118
Ultimate Laptop Shop
– #06-25 Funan Centre. Tel: 3386235
– #05-45 Sim Lim Square. Tel: 3396243

FASHION

Ad Hoc, #02-40 Hilton Hotel Shopping Gallery.
Tel: 7375112
Anne Klein, #03-08 Le Meridien Shopping Centre.
Tel: 7338817.
Aquascutum, #01-14 Raffles Hotel Shopping Ar-
cade. Tel: 3343248
BabyGuess, #01-03/04 Forum The Shopping Mall.
Tel: 7343957
Boutique Celine, #01-02A Shaw Centre.
Tel: 7360511
Boutique Lacoste
– #02-35 Wisma Atria. Tel: 2359796
– #01-08 Centrepoint. Tel: 2358000
– 22 Orange Grove Road, #01-07. Tel: 7341018
Boutique Lanvin
– #02-16/17 Wisma Atria. Tel: 7370155
– #01-30/31, Ngee Ann City. Tel: 7346245
Burberrys
– Daimaru, Liang Court. Tel: 3391111
– DFS Meridien Shopping Centre. Tel: 2359700
– Isetan Wisma Atria. Tel: 7387118
– #01-10 Ngee Ann City. Tel: 7351283
– Sogo, Raffles City Shopping Centre. Tel: 3396682
Bylines, #02-33 Plaza Singapura. Tel: 3371441
Byblos, #01-K1/01A Forum The Shopping Mall.
Tel: 7377940
Caserini
– #02-20 Wisma Atria. Tel: 2351488
– #01-26 Chinatown Point. Tel: 5323633
– #01-07 Raffles City. Tel: 3388622

- #02-132 Marina Square. Tel: 3398168
- #02-143A Marina Square. Tel: 3395007
- #02-02 Centrepoint. Tel: 7360607

Cacharel, #01-05 Scotts Shopping Centre.
Tel: 7343285

Christian Dior, #02-42 Wisma Atria. Tel: 7340374

Claude Montana, #02-28 Hilton Hotel Shopping Gallery. Tel: 7344652

Club 21
- #03-16 Meridien Hotel. Tel: 7328675
- #03-01/04 Meridien Hotel. Tel: 2350753
- #02-09/11 Hilton Hotel Shopping Gallery. Tel: 7324531
- #02-08 Wisma Atria. Tel: 7344347

Dolce & Gabbana, #01-02 The Promenade. Tel: 7341866

Dress Shop, #02-03 Raffles Hotel Shopping Arcade. Tel: 3384806

Ellesse Boutique, #03-38 Centrepoint. Tel: 7360151

Emanuel Ungaro, #01-31 Paragon by Sogo. Tel: 7375971

Emporio Armani, #02-02 HPL House. Tel: 7345766

Ermenegildo Zegna, #02-21/23 Wisma Atria. Tel: 7328959

Escada
- #01-27/30 Paragon by Sogo. Tel: 7384043
- #02-24/27 Wisma Atria. Tel: 7332708
- #02-00 Shaw House. Tel: 7340686

Esprit
- #B1-09 Wisma Atria. Tel: 7344448
- #02-00 Raffles City. Tel: 3388695
- #01-07 Scotts Shopping Centre. Tel: 7382696
- #270 Orchard Road. Tel: 7329890

Etienne Aigner
- #01-02 Shaw Centre. Tel: 7376141
- #B1-08 Palais Renaissance. Tel: 2355184
- #01-36D Paragon by Sogo. Tel: 7384039
- #01-12 Raffles Hotel Shopping Arcade. Tel: 3342108
- #02-300 Metro Marina. Tel: 3395952
- #02-00 Wisma Atria. Tel: 7322750
- #01-02 Orchard Building. Tel: 7330411
- #01-00 Raffles City. Tel: 3360736

F J Benjamin
- 6B Orange Grove. Tel: 7370155
- #01-04 Palais Renaissance. Tel: 7347118

Fendi
- #02-07 Hilton Hotel Shopping Gallery. Tel: 7343907
- #02-37/38 Wisma Atria. Tel: 7386080

Fifth Avenue, #B1-13 Wisma Atria. Tel: 7389737

Flyers
- #03-26/27 Centrepoint. Tel: 7346657
- #01-16/18 International Building. Tel: 7344301

Fontana, #02-03 Hilton Hotel Shopping Gallery. Tel: 7385512

G Gigli, #01-22 Forum The Shopping Mall. Tel: 7378916

Gianfranco Ferre, #02-24/25 Hiton Hotel Shopping Gallery. Tel: 7385560

Gianni Versace
- #02-01/02 Palais Renaissance. Tel: 7338840

- #02-28/29 Ngee Ann City. Tel: 7338840

Giorgio Armani, #01-11/12 Hilton Hotel. Tel: 7344025

Givenchy, #01-12 Paragon by Sogo. Tel: 7345881

Glamourette Ladies & Mens, #02-02 The Promenade. Tel: 7343137

Gottex, #03-26 Wisma Atria. Tel: 7341495

Gucci of Italy
- #01-01/02 Paragon by Sogo. Tel: 7342528
- #01-01/02 Hilton Hotel. Tel: 7323298
- #01-04 Palais Renaissance. Tel: 7347118

Guess?
- #02-15 Wisma Atria. Tel: 7381723
- ##01-12/15 Scotts Shopping Centre. Tel: 7384253
- #02-124 Marina Square. Tel: 3391082
- #B1-25/28 Ngee Ann City. Tel: 7357363

Hermès
- #01-02A Liat Towers. Tel: 7341353
- Daimaru, Liang Court. Tel: 3391111

Hugo Boss
- #02-07 Palais Renaissance. Tel: 7330322
- #01-03 Ngee Ann City. Tel: 7350233
- #02-25 Raffles Shopping Arcade. Tel: 3361033

Istante, #02-07 Ngee Ann City. Tel: 7341318

Ken Done
- B1-51 Ngee Ann City. Tel: 7355545
- #02-07/08 Palais Renaissance. Tel: 7345313
- Tudor Court Shopping Gallery. Tel: 7341252
- #02-50 Hotel Meridien Shopping Centre. Tel: 7345817

KL by Karl Lagerfeld
- #01-24 Paragon by Sogo. Tel: 7345817
- #01-05 Palais Renaissance. Tel: 7327155

Knickerbox, #03-24 Wisma Atria. Tel: 2350151

Link
- #03-03 Palais Renaissance. Tel: 2354648
- #02-04 Ngee Ann City. Tel: 7351516

Liz Clairborne Boutique, #02-09/11 Scotts Shopping Centre. Tel: 7388830

Louis Feraud, #B1-09 The Promenade. Tel: 7321025

Man And His Woman, #03-17 Le Meridien Shopping Centre. Tel: 7379492

Max Mara
- #01-35/36 Forum The Shopping Mall. Tel: 7385561
- #03-11 Meridien Hotel. Tel: 2355186

Melwani, #01-25 Paragon by Sogo. Tel: 7322556

Missoni
- #02-38 Hilton Shopping Gallery. Tel: 2353396
- #02-13 Raffles Hotel Shopping Arcade. Tel: 3380370
- #01-12 Palais Renaissance. Tel: 7330466

Mondi
- #02-14/15 The Promenade. Tel: 7381101
- #03-42, Centrepoint. Tel: 2350338

Moschino, #02-20/21 Hilton Hotel Shopping Gallery. Tel: 7321375

Mothers In Vogue
- #B1-06 The Promenade. Tel: 7325320
- 24 Raffles Place #02-03. Tel: 5385169
- #02-16 Park Mall. Tel: 3380060

Naf Naf Boutique, #01-09 Park Mall. Tel: 3343585
Oshkosh B' Gosh
– #B1-31 Wisma Atria. Tel: 7370174
– #01-19 Forum The Shopping Mall. Tel: 7326167
– #02-123 Marina Square. Tel: 3397428
Paul Smith, #02-39 Hilton Hotel. Tel: 7378861
Petite Cherie Boutique
– #02-15/16 Forum The Shopping Mall.
Tel: 7345223
– #02-40/41 Centrepoint. Tel: 7349658
Polo Ralph Lauren
– #01-02 The Promenade. Tel: 7320606
– #02-40 Wisma Atria. Tel: 2354113
Richards the Working Wardrobe
– #03-15 Wisma Atria. Tel: 7370953
– #01-01 Forum The Shopping Mall.Tel: 7371259
Renoma, #01-01 International Building.
Tel: 7375024
Romeo Gigli, #03-12 Meridien Hotel. Tel: 7385453
SAGA, #03-01 Park Mall. Tel:3372818.
Salvatore Ferragamo
– #B1-03/04 Palais Renaissance. Tel: 7361501
– #01-36C Paragon by Sogo. Tel: 7383206
Singora, #02-37 Hilton Hotel Shopping Gallery.
Tel: 7370768
SoHo Glamourette, #B1-07/08 The Promenade.
Tel: 7333359
Sonia Rykiel
– #01-33 Paragon by Sogo. Tel: 2359300
– Orchard Isetan Wisma Atria. Tel: 7379750
Studio E. Fx
– #03-03 Wisma Atria. Tel: 2359587
– #02-30 Raffles City. Tel: 3365221
– #B1-03 Ngee Ann City. Tel: 7357759
– Takashimaya, Ngee Ann City. Tel: 7357962
Style Singapore, #01-01 Park Mall. Tel: 3341216
Tee Stop, #03-53 Far East Shopping Centre.
Tel: 2350658
Thomas Wee
– 11 Stamford Road #01-12. Tel: 3381310
– #02-25 Orchard Point. Tel: 7342066
Timberland
– #01-33 Wisma Atria. Tel: 7372639
– #01-42 Forum The Shopping Mall. Tel: 7324629
Valentino, #01-17/18 Hilton Hotel. Tel: 2353152
Versus, #03-03 Palais Renaissance. Tel: 2354648

GOLD & JEWELLERY

A&E Gems, #01-55 Lucky Plaza. Tel: 2350583
Asia Jewellery, #01-43/46 Centrepoint.
Tel: 2351889
BP de Silva Jewellers, #02-227/228 Marina
Square. Tel: 3394318
Batu Pahat Goldsmith, 1 Upper Dickson Road.
Tel: 2931731
Beaumont Jewellery, #03-119 Far East Plaza.
Tel: 2352949
Bits & Pieces
– #02-33 Far East Plaza. Tel: 7382016
– #03-117A Marina Square. Tel: 3385449

– #10-03 Park Mall. Tel: 3394459
Bvlgari, #01-08 Hilton Hotel Shopping Gallery.
Tel: 7371652
C K Jewellery, #B1-120 Lucky Plaza. Tel: 7331740
C.T. Hoo, #01-22 Tanglin Shopping Centre.
Tel: 7375447
Cartier, #01-04 Hilton Shopping Gallery.
Tel: 2350295
GM de Silva Jewellers, #01-34 Specialist Shopping
Centre. Tel: 7375637
Je t'aime, 120 Oxley Rise. Tel: 7342275
K.M. Oli Mohamed
– #01-29/31 Peninsula Plaza. Tel: 3369134
– #03-30 Lucky Plaza. Tel: 7378750
Kampooli Jewellers, #01-07 Plaza Singapura.
Tel: 3361381/3361390
Larry Jewellery
– #01-10 Orachrd Towers. Tel: 7323222
– #01-18 Lucky Plaza. Tel: 7347107
– #01-38 Raffles City. Tel: 3369648
les must de Cartier Boutique, #01-04 Hilton
Shopping Gallery. Tel: 2350295
Little India Goldsmiths, Blk 664 Buffalo Road.
Tel: 2945000
Mee Kwong Chye Goldsmith, #01-11/12 Pidemco
Centre. Tel: 5342333
Poh Heng
– 27-28 North Canal Road. Tel: 5354933
– #01-17 People's Park Complex. Tel: 5350960
– #01-08 Northpoint Shopping Centre. Tel: 7562691
Poh Seng Jewellers, 225 South Bridge Road.
Tel: 2237227
Singapore Showcase
– Design Centre Branch, 141 North Bridge Road.
Tel: 3316115/7
– Airport Terminal 2, #026-084 Terminal 2
Departure/Transit Lounge, Singapore Changi Air-
port. Tel: 5458279
Tiffany
– #01-05 Raffles Hotel. Tel: 3340168
– Level 1 & 2 Unit 5/6, Tower B, Ngee Ann City.
Tel: 7358823

SILK

Asher Fabrics, 89 Arab Street. Tel: 2936892
China Silk House
– #02-11/13 Tanglin Shopping Centre. Tel: 2355020
– #02-01 Centrepoint. Tel: 7330555
– #02-77/78 Lucky Plaza. Tel: 2353528
– #01-03 Scotts Shopping Centre. Tel: 2354696
– #03-226 Marina Square. Tel: 3398698
– #01-10/11 Capitol Building. Tel: 3344500
– #01-26 Raffles Hotel Shopping Arcade.
Tel: 3366663
Design-Thai, #B1-19/21 Tanglin Shopping Centre. Tel: 2355439
Jim Thompson Silk Shop, Orchard Parade Hotel.
Tel: 2354379
Malaya Silk Store, #01-01/02 Orchard Shopping
Centre. Tel: 2352467

Melati Moda, Blk 1 Joo Chiat #02-1029.
Tel: 7436520
The Ming Shop, #01-03 Orchard Towers.
Tel: 7372656

WATCHES

A.D. Time International, #08-02 Bright Chambers,
108 Middle Road. Tel: 3341577
All Watches, #B1-128 Lucky Plaza. Tel: 7327673
BMI, Service Centre, #17-05 Orchard Towers.
Tel: 7373566
City Chain Stores
– #01-13 Plaza Singapura. Tel: 3362805
– #01-130 Marina Square. Tel: 3393878
– #B1-49/67 Parkway Parade. Tel: 4471384
– #01-03 Centrepoint Shopping Centre. Tel: 2353370
Dickson
– #01-03 Promenade. Tel: 7328900
– #01-05 Centrepoint. Tel: 7345822
The Hour Glass
– #01-36B Lucky Plaza. Tel: 7342420
– #01-10 Palais Renaissance. Tel: 7331262
– #01/21/22 Centrepoint. Tel: 7341598
– #01-01/02 Peninsula Plaza. Tel: 3378309
– 268 Orchard Road, #18-01. Tel: 7379103
– #01-09/11 Scotts Shopping Centre. Tel: 2357198
Rolex, #01-01 Tong Building, 302 Orchard Road.
Tel: 7379033.
Sincere
– #01-22 Lucky Plaza. Tel: 7374593
– #02-220 Marina Square. Tel: 3384006
– #01-12 Tower B, Ngee Ann City. Tel: 7330618
SwissAm, #05-234/236 Faber House, 230 Orchard
Road. Tel: 2357308
Welltime Singapore, #12-01 Wisma Atria Shopping Centre. Tel: 2357911

DEPARTMENT STORE

Chomel
– #01-41/42 Centrepoint. Tel: 7375714
– #03-218 Marina Square. Tel: 3393032
– #02-19/23 Orchard Point. Tel: 7388197
– #02-01/02 Paragon by Sogo. Tel: 7349631
– #01-45 Raffles City. Tel: 3392707
– #01-01 Scotts Shopping Centre. Tel: 7344277
– #01-08/09 Wisma Atria. Tel: 7347549
– #01-06/08 Change Alley. Tel: 5386383
– #B1-06/08 Ngee Ann City. Tel: 7387275
– #01-18/19 Liang Court. Tel: 3390373
Daimaru, #04-10 Liang Court. Tel: 3391111
Emporium Holdings, Tel: 4593838; operates over
15 stores around the island.
Galeries Lafayette
– #05-03/04 Liat Towers. Tel: 7329177
– #01-03/05 OUB Centre. Tel: 5357069
Isetan
– Wisma Atria Shopping Centre. Tel: 7337777
– Shaw Centre. Tel: 7331111
– Parkway Parade. Tel: 3455555

John Little
– Specialists Shopping Centre. Tel: 7372222
– Northpoint Shopping Centre. Tel: 7529288
K-Mart
– Marina Square. Tel: 3381323
– #05-00 Lucky Plaza. Tel: 7376033
Lane Crawford, #05-00 Lane Crawford Place, 501
Orchard Road. Tel: 7353332
Metro
– Far East Plaza. Tel: 7333322
– #05 Lucky Plaza. Tel: 7376033
– #02-300 Marina Square. Tel: 3372868
– #04 Paragon By Sogo, Tel: 2352811
Metro Factory Outlet
– #02-37 Centrepoint. Tel: 7345489
– #01-46 Chinatown Point. Tel: 5345721
OG Departmental Store
– People's Park. Tel: 5357788
– Plaza Singapura. Tel: 3382211
– 224/228 Orchard Road. Tel: 7374488
Robinson's, #05-05 Centrepoint. Tel: 7330888
Sogo
– Raffles City Shopping Centre. Tel: 3391100
– 12 Tampines Central 1, #01-01 Tampines DBS
Centre. Tel: 7882212
St. Michael's
– Levels 1 & 2 Centrepoint. Tel: 7341800
– #03-21/22 Scotts Shopping Centre. Tel: 2355603
– #01-44 Raffles City Shopping Centre.
Tel: 3399013
– #01-03 Clifford Centre, Raffles Place.
Tel: 5326469
– #03-236 Marina Square. Tel: 3365701
– 3–5 Holland Village. Tel: 4620061
– #02-16 Northpoint Shopping Centre. Tel: 7535211
Stock-Mart
– #01-16 Bukit Timah Plaza. Tel: 4689364
– #02-28 Centrepoint. Tel: 2350446
– #02-24 Clifford Centre. Tel: 5327791
– #B1-03 Lucky Plaza. Tel: 7348419
– #03-100 Marina Square. Tel: 3387605
– #02-34A Parkway Parade. Tel: 4470756
– #01-63 Thomson Plaza. Tel: 4548802
– #01-33 Raffles City. Tel: 3399871
Takashimaya, 391 Orchard Road, Ngee Ann City.
Tel: 7381111
Tangs, 320 Orchard Road. Tel: 7375500
Tangs Studio, Level 2-4, Ngee Ann City.
Tel: 7370033
Watson's, Tel: 2249808; branches all over the island
Yaohan
– Plaza Singapura. Tel: 3374061
– Parkway Parade. Tel: 3449011
– Thomson Plaza. Tel: 4546511
– Bukit Timah Plaza. Tel: 4685851

LOCAL FLAVOURS

Tanjong Pagar Conservation Area. For traditional
craft – clogs, ceramics, paper umbrellas, lacquer,
rosewood carvings. This shopping enclave is also

dotted with tea-houses and eateries serving Chinese and other cuisines. Getting there: Get off at Tanjong Pagar MRT Station.

Bugis Village, opposite Bugis MRT Station, Tel: 5397671. *Pasar Malam* offering local merchandise. Also street hawker fare and an outdoor beer garden. Getting there: Get off at Bugis MRT Station.

Emerald Hill, opposite Somerset MRT Station. Focusing on the Straits Chinese heritage in Singapore, the shops in Peranakan Place houses a range of goods, both traditional and modern. There is also a pub serving Peranakan dishes and a museum showcasing a typical Straits-Chinese home. Getting there: Get off at Somerset MRT Station.

GST

The Goods and Services Tax imposes a 3 percent sales tax on all goods. To qualify for a visitor refund scheme, visitors must spend at least S$500 from a single retailer or retail chain. The goods must be for export purpose. The refund may be made either by cheque or through your credit card. Claim forms and the correct procedure on how to make a claim can be obtained at all participating retailers.

SPECIAL INFORMATION

CHILDREN

Singapore has plenty to offer children apart from typical Asian love. They are always welcome here.

The Singapore Zoological Gardens is one of the best in the world, and who could resist breakfast with an orang-utan, or feeding time at the polar bear enclosure. There are also planned itineraries designed for children at the zoo.

Children will be enthralled by the 'All Star Birdshow' at the Jurong Bird Park, as well as great hornbills perched on a keeper's arm or falcons swooping for prey at the 'King of the Skies' show.

Crocodiles perform in Jurong Crocodile Paradise, beside the Birdpark, at 730 East Coast Parkway and 790 Upper Serangoon Road.

Sentosa Island is full of fun things to do, from roller skating to roller coaster, and the stunning new Underwater World. So a day can easily be spent there, perhaps going by cable car or bus, and returning by ferry for a different experience.

Let off steam on the beach at the East Coast, or shoot down slides and enjoy the pools at the water

parks. There are bicycles for hire here, as well as an enormous playground. Changi beach is another wonderful stretch of sand. There's a huge park at Pasir Ris where picnics are a good idea.

The Singapore Science Centre has hundreds of hands-on exhibits as well as a planetarium and an omnimax theatre for mesmerising movies to occupy youself and the children.

When parents are in the shopping centres, kids of all ages can join in the spending at Toys R Us at Parkway Parade, Forum The Shopping Mall and Northpoint Shopping Centre.

LANGUAGE

The national language and that of the National Anthem is Malay. However, documents, notices and T.V. announcements are also made in the other official languages: Mandarin, Tamil and English.

The lingua franca is English although actually most Singaporeans speak 'Singlish' lah, isn't it? Peppered with the odd word of Malay or expressions from various Chinese dialects, Singlish is an attractive variation of the Queen's version.

PHOTOGRAPHY

In tropical places, better results are obtained by protecting your camera and film from excessive exposure to heat and humidity. Do not leave your camera in the sun or in a hot car because heat gives the film a green overtone. Use a haze filter for better colour and store your equipment in a dry cool place such as an air-conditioned hotel room.

Do not leave unexposed films in luggage as incoming and outgoing baggage is subjected to a liberal use of X-ray. For the same reason do not mail unprocessed films.

Some oldtimers believe that a photograph may carry away one's soul and will protest if someone tries to invade their world with a snapshot. The solution, in this case, lies in a telephoto lens; the scene is more spontaneous that way, too.

If urgent, processing of colour films can be done within the hour, monochrome takes three working days and Kodachrome two weeks. Singapore is undoubtedly one of the best places in the world for purchasing leading-brands of cameras, lenses and equipment duty-free.

USEFUL ADDRESSES

STPB OFFICES

Head Office:
Singapore Tourist Promotion Board, Raffles City Tower #36-04, 250 North Bridge Road, Singapore 0617. Tel: 3396622; Telex: STBSIN RS 33375; Telefax: 3399423. Open: Mondays–Fridays: 8.30am–5pm. Saturdays: 8.30am–1pm (closed on Sundays & public holidays)

ASIA

Osaka: 1st Floor, Sumitomo Seimei Nishi-Honmachi Building, 1-Chome, 6-5 Nishi-Honmachi, Nishi-Ku Osaka 550, Japan. Tel: 81-6-5383389; Telefax:81-6-5383384.
Seoul: 9th Floor, Young Poong Building, 33 Sorin-Dong, Chongro-ku, Seoul, Republic of Korea. Tel: 82-2-3995570; Telefax: 82-2-3995574.
Taipei: Unit H 6th Floor, Hung Tai Center, 168 Tun Hwa North Road, Taipei, Taiwan. Tel: 886-2-785280; Telefax: 886-2-7191049.
Tokyo: 1st Floor, Yamato Seimei Building, 1 Chome, 1-7 Uchisaiwai-cho, Chiyoda-ku, Tokyo 100, Japan. Tel: 81-3-5933388; Telefax: 81-3-5911480.

AUSTRALIA/NEW ZEALAND

Auckland: c/o Walshes World, 2nd Floor, Dingwall Building, 87 Queen Street, P.O.Box 279, Auckland 1, New Zealand. Tel: 64-9-793708; Telex: WALWOR NZ 21437; Telefax: 64-9-3022420.
Perth: 8th Floor, St Georges Court, 16 St Georges Terrace, Perth, WA 6000, Australia. Tel: 61-9-3258578/3258511; Telex: AA 197542; Telefax: 61-9-2213864.
Sydney: Suite 1604, Level 16, Westpac Plaza, 60 Margaret Street, Sydney, NSW 2000, Australia. Tel: 61-2-2413771/2; Telex: STBSYD AA127775; Telefax: 61-2-2523586.

EUROPE

Frankfurt: Singapore Tourist Promotion Board (Fremdenverkehrsburo von Singapur) Poststrasse 2-4, D-6000 Frankfurt/Main, Federal Republic of Germany. Tel: 49-69-231456/7; Telex: STBF D4189742; Telefax: 49-69-233924.
Italy: Singapore Tourist promotion Board (Ente Nazionale del Turismo di Singapore), c/o Mr Patrick Trancu, Theodore Trancu & Associates, Via Pisacane 1, 20129 Milan, Italy. Tel: 39-2-7490187; Telefax: 39-2-7381032.
London: 1st Floor, Carrington House, 126–130 Regent Street, London W1R 5FE, United Kingdom. Tel: 44-71-437-0033; Telex: STBLON G893491; Telefax: 44-71-734-2191.
Paris: Singapore Tourist Promotion Board (L'Office National du Tourisme de Singapour), Centre d'Affaires Le Louvre, 2 Place du Palais-Royal, 75044 Paris Cedex 01, France. Tel: 33-1-42971616; Telefax: 33-1-42971617; Telex: SINGPAR 213593F.
Zurich: Singapore Tourist Promotion Board (Fremdenverkehrsburo Von Singapur), Hochstrasse 48, CH-8044, Zurich, Switzerland. Tel: 41-1-2525454; Telefax: 41-1-25225303.

USA AND CANADA

Chicago: 333 North Michigan Avenue, Suite 818, Chicago, Illinois 60601, USA. Tel: 1-312-2200099; Telex: 798975 SINGPOR TB CGO; Telefax: 1-312-2200020.
Los Angeles: 8484 Wilshire Boulevard, Suite 510, Beverly Hills, California 90211, USA. Tel: 1-213-8521901; Telex: SING-UR 278141; Telefax: 1-213-8520129.
New York: 590 Fifth Avenue, 12th Floor, New York, NY 10036, USA. Tel: 1-212-3024861; Telex: SING-UR 220843; Telefax: 1-212-3024801.
Toronto: 175 Bloor Street East, Suite 1112, North Tower, Toronto, Ontario, M4W 3R8, Canada. Tel: 1-416-3239139; Telex: 1-06-217510 SINGA POR TOR; Telefax: 1-416-3233514.

BANKS

ABN Amro Bank, 18 Church Street. Tel: 5355511
Allied Irish Banks PLC, #11-01 Hongkong Bank Building, 21 Collyer Quay. Tel: 2258666
American Express Bank Ltd, #03-00 Hitachi Tower, 16 Collyer Quay. Tel: 5384833
ANZ Bank, 10 Collyer Quay, #17-02/05 Ocean Building. Tel: 5358355
Arab Bank, 80 Raffles Place, #55-00 UOB Plaza. Tel: 5330055
Ban Hin Bank Bhd, 105 Cecil St, #01-00. Tel: 2272133
Ban Hin Lee Bank, 15 Phillip Street, #01-00 Tan Ean Kiam Building. Tel: 5337022
Bangkok Bank, 180 Cecil Street, Bangkok Bank Building. Tel: 2219400
Bank Brussels Lambert, 1 Raffles Place, #42-00 UOB Centre. Tel: 5324088
Bank Bumiputra, Wing On Life Building, 150 Cecil Street, #03-01/02. Tel: 2222133
Bank Indonesia, #08-01 The Arcade. Tel: 2232700
Bank of America, 78 Shenton Way, Ong Building. Tel: 2236688
Bank of China, 4 Battery Road #05-00. Tel: 5352411

Bank of East Asia, 137 Market Street. Tel: 2241334

Bank of Hawaii, 4 Shenton Way, #19-01 Shing Kwan House. Tel: 2210500

Bank of India, 108 Robinson Road. Tel: 2220011

Bank of Korea, 24 Raffles Place, #20-02A Clifford Centre. Tel: 5323522

Bank of Montreal, 150 Beach Road, #26-01 Gateway West. Tel: 2963233

Bank of New York, 10 Collyer Quay, #14-02/03 Ocean Building. Tel: 5359188

Bank of New Zealand, 65 Chulia Street, #13-05/07 OCBC Centre. Tel: 5355744

Bank of Nova Scotia, 10 Collyer Quay, #15-01/04 Ocean Building. Tel: 5358688

Bank of Singapore, 101 Cecil Street, #01-02 Tong Eng Building. Tel: 2239266

Bank of Tokyo, 16 Raffles Quay, #01-06 Hong Leong Building. Tel: 2208111

Banque Française du Commerce Exterieur, #35-01 Shell Tower. Tel: 2241455

Banque Indosuez, 6 Raffles Quay, #17-00 Denmark House. Tel: 5354988

Banque National de Paris, #03-00 Tung Centre, Collyer Quay. Tel: 2240211

Barclays Bank, 50 Raffles Place, #23-01 Shell Tower. Tel: 2248555

Chase Manhattan Bank, 50 Raffles Place, Shell Tower. Tel: 5304111

Chung Khiaw Bank, 10 Anson Road, #01-01 International Plaza. Tel: 2228622

Citibank NA, 1 Shenton Way, #-02-03. Tel: 2255221

Commerzbank A G, Shenton Way, #32-01 Treasury Building. Tel: 2234855

Credit Suisse, 80 Raffles Place, #48-00 UOB Plaza 1. Tel: 5386322

Deutsche Bank A G, #01-01 Treasury Building. Tel: 2244677

Development Bank of Singapore (DBS), 6 Shenton Way, DBS Building. Tel: 2201111

Dresdner Bank A G, 20 Collyer Quay, #22-00 Tung Centre. Tel: 2228080.

Far Eastern Bank, 156 Cecil Street, #01-00 Far Eastern Building. Tel: 2219055

Four Seas Bank, 10 Robinson Road, #05-00. Tel: 2249898

Hongkong And Shanghai Banking Corp, 21 Collyer Quay, #19-00. Tel: 5305000

Indian Bank, 2 D'Almeida Street. Tel: 5343511

Indian Overseas Bank, IDB Building, 64 Cecil Street. Tel: 2251100

Industrial & Commercial Bank, 2 Shenton Way, #03-01 ICB Building. Tel: 2211711

International Bank of Singapore, 50 Collyer Quay, #02-01 Overseas Union House. Tel: 2234488

Keppel Bank, 10 Ho Ching Road, #06-00. Tel: 2228222

Korea Exchange Bank, 2 Finlayson Green, #01-00 Asia Insurance Building. Tel: 2241633

Kwangtung Provincial Bank, 60 Cecil Street, Kwangtung Provincial Bank Building. Tel: 2239622

Lee Wah Bank, 1 Coleman Street, #01-14 The Adelphi. Tel: 3343368

Malayan Banking Berhad, 2 Battery Road, #B1-00 Malayan Bank Chambers. Tel: 5352266

May Bank, 2 Battery Road, #01-00 Malayan Bank Chambers. Tel: 5352266.

Merrill Lynch International Bank, 2 Raffles Link, #03-00. Tel: 3343368

Mitsubishi Bank, #01-02 Tung Centre. Tel: 2205666

National Bank of Canada, #11-04/06 Odeon Towers. Tel: 3393455

Oversea-Chinese Banking Corpn, 65 Chulia Street, #12-00 OCBC Centre. Tel: 5357222

Overseas Union Bank, 1 Raffles Place, OUB Centre. Tel: 5338686

Post Office Savings Bank, 73 Bras Basah Road. Tel: 3393333

PT Bank Negara Indonesia, 158 Cecil Street, #03-00. Tel: 2257755

Royal Bank of Canada, 140 Cecil Street, #01-00 PIL Building. Tel: 2247311

Royal Bank of Scotland PLC, 6 Battery Road, #18-01 Chartered Bank Building. Tel: 2251233

Sakura Bank, 16 Raffles Quay, #01-04 Hong Leong Building. Tel: 2209761

Security Pacific National Bank, 50 Raffles Place, #01-03 Shell Towers. Tel: 2243363

Société Génerale, 105 Cecil Street, #24-01 The Octagon. Tel: 2227122

Standard Chartered, #09-00/11-00 Plaza by the Park. Tel: 2258888

Sumitomo Bank, 6 Shenton Way, #17-01 DBS Building. Tel: 2201611

Swiss Bank Corporation, 6 Battery Road, #35-02 Chartered Bank Building. Tel: 2242200

Tat Lee Bank, 63 Market Street, Tat Lee Bank Building. Tel: 5339292

United Malayan Banking Corp Bhd, #01-00 Wing On Life Building. Tel: 2253111

United Overseas Bank Ltd, 80 Raffles Place, UOB Plaza 1. Tel: 5339898

AIRLINES

Aeroflot Soviet Airlines, 15 Queen Street, #01-02 Tan Chong Tower. Tel: 3361757

Aerolineas Argentinas, Blk 1 Sultan Gate #01-01. Tel: 2917300

Air Canada, 100 Orchard Road, #02-43/4 Meridien Shopping Centre. Tel: 7328555

Air China, 51 Anson Road, #01-53. Tel: 2252177

Air France, 400 Orchard Road, #14-05 Orchard Towers. Tel: 7377166

Air India, 5 Shenton Way, #17-01 UIC Building. Tel: 2259411

Airlanka, 140 Cecil Street, #02-00/B PIL Building. Tel: 2257233

Air Mauritius, 135 Cecil Street, #04-02 LKN Building. Tel: 2223033

Air New Zealand, 10 Collyer Quay, #024-07/08 Ocean Building. Tel: 5358266

Air Niugini, 101 Thomson Road, #01-05/06 United Square. Tel: 2504868
Air Seychelles, 1 Newton Road, #01-31. Tel: 2557373
Airlanka, 140 Cecil Street, #02-00/B PIL Building. Tel: 2236026
Alitalia, 435 Orchard Road, #20-01 Wisma Atria. Tel: 7376966
All Nippon, 139 Cecil Street, #01-01 Cecil House. Tel: 2248173
American Airlines Inc, Blk 3 Seah Street, #01-04. Tel: 3390001
Asiana Airlines, 135 Cecil Street, #01-00 LKN Building. Tel: 2253866
Balkan Bulgarian Airlines, 3 Coleman Street, #03-28 Peninsula Shopping Centre. Tel: 3395991
Bangladesh Biman Airlines, 15 McCallum Street, #01-02 Nat West Centre. Tel: 2217155
British Airways, #01-56 United Square. Tel: 2538444
Cathay Pacific Airways, 10 Collyer Quay, #16-01 Ocean Building. Tel: 5331333
China Airlines, 400 Orchard Road, #01-29 Orchard Towers. Tel: 7372211
Delta Airlines, 101 Thomson Road, #01-08/09 United Square. Tel: 3522816
Emirates, 435 Orchard Road, #09-06 Wisma Atria. Tel: 2351911
Eva Airways, 70 Anson Road, #01-00. Tel: 2261533
Finnair, 541 Orchard Road, #08-01 Liat Towers. Tel: 7333377
Garuda Indonesia Airways, 101 Thomson Road, #13-03 United Square. Tel: 2502888
Gulf Air, 50 Cuscaden Road, #07-03. Tel: 7382511
Indian Airlines, #01-03 Marina House. Tel: 2254949
Japan Airlines (JAL), 16 Raffles Quay, #01-01 Hong Leong Building. Tel: 2210522
Japan Air Systems, 137 Cecil Street, #01-02 ICS Building. Tel: 2261525
Kampuchea Airlines, 6001 Beach Road, #13-08 Golden Mile Tower. Tel: 2998696
KLM Royal Dutch Airlines, 333 Orchard Road, #01-02 Mandarin Hotel Arcade. Tel: 7377622
Korean Air Lines, Collyer Quay, #01-02 Ocean Building. Tel: 5342111
Ladeco Chilean Airlines, 101 Thomson Road, #01-10. Tel: 2562253
LOT Polish Airlines, 94 Tanjong Pagar Road. Tel: 2210344
Lufthansa German Airlines, 390 Orchard Road, #05-01/02 Palais Renaissance. Tel: 7379222
Malaysian Airlines System (MAS), 190 Clemenceau Avenue, #02-09 Singapore Shopping Centre. Tel: 3366777
Middle East Airlines, TTM Travel Agency, 10 Collyer Quay, #06-01 Ocean Building. Tel: 5335252
Myanmar Airways, 111 North Bridge Road, #03-22 Peninsula Plaza. Tel: 3347322
Northwest Airlines, Odeon Towers. Tel: 3363371
Olympic Airways, 9 Penang Lane, #08-17. Tel: 3366061
Pakistan International Airlines, #01-01/04 United

Square, 101 Thomson Road. Tel: 2512322
Philippine Airlines, #01-02 Parklane Shopping Mall. Tel: 3371105
Qantas Airways, #04-02 The Promenade. Tel: 7373744
Royal Brunei Airlines, 25 Scotts Road, #01-4A/B/5 Royal Holiday Inn Crowne Plaza. Tel: 2354672
Royal Jordanian, 15 Beach Road, #03-11 Beach Centre. Tel: 3388188
Royal Nepal Airlines, 3 Coleman Street, #03-07/08. Tel: 3395535
Sabena World Airlines, #02-04 CIAS Cargo Complex. Tel: 5425580
Saudi Arabian Airlines, No 1 Sultan Gate Place, #01-01 Beach Road. Tel: 2917322
Scandinavian Airlines System, #23-01/04 Gateway East, 152 Beach Road. Tel: 2941611
Sempati Air, 541 Orchard Road, #08-04 Liat Towers. Tel: 7386830
Silkair, #03-00 SATS Building. Tel: 5428111
Singapore Airlines, 77 Robinson Road. Tel: 2238888/5456666
South African Airways, 171 Tras Street, #01-179 Union Building. Tel: 2277911
Swissair, 304 Orchard Road, #03-18 Lucky Plaza. Tel: 7378133
Tarom Romanian Air Transport, 3 Coleman Street, #03-07/08 Peninsula Shopping Complex. Tel: 3381467
Thai Airways International, 100 Cecil Street, #02-00 The Globe. Tel: 2242011
Trans World Airlines (TWA), 7500A Beach Road, #09-324 The Plaza. Tel: 2936833
Turkish Airlines, 545 Orchard Road, #02-21 Far East Shopping Centre. Tel: 7324556
United Airlines, 16 Raffles Quay, #44-02 Hong Leong Building. Tel: 2200711
UTA French Airlines, 400 Orchard Road, #14-05 Orchard Towers. Tel: 7370551
Vietnam Airlines, 15 Beach Road, #02-11 Beach Centre. Tel: 3393552

USEFUL NUMBERS

Fire, Ambulance	995
Police	999
Flight Information	5424422
Meterological Office	5427788
Postal Service	165
Telephone Directory Assistance	104
Assistance in Calling (local calls)	100
Time Announcing Service	1711
Singapore Bus Service	2848866
Singapore Tourist Promotion Board	3396622
Railway Administration	2225165
Overseas Call Booking	104

Argentina: 302 Orchard Road, #15-03 Tong Bldg. Tel: 2354231. Open: 9am–3pm, Mon–Fri.

Australia: 25 Napier Road. Tel: 7379311. Open: 8.30am–12.30pm, 1.30pm–4.30pm, Mon–Fri.

Austria: 1 Scotts Road, #22-04 Shaw Centre. Tel: 2354088. Open: 8am–4pm, Mon–Fri.

Bangladesh: 101 Thomson Road, #06-07 United Square. Tel: 2506323/2505539. Open: 9am–11.30am, 2.30pm–5pm, Mon–Fri.

Belgium: 10 Anson Road, #09-24 International Plaza. Tel: 2207677. Open: 8.30am–12.30pm, 1.30pm–4pm, Mon–Fri.

Brazil: 101 Thomson Road, #10-05. Tel: 2566001. Open: 10am–1pm, 2pm–5pm, Mon–Fri.

Britain: 30 Napier Road. Tel: 4739333. Open: 8.30am–1pm, 2pm–5pm, Mon–Fri.

Brunei: 325 Tanglin Road. Tel: 7339055. Open: 8.30am–4.30pm, Mon–Fri.

Bulgaria: 15 Scotts Road, #09-09 Thong Teck Bldg. Tel: 7371111. Open: 9am–12.30pm, 1.30pm–4.30pm, Mon–Fri.

Canada: 80 Anson Road, 14th & 15th Storey, IBM Towers. Tel: 2256363. Open: 8am–12.30pm, 1.30pm–4.30pm, Mon–Fri.

Chile: 105 Cecil Street, #14-01 The Octagon. Tel: 2238577. Open: 9am–2pm, Mon–Fri.

China: 70-76 Dalvey Road. Tel: 7343361. Open: 9am–12pm, Mon–Fri.

Cyprus: 6 Kung Chong Road. Tel: 4748473. Open: 9.30am–12.30pm, 2pm–4.30pm, Mon–Fri.

Denmark: 101 Thomson Road, #13-01/02 United Square. Tel: 2503383. Open: 8.30am–4pm, Mon–Thurs, 8.30am–1.30pm, Fri.

Egypt: 75 Grange Road. Tel: 7371811. Open: 9am–3pm, Mon–Fri.

Finland: 101 Thomson Road, #21-02/03 United Square. Tel: 2544042. Open: 8.30am–12.30pm, 1pm–4pm, Mon–Fri.

France: 5 Gallop Road. Tel: 4664866. Open: 9am–2pm, Mon–Fri.

Germany (Federal Republic of): 545 Orchard Road, #14-01 Far East Shopping Centre. Tel: 7371355. Open: 8am–1pm, 2pm–4pm, Mon–Thur, 8am–2pm, Fri.

Greece: 19 Keppel Road, #05-04. Tel: 2212364. Open: 9am–5pm, Mon–Fri, 9am–1pm, Sat.

Honduras: 10 Anson Road, #33-05. Tel: 2272170. Open: 9.30am–12.30pm, 2pm–5pm, Mon–Fri.

Hungary: 101 Thomson Road, #22-05 United Square. Tel: 2509215. Open: 9.30am–5pm, Mon–Fri.

Iceland: Lower Kent Ridge Road. Tel: 7765598. Open: 9am–5pm, Mon–Fri.

India: 31 Grange Road. Tel: 7376777. Open: 9am–1pm, 1.30pm–5pm, Mon–Fri.

Indonesia: 7 Chatsworth Road. Tel: 7377422. Open: 8.30am–12.30pm, 2pm–4.30pm, Mon–Fri.

Ireland: 346 River Valley Road, #13-00. Tel: 7323430. Open: 9am–5pm, Mon–Fri, 9am–12.30pm, Sat.

Israel: 58 Dalvey Road. Tel: 2350966. Open: 8.30am–4.30pm, Mon–Fri.

Italy: 101 Thomson Road, #27-02/03 United Square. Tel: 2506022. Open: 8am–2pm, Mon–Fri.

Japan: 16 Nassim Road. Tel: 2358855. Open: 8.30am–12.30pm, 2pm–4.30pm, Mon–Fri.

Korea (Democratic People's Republic of): 7500A The Plaza, Beach Road, #09-322. Tel: 2991650. Open: 9.30am–5.30pm, Mon–Fri.

Korea (Republic of): 101 Thomson Road, #10-03 United Square. Tel: 2561188. Open: 8.30am–12.30pm, 2pm–4.30pm, Mon–Fri; 8.30am–12.30pm, Sat.

Malaysia: 301 Jervois Road. Tel: 2350011. Open: 8.45am–3.30pm, Mon–Fri.

Malta: 20 Maxwell Road, #07-01. Tel: 2222100. Open: 9am–5pm, Mon–Fri, 9am–12pm, Sat.

Mexico: 152 Beach Road, #06-07 Gateway East. Tel: 2982678. Open: 9am–3pm, Mon–Fri.

Myanmar: 15 St. Martin's Drive. Tel: 2358763. Open: 9am–1pm, 2pm–5pm, Mon–Fri.

Netherlands: 541 Orchard Road, #13-01 Liat Towers. Tel: 7371155. Open: 9am–12pm, 1.30pm–3pm, Mon–Fri.

New Zealand: 13 Nassim Road. Tel: 2359966. Open: 8.30am–12.30pm, 1.30pm–4.30pm, Mon–Fri.

Norway: 16 Raffles Quay, #44-01 Hong Leong Building. Tel: 2207122. Open: 10am–2pm, Mon–Fri.

Pakistan: 20A Nassim Road. Tel: 7376988. Open: 9.30am–5pm, Mon–Fri.

Panama: 16 Raffles Quay, #41-06 Hong Leong Building. Tel: 2218677. Open: 9am–12pm, 2pm–4pm, Mon–Fri.

Papua New Guinea: 11 Dhoby Ghaut, #09-10 Cathay Building. Tel: 3367677. Open 9am–1pm, 2pm–4pm, Mon–Fri.

Peru: 390 Orchard Road, #12-03 Palais Renaissance Building. Tel: 7388595. Open: 9am–1pm, 2pm–5pm, Mon–Fri.

Philippines: 20B Nassim Road. Tel: 7373977. Open: 9am–12pm, 2pm–5pm, Mon–Fri.

Poland: 100 Beach Road, #33-11/12 Shaw Towers. Tel: 2942513. Open: 9am–4pm, Mon–Fri.

Portugal: 55 Waterloo Street, #09-03A. Tel: 3341231. Open: 8am–12pm, Mon–Fri.

Romania: 48 Jln Harom Setangkai. Tel: 4683424. Open: 8am–2pm, Mon–Fri.

Russian Federation: 51 Nassim Road. Tel: 7370048. Open: 8am–3pm, Mon–Fri.

Saudi Arabia: 10 Nassim Road. Tel: 7345878. Open: 9am–4pm, Mon–Fri.

Seychelles: 195A Goldhill Centre. Tel: 2522088. Open: 9am–5pm, Mon–Fri, 9am–12pm, Sat.

South Africa: 331 North Bridge Road, #15-00 Odeon Towers. Tel: 3393319. Open: 9am–12pm, 2pm–5pm, Mon–Fri.

Spain: 15 Scotts Road, #05-08/09 Thong Teck Bldg. Tel: 7329788. Open: 9.30am–12pm, 2pm–4pm, Mon–Fri.

Sri Lanka: 51 Newton Road, #13-07 Goldhill Plaza. Tel: 2544595. Open: 9am–1pm, 2pm–5.15pm, Mon–Fri.

Sweden: 111 Somerset Road, #05-08 PUB Bldg, Devonshire Wing. Tel: 7342771. Open: 8.30am–12.30pm, 1.30pm–5pm, Mon–Fri.
Switzerland: 1 Swiss Club Link. Tel: 4685788. Open: 9am–1pm, Mon–Fri.
Taipei: 460 Alexandra Road, PSA Building, #23-00. Tel: 2786511. Open: 9am–12.30pm, 1.30pm–4.30pm, Mon–Fri, 9am–12pm, Sat.
Thailand: 370 Orchard Road. Tel: 7372644. Open: 9am–12.30pm, 2pm–5pm, Mon–Fri.
Turkey: 20B Nassim Road. Tel: 7329211. Open: 9am–12.30pm, 2pm–6pm, Mon–Fri.
USA: 30 Hill Street. Tel: 3380251. Open: 8.30am–5pm, Mon–Fri.
Vietnam: 10 Leedon Park. Tel: 4683747. Open: 9am–noon, Mon–Sat.

FURTHER READING

GENERAL

Ministry of Communications and Information: *Singapore Facts and Figures 1990.* and *Singapore 1990.*
Norman Edwards & Peter Keys: *Singapore, A Guide to Buildings, Streets, Places.* Times Books International.
Jane Beamish & Jane Ferguson: *A History of Singapore Architecture, The Making of a City.* Graham Brash.

HISTORICAL

C.M. Turnbull: *A History of Singapore 1819–1975.* Oxford University Press.
Noel Barber: *Sinister Twilight.* Coronet. Fascinating account of the fall of Singapore.
Straits Affairs. The Malay World and Singapore. 'Glimpses of the Straits Settlements and the Malay Peninsula in the Nineteenth Century' as seen through the Illustrated London News and other contemporary sources. Compiled by J.M.Tate. John Nicholson Ltd.

FICTION

Noel Barber: *Tanamera.* Coronet. Good read, fiction set in the colonial period.
Goh Sin Tub: *The Nan-mei-su Girls of Emerald Hill.* Heinemann Asia. Local writer, story set in Emerald Hill during the war.

Philip Jeyaretnam: *First Loves.* Times Books International. Growing up in Singapore, an interesting insight by a prize-winning author.
Philip Jeyaretnam: *Raffles Place Ragtime.* Times Books International. About love, ambition and social expectations in Singapore.
Catherine Lim: *Little Ironies, Stories of Singapore.* Heinemann Asia. Ups and downs of Singapore life recounted with great perception.
Rex Shelley: *The Shrimp People.* Times Books International. Award-winning evocative story on the Eurasians in Singapore.

CLASSICAL

Joseph Conrad: *Lord Jim.* Penguin.
Anthony Burgess: *The Malayan Trilogy.* Penguin. Not strictly Singapore, but a must for those interested in this part of the world.
Somerset Maugham: *Collected Short Stories.* Mandarin. More Malaya, but a fascinating insight into life in the colonies.

MORE ON SINGAPORE

David Brazil: *Street Smart Singapore.* Times Books International
The Secret Map of Singapore. Ropion, Blaisdell, Mowe
Singapore's 100 Best Restaurants 1991. Compiled by the Editors of Singapore Tatler. Illustrated Magazine Publishing Co. Ltd.

NATURAL HISTORY

An excellent series of small handbooks on Singapore has been published by The Singapore Science Centre. Each volume costs just S$5 and the subjects range from Wayside Trees, Ferns and Common Birds to Seashore Life and Freshwater Fish.
Christopher Hails and Frank Jarvis: *Birds of Singapore.* Times Editions. A beautiful, comprehensive guide to the subject.

COOKERY BOOKS

Mrs. Lee Chin Koon: *Mrs Lee's Cookbook.* Eurasia Press. A delightful introduction to Nonya cuisine and culture.
Jacki Passmore. *Asia. The Beautiful Cookbook.* Merehurst Press. A gorgeous book of stunning photographs, interesting explanations and delicious recipes from all over Asia.
Margaret Chan's Foodstops. Landmark Books. Comprehensive listings of the what to eat and where to eat them, in Singapore.

GETTING THERE

BY ROAD

Buses to Johor Bahru (JB) depart every 10 minutes from the Ban San Street terminus in Singapore (S$1.50). Alternatively, you can catch the No. 170 bus every 15 minutes from Queen Street or various stops along Bukit Timah Road (S$0.80).

Share and charter taxis to Johor also leave from Queen Street (about S$6 per person or $24 for the whole taxi). Otherwise you can take a regular Singapore taxi to the Woodlands border post and walk across the 1km causeway.

The long-distance taxi station in JB is situated on Jalan Wong Ah Fook; the bus station on Jalan Trus Johor Bahru.

BY RAIL

There are daily trains from Keppel Station in Singapore to Johor Bahru Station on Jalan Tun Abdul Razak. Departures at 10am, 11.20am, 12.30pm, 4pm and 6pm. Trains from JB to Singapore depart at 2.10pm, 3pm and 7.15pm. You should allow one hour for ticket purchase and customs formalities before departure. Likewise, you can catch trains heading northward to Kuala Lumpur, Butterworth (Penang) and Bangkok. For information call 2225165 in Singapore or 07-224727 in Johor.

BY SEA

Ferrylink operates car and passenger boats between Changi Point in Singapore and Tanjung Belungkor in eastern Johor state. Ferries leave Singapore each day at 9am, noon and 4.15pm and leave Belungkor at 10.30am, 1.30pm and 5.45pm. An adult return ticket from Singapore is S$24 and from Belungkor M$27. Vehicle fare for a regular sized car is S$32 from Singapore and M$36 from Belungkor. For information and reservations call 5453600 in Singapore.

BY AIR

There are no flights between Singapore and Johor. However, Senai International Airport in Johor offers connections to all major cities in Malaysia through Malaysia Airlines (MAS) domestic services. MAS also provides a direct flight to/from Hong Kong. The MAS office in Johor Bahru is Suite 1.1, Level 1, Menara Pelangi, Taman Pelangi, 80400 Johor Bahru. Tel: 341001, Fax: 340043. The airport number is 594737.

TRAVEL ESSENTIALS

VISAS & PASSPORTS

Valid passports and a health certificate of vaccination against yellow fever are required if travelling from an infected area. Citizens of Commonwealth countries (except India), Ireland, Switzerland, the Netherlands, San Marino and Liechtenstein do not require a visa. The following countries don't need a visa for a visit not exceeding three months: Austria, Belgium, Brunei, Denmark, Finland, France, Germany, Iceland Indonesia, Ireland, Italy, Japan, Liechtenstein, Luxembourg, Netherlands, Norway, Philippines, Singapore, South Korea, Sweden, Switzerland, Thailand, Tunisia and the United States.

Immigration requests that your passport be valid for at least 6 months after arrival. The most common visa will be for 14 days, but you can request 30 days. If you wish to extend your stay – and are from one of the countries enjoying diplomatic relations with Malaysia – you may do so at the Immigration Dept, Wisma Persekutuan Johor, Blok B, Tingkat 1, Jln. Air Molek, 80550 Johor Bahru. Tel: 07-244255.

MONEY MATTERS

The Malaysian currency is the *ringgit* or Malaysian dollar, which is divided into 100 sen. The amount of Malaysian dollars you are allowed to bring in or take out of Malaysia is unlimited. At the time of going to press, the exchange rates were: M$2.54 to US$1 and M$1.65 to A$1. The Singapore and Brunei dollar are worth about 60 percent more than the Malaysian ringgit, and no longer circulate freely in Malaysia. You may be able to use Singapore dollars in Johor, but they are counted as having the same value as the *ringgit*.

Banks and licensed money changers offer better rates than do hotels and shops, where a service charge may be levied (usually 2–4 percent). Make sure that you have enough cash before you leave for smaller towns or remote areas in Johor state.

Banks in Johor follow the non-Islamic work week. They are open 9.30am–3.30pm Mon–Fri and 9.30am–noon Sat. Banks are closed on Sunday.

Travellers' Cheques and Credit Cards: In the

more flashy quarters of Johor Bahru – especially in department stores, first-class restaurants and hotels – travellers' cheques change hands easily. Have your passport ready when changing cheques. Off the beaten track, you may find it harder to change TCs. Credit cards are widely accepted at the same sort of establishments. Popular cards include American Express, Diners Club, JCB, Mastercard and Visa.

In general, costs in Malaysia are considerably lower than in Europe, North America and Singapore (except for some imported goods), and higher than countries like Thailand and Indonesia.

HEALTH

Travellers have little to worry about in a country where the health standards are ranked amongst the highest in Asia. Water in Johor Bahru is generally safe for drinking, but it's wiser to drink it boiled. Bottled water is widely available. Avoid drinking iced water from roadside stalls. Remember that it's important to drink enough to avoid dehydration in the tropical heat; drink more than you would normally if you're coming from a cold country.

The sun is deceptively strong here: one hour of sunbathing a day for the first few days will get you a lasting tan without giving you sunstroke.

If you are visiting remote jungle areas of Johor state, it's advisable to take malaria tablets; your doctor will know which type is suitable for the region. To help keep mosquitoes at bay, use insect repellents, mosquito coils and nets at night.

Treat open cuts and scratches immediately as infection in humid climates can delay healing, and at worst, cause tropical ulcers. If you are swimming in the sea near coral reefs, don't touch shells, snakes and other creatures – they may be poisonous! It's also a good idea to wear plastic shoes or flippers to avoid cutting yourself on the coral.

Medical supplies are widely and readily available throughout Johor state, and all large towns have government polyclinics as well as private clinics. In addition, all major towns have government-run and private specialist hospitals.

In an emergency, call 999 for ambulance, fire or the police.

SAFETY

Even though Johor is a relatively crime-free destination, it's wise to follow basic safety rules while visiting. Stay in brightly lit areas at night, never carry too much cash on your person, and keep travellers' cheque numbers apart from the cheques. Most hotels have security services and many of them have safes for valuables. In the event of loss, you can call the Tourist Police Unit at 232222.

WHAT TO WEAR

In the tropical climate of Malaysia, informal wear is suitable and comfortable. However, since this is predominantly a Muslim and conservative country, observance of local customs is important.

Away from the beach or pool, women should not wear dresses, skirts or shorts that are too short, and you should always wear a bra. Likewise, shorts are not a good idea in cities, towns and villages. While visiting mosques, a woman's legs should be covered to below the knee; some mosques will provide scarves for the head and arms. Men may wear T-shirts or cotton shirts with short sleeves, and open sandals.

Topless or nude sunbathing is strictly frowned upon. When visiting government offices and passing through immigration points, long trousers and skirts are looked upon favourably.

WHAT TO BRING

There is very little need to worry about leaving something important behind when you visit Johor. Toiletries, medicines, clothes, photographic film, suntan lotion and straw hats are all readily available in Johor Bahru. In fact, the best advice is to take as little as possible so that you can travel lightly and comfortably.

CUSTOMS

Import duties seldom affect the average traveller, who may bring in 225 grammes of tobacco or cigars, or 200 cigarettes, one-quart of liquor as well as personal cameras, watches, cassette players, cosmetics etc. If you wish to bring in a dutiable item, you may be asked to pay a deposit (usually 50 percent of the item's value) which will be refunded on departure. Ensure you get an official receipt for any tax or deposit paid. Pornography and weapons are strictly prohibited. Possession of narcotics and other illegal drugs carries the death sentence, and firearms are subject to licensing.

GETTING ACQUAINTED

TIME ZONE

Malaysia's standard time is 8 hours ahead of Greenwich Mean Time (or 7 hours ahead of British Summer Time), the same as Singapore.

CLIMATE

Johor's weather is generally warm, humid and sunny year round, with temperatures wavering 32°C during the day and 22°C at night.

LANGUAGE

Malay is the mother tongue of more than 150 million Asians, including the majority of people in Johor state. Though formal Malay is a complex language demanding some time of serious study, the construction of 'Basic Malay' is fairly simple, with many things about the language conducive to learning. Malay is written in the Latin alphabet and – unlike some Asian tongues – is not a tonal language.

ELECTRICITY

The Malaysian current is 220 volts, 50 cycles. Adaptors for 110-volt, 60 cycles appliances can be bought at electrical shops throughout Johor, or ask to borrow one at your hotel.

BUSINESS HOURS

Business hours in Johor are confusing. State and municipal government retain the traditional Muslim system: offices are open Saturday to Wednesday and half a day on Thursday. The work day begins at 8am and ends at 4pm (12.45pm Thursday). Thursday afternoon and Friday are the weekend.

Federal offices, on the other hand, are open Monday to Friday and half a day on Saturday (same hours as above). Saturday afternoon and Sunday are the weekend. Most private offices and shops follow the federal system (Sunday weekend). Offices tend to favour a nine-to-five routine. Shops are open 9.30am–7pm. Supermarkets and department stores are open 10am–10pm. The state government was all set to introduce a common Sunday weekend in 1994, but seem to be backing down under pressure from Islamic experts and theologians.

COMMUNICATIONS

POSTAL SERVICES

Malaysia has one of the most efficient postal services in Asia. The main post office in Johor Bahru is situated between the Sultan Ibrahim Building and the Mahkamah Courthouse. All post offices in Johor are open 8am–5pm. Mon–Sat; closed on Sunday. Most international hotels also provide postal services; and stamps and aerogrammes are often sold at the small Indian sweet and tobacco stalls.

TELEPHONE & TELEGRAM

Public phones can be found in most towns, often located in front of restaurants. Many use telephone cards which are sold at post offices and small shops. The cost of local phone calls is 10 sens for every three minutes. Long-distance and international calls can be made from a post office or hotel.

The telephone prefix (area code) for Johor state is 07. To dial Singapore from Johor you must place 02 before the local number.

International Direct Dialling (IDD) is available in most international hotels, as are secretarial and facsimile services.

Other useful numbers:
Trunk call assistance	101
Connection difficulties	102
Directory enquiries	103
Telegrams	104
Weather report (Monday-Friday)	1052
Emergency (police/fire/ambulance)	999
Tourist Police	232222

Getting Around

Where to Stay

PUBLIC TRANSPORT

Taxi: Taxis remain one of the most popular and cheap means of transport, especially on a shared basis. You can hail them by the roadside, hire them from authorised taxi stands, or book them by phone, in which case, mileage is calculated from the stand or garage from which the vehicle is hired.

Most taxis are fitted with meters. At the start of the journey, the meter reads M$1.50 and turns over 10 sen for every 100 metres. A surcharge of 50 percent is imposed late at night (1am–6am). Some night drivers are reluctant to use their metres and prefer to fix a price to the destination: this is where you'll need your bargaining skills! You can also negotiate a day price with town taxis.

Car rental: Having your own transport gives you the freedom to explore places off the beaten track. Cars are usually rented with unlimited mileage. The daily rates vary from M$148 per day for economy cars, to M$428 per day for super luxury class. Weekly rates range from M$880 to M$2,568. An international, national or state driving licence is required by visitors who wish to drive in Malaysia. Insurance is highly recommended and costs an additional M$15-$25 per day. Personal injury insurance costs M$6 per day. The principal car rental firms serving Johor are listed below:

Avis Rent-A-Car, Ground Floor, Tropical Inn. Tel: 237971, Fax: 237970.
Budget Rent-A-Car, Orchid Plaza. Tel: 243951, Fax: 243953.
Hertz Rent-A-Car, 35 Jln Ibrahim. Tel: 237520, Fax: 242084.

The following list of hotels is by no means exhaustive, but will give the visitor some idea of what is available in Johor state.

JOHOR BAHRU

Causeway Inn, 6A-F Jln Meldrum, Tel: 248811, Fax: 248820. Air-conditioned rooms with king-size beds and TV's, conference and banquet facilities.
Crystal Crown Hotel, Jln Tebrau, Tel: 334422, Fax: 343582, 345505. 250 rooms, lounge, karaoke club, coffee house and Chinese restaurant. Conference/banquet facilities, health centre, swimming pool.
Crystal Inn, 36 Jln Zabedah, Tel: 415222, Fax: 418188. 56 air-conditioned rooms with TV's. Restaurant serving Western and Malaysian cuisine.
First Hotel, Jln. Station, Tel: 222888, Fax: 248868. 42 air-conditioned rooms, coffee house, health centre.
Holiday Inn Crowne Plaza, Jln Dat Sulaiman, Tel: 323800, Fax: 318884. 350 rooms, coffee house and restaurants serving Chinese, Indian, Italian cuisine, polo lounge. Business centre, swimming pool, squash courts, health centre, disco, shops, travel service.
Johor Hotel, 69 Jln Sultan Ibrahim, Tel: 224395. 33 rooms, bath/shower.
Merlin Tower Hotel, 10 Jln. Bukit Meldrum, Tel: 237400/1, Fax: 248919. 104 air-conditioned rooms, coffee house, restaurant, pub.
Peninsula Hotel, 6A Jln Abiad Taman Tebrau Jaya, Tel: 323277/88, Fax: 332337. 38 air-conditioned rooms.
Puteri Pan Pacific, Jln Salim, Tel: 233333. 500 rooms, full room facilities and service, coffee shop and restaurants serving Malay, Chinese and Italian cuisine, bars. Business and fitness centres, swimming pool, tennis and squash courts.
Regent Elite Hotel, 1 Jln Siew Nam, Tel: 243811. 76 rooms, air-conditioned, restaurant, disco, nightclub.
Straits View, 1D Jln Scudai, Tel: 241400, Fax: 242698. Air-conditioned rooms with private bath, IDD and TV's. In-house videos, coffee house and seafood restaurant, function hall.
Tropical Inn, 15 Jln Gereja, Tel: 247888. 160 rooms, air-conditioned, TV, hot water, bath/shower, restaurant, coffeehouse, bar lounge, health centre, beauty salon, disco, nightclub, car rental.

Wato Inn, 15R-T/223694 Jln Bukit Meldrum, Tel: 221328. 22 rooms, air-conditioned, bath/shower, TV, bar, car rental.

BATU PAHAT

Dragon Hotel, 1 Jln Puteri, Tel: 441834, Fax: 441977. 41 rooms, air-conditioned, telephone, hot water.

Garden Hotel, 29 Jalan Jenang, Tel: 415999, Fax: 415759. 85 air-conditioned rooms with private bathrooms. In-house videos, karaoke lounge, 24-hour coffee shop and Japanese restaurant. Conference facilities, shopping centre nearby.

Hotel Carnival, 2 Jln Fatimah, Tel: 415122/412949, Fax: 410611. 60 air-conditioned rooms with TV's. In-house videos, coffee house and Chinese restaurant. Conference/banquet facilities.

Landmark Hotel, 1 Jln Omar, Tel: 420001, Fax: 420088. 55 air-conditioned rooms, in-house video, coffee house and lounge. Conference and banquet facilities available.

Sentosa Hotel, 15 Jln Penjaja, Tel: 445055.

DESARU

Desaru Garden Beach Resort, Tanjung Penawar, Kota Tinggi, Tel: 821101/7, Fax: 821480/821237. 100 rooms plus chalets, golf lodge, dormitory-style accommodation and camp site facilities and services, coffee house, Japanese and seafood restaurants, bar lounge, karaoke, shops, tennis and volleyball courts, swimming pool, sea sports, golf course.

Desaru Golf Hotel, Tanjung Penawar, Kota Tinggi, Tel: 821101/7, Fax: 821480. 98 rooms, swimming pool, restaurant serving Malay, Chinese and Western food, bar lounge, billiards, video games, board games, horse-riding, cycling, jogging, jungle treks, scuba diving instruction (padi), tennis, table tennis, volleyball, 18-hole golf course.

Desaru Holiday Resort, Tanjung Penawar, Kota Tinggi, Tel: 821240. 35 chalets on beach, from simple 3-bed chalets with sitting room and verandah (TV on request), to family chalets with cooking facilities, all chalets with air-conditioning; restaurant, water sports, golf by arrangement, cycling.

Desaru View Hotel, P.O. Box 50, 81970 Kota Tinggi Tel: 821101/7 (in Singapore: 2232157), Fax: 821480. 134 international-standard rooms. Three restaurants, pool bar, horse-riding, water sports, conference facilities.

KLUANG

Anika Hotel, 298 Jln Haji Manan Lian Seng Gdn, Tel: 724977, Fax: 725870. 90 air-conditioned rooms with TV's and mini bars. In house videos, lounge, snooker room, disco, coffee house and Chinese restaurant. Conference/banquet facilities, health club.

Kluang Rest House, Jln. Pejabat Kerejaan, Tel: 721567. 14 rooms, air-conditioned.

Regal Hotel, 42 Jln. Dato Captain, Tel: 724922. 36 rooms, air-conditioned, telephone, hot water.

KOTA TINGGI

Waterfall Chalets, Kota Tinggi Waterfall, Tel: 831146. Chalets with hot water, some self-catering, restaurant.

MUAR

Hotel Sri Pelangi, 79 Jln Sisi, Tel: 918088, Fax: 926999. 82 air-conditioned rooms with TV, IDD.

MERSING

East Coast Hotel, 43A-1 Jln. Abu Bakar, Tel: 791337. Basic rooms.

Mersing Hotel, Jln. Dato Mohd Ali, Tel: 791004. 23 rooms, 13 of which are air-conditioned.

Mersing Merlin Inn, 1 Km Endau Road, Tel: 791311/2/3, Fax: 793177. 34 air-conditioned rooms, TV, hot water, bath/shower, room service, continental restaurant, swimming pool, disco.

Sri Mersing Chalet, Pantai Air Papan, Tel: 794194.

SEGAMAT

Segamat Merlin Inn, 26 Jln Ros, Tel: 919911/2/3, Fax: 919914. 85 rooms, fried chicken fast food restaurant, bar.

JOHOR ISLANDS

All islands accessible from Mersing ferry point.

PULAU BESAR

Besar Beach Resort. Chalets, restaurant, sea sports.

Hillside Chalet Island Resort, booking office: Suite 125, 1st floor, Johor Tower, Johor Bahru, Tel: 236603, Fax: 244329. Wooden chalets each containing two queen sized beds with attached bathroom. Cooled by ceiling fans. Beach and hillside chalets available.

Radin Island Pulau Besar Resort. Bookings from office near jetty, or write to 5 Jln. Abu Bakar, Mersing, Tel: 794152/791413. Coconut-framed huts, bungalows, sea sports, jungle treks, restaurant, seafood, barbecues on request.

PULAU RAWA

Rawa Safaris Island Resort. Bookings and boats from Mersing, Tel: 791204, Fax: 793848. Wooden chalets and bungalows, some with attached bathroom, electricity till midnight, lanterns provided, restaurant, seafood, barbecues, windsurfing, canoeing, scuba diving, snorkelling, fishing, equipment for hire, aqua and other shops.

PULAU SIBU

Sea Gypsy Village Resort, Sibu Island, Tel: 793125. Chalets, private bathroom, restaurant, sea sports, fishing.
Sibu Island Cabanas, Sibu Island, Tel: 311920/ 317216, Fax: 321251/311920. 14 chalets, fancooled, private bathroom, restaurant, sea sports, indoor games, fishing.

FOOD DIGEST

WHAT TO EAT

The different people that comprise Malaysia's multiracial population provide the country with enough flavours to please every palate. The most popular cuisines are Malay, Chinese and Indian. Thai food is also well represented and Western cuisine is increasingly popular, especially American fast-food outlets.

Variety isn't restricted to taste, but extends to the many dining environments. These range from plush air-conditioned restaurants with a formal setting and attentive waiters, to Chinese coffee shops and open-air foodstalls. During your stay in Johor you should eat at roadside stalls at least once, for it's here that some of the region's most famous and tasty foods are cooked.

Malay food is generally rich and spicy, though not as hot as Thai and Indian food. White rice (*nasi*) is the staple grain. Seafood, chicken and meat (except pork) are cooked in a variety of ways. Coconut forms the basis for many dishes. The 'milk' is a popular drink, while the meat is usually grated and squeezed to provide the juice for a tasty sauce. Perhaps the best known of all Malay dishes is *satay*, tender slivers of meat on wooden skewers, which are barbecued over charcoal and served with a peanut sauce.

Other tasty dishes include *tahu goreng*, fried cubes of soya bean curd with fresh bean sprouts; *gado gado*, a salad of raw vegetables topped with a rich peanut sauce; *laksa*, a type of spicy soup made of fine noodles and fish stock; *mee rebus* (boiled noodles) and *mee siam* (Thai-style noodles).

Chinese cuisine is everywhere in JB, and you will find it has influenced many of the Malay dishes. Therefore Malays cook noodles and the Chinese use chilli – it's a mutual exchange, except for the forbidden pork, so loved by the Chinese. Many people claim that Indian food in Malaysia is better than that in India. There are three traditions of Indian food represented here: North Indian food, which has rich, creamy sauces and uses the tandoor oven; Muslim Indian food, which serves spicy foods such as *rojak*; and South Indian Hindu food, which, near the local temple, is purely vegetarian.

SHOPPING

The toast of Johor Bahru shopping is the new **Plaza Kota Raya** beside the Pan Pacific Hotel, where you can get just about anything you can think of: clothes, electronics, videos, craft items, home furnishings, fast food, etc.

But it's not the only large shopping centre in JB. Holiday Plaza is said to be one of the longest shopping arcades in Asia, designed not only for shopping, but also for entertainment and sports. **Plaza Pelangi** has 150 stores offering the tourist handicrafts, batik and duty-free items. Other major shopping centres are **Wisma Abad Complex**, **Tun Abdul Razak Complex**, **Sentosa Complex** and **Merlin Tower** shopping centre.

For Malaysian arts and crafts, visit the **Handicraft Development Corporation**'s showroom and work area on the road to **JARO**, which has a good selection of Asian crafts upstairs and its rattan and leather bookbinding workshops downstairs. Or you can visit **Johorcraft Village**, Lot 2135 M.S. Jln JB, Kota Tinggi. Tel: 07-836393, Fax: 07-836394. Here you can not only buy craft and ceramic items but also be informed with demonstrations and entertained with cultural performances.

There are fascinating **bazaars** near the Central Market. And once the sun has gone down, several streets become open-air night markets (*pasar malam*) which make for an interesting entertainment.

USEFUL ADDRESSES

TOURIST INFORMATION

The Malaysia Tourism Promotion Board (MTPB) has offices throughout Malaysia. Their office in Johor Bahru should be contacted for general information on Malaysia. For detailed information on Johor state, it may be better to contact the state-run Department of Tourism.

MTPB (Singapore), 10 Collyer Quay, #01-03 Ocean Bldg, Singapore 0104. Tel: 532-6321 or 532-6351, Fax: 535-6650.
MTPB (Southern Region Office), No. 52, Ground Floor, Kompleks Tun Razak, Jln. Wong Ah Fook, 80000 Johor Bahru, Johor. Tel: 223590, Fax: 235502.
State Department of Tourism Johor, 4th floor, Sultan Ibrahim Building, Bukit Timbalan, 80503 Johor Bahru, Negeri Johor Darul Ta'zim. Tel: 234935 or 241957 ext 130, Fax: 237554.

TRAVEL AGENTS

A number of tour operators and travel companies in Singapore and Johor Bahru offer day trips to points of interest in Johor state. The reputable agents are registered with the Malaysia Tourism Promotion Board (MTPB) or the Singapore Tourist Promotion Board (STPB). Below is a short list of registered agents.

SINGAPORE

Malaysian and Singapore Travel Centre, #04-15 Tanglin Shopping Centre, Singapore 1024. Tel: 2354411, Fax: 2353033.
Siakson Coach Tours, 3 Miller Street, Siakson Building, Singapore 0718. Tel: 3318207, Fax: 3374814.
Singapore Sightseeing, Unit 8, Basement, Equatorial Hotel, 429 Bukit Timah Road, Singapore 1025. Tel: 2355703, Fax: 2350175.

JOHOR BAHRU

East Coast Adventure, Room 402, 4th floor, Bangunen Kergesama, Jln Dhobi, 80000 Johor Bahru. Tel: 242505, Fax: 232571.
Wat Seng Travel and Tours, 1-A Jln Rugayah Barat, 83000 Batu Pahat. Tel: 441998, Fax: 410851

GETTING THERE

Thousands of people make the voyage between Singapore and the Riau islands each day. There are frequent sailings from the new high-tech ferry terminal at the World Trade Centre (WTC) in Singapore, including dozens of daily services to Sekupang and Batu Ampar on the north coast of Batam, and two daily trips to Tanjung Pinang on the southwest coast of Bintan.

Boats to Batam depart every 15 to 30 minutes from the WTC docks between 7.40am to 6.40pm each day (Singapore time). The last ferry back to Singapore leaves Sekupang at 6.20pm and Batu Ampar at 7.30pm (both Indonesia time). The boats are fast and comfortable, with refreshment counters, outside viewing decks and in-house movies. Tickets cost S$18 one way and S$32 return and can be purchased from computerized check-in counters on the ground floor at WTC. People who travel frequently between Singapore and Batam can apply for a 'smart card' for easier customs and immigration at both ends. For more information on Riau ferries contact DINO Shipping (Tel: 2702228) or Indo Falcon (Tel: 2706778 or 2783167).

Ferries to Tanjung Pinang depart WTC at 10am and 3pm each day (Singapore time). In the reverse direction, ferries leave Tanjung Pinang at 9.30am and 2pm (Indonesian time). The two-hour crossing costs S$51 one way and S$73 return. Tickets can be purchased at shipping agency offices on the second floor at WTC. For more information contact DINO Shipping (Tel: 2702228) or Auto Batam (Tel: 2714866) in Singapore.

As an alternative, you can also travel to Batam and Bintan via Johor Bahru on boats operated by Sinar line. Ferries depart each day from the JB waterfront (Pasir Gudang port). The fare is Rp50,000.

Beyond Riau: If you wish to explore other parts of Indonesia, it's possible to travel by steamer from Tanjung Pinang. This is an 'unforgettable' trip across the Java Sea aboard a crowded ship with primitive sanitation facilities – recommended only for the hardy. Cabins must be booked one to two weeks in advance. However, deck class can be obtained at short notice. It's advisable to leave Singapore two days before departure so that you have plenty of time to explore Tanjung Pinang and other parts of Bintan.

There are two choices: a private ship called the *MV Bintan Peramata* which departs each Friday at 8am; or an Indonesian government owned boat called the *MV Rinjani* (PELNI line) which is supposed to sail every Tuesday at 8am. There are many different fares, ranging from Rp38,000 to Rp111,500. The journey takes about 22 hours, with arrival at around 10am the following day at Tanjung Priok in Jakarta. For more information contact PT Netra Service Jaya in Tanjung Pinang (Tel: 21384) or the PELNI office in Singapore (Tel: 2726811).

For the time being, there are no flights between Singapore and Batam or Bintan. However, it is possible to fly from the Riau archipelago to other parts of Indonesia.

Sempati Air offers daily flights from Hang Nadim Airport on Batam island to Jakarta, Medan, Bandung, Semarang, Surabaya, Yogyakarta, Denpasar and Balikpapan. In addition Merpati Airlines flies from Kijang Airport on Bintan Island to Jakarta.

Batam:
Sempati Air, New Holiday Hotel, Jln Imam Bonjal, Nagoya P Batam. Tel: (778) 454762/454763/454764/459619/459201/455074. Airport office: Bandara Hang Nadim. Tel: (778) 459982/310091/310092 ext 114.

Singapore:
Sempati Air, #08-04, 541 Orchard Road. Tel: (65) 7345077. Airport office: 035-45 Changi airport. Tel: (65) 5429931/5452772, Fax: (65) 5427809.

Merpati Airlines, #08-08 Park Mall, 9 Penang Road. Tel: (65) 3362558, Fax: 3391140.

TRAVEL ESSENTIALS

All travellers to Indonesia must be in possession of a passport valid for at least six months after arrival and with proof (tickets) of onward passage.

Visas have been waived for nationals of countries for a visit not exceeding two months. Those countries are: Argentina, Australia, Austria, Belgium, Brazil, Brunei, Canada, Chile, Denmark, Egypt, Finland, France, Germany, Greece, Iceland, Ireland, Italy,

Japan, Kuwait, Liechtenstein, Luxembourg, Malaysia, Malta, Mexico, Morocco, Netherlands, New Zealand, Norway, Philippines, Saudi Arabia, Singapore, South Korea, Spain, Sweden, Switzerland, Taiwan, Thailand, Turkey, United Kingdom, United States of America and Venezuela, United Arab Emirates and Yugoslavia.

For citizens of countries other than those listed above, tourist visas can be obtained from the Indonesian Embassy in Singapore or any other overseas mission. Two photographs are required and a small fee is charged.

MONEY MATTERS

Indonesia's currency is the rupiah. The exchange rates at time of press were Rp2,102 to the US dollar and Rp1,562 to the Singapore dollar. It should also be pointed out that Singapore banknotes can be used to pay for many goods and services in the Riau islands. However, you should always have a ready supply of *rupiah* just in case.

Changing Money: Foreign currency is best exchanged at major banks or leading hotels (though hotel rates are slightly less favorable than bank rates). There are also limited numbers of registered money changers in Batam and Bintan (major ferry terminals have money changing kiosks), but avoid unauthorized changers who operate illegally. Banks in smaller towns are not necessarily conversant with all foreign banknotes, so it's advisable to change money before you head for rural areas. Your *rupiah* may be freely converted to foreign currencies when you are leaving the country.

Traveller's cheques: Traveller's cheques are a mixed blessing. Major hotels, banks and some shops will accept them, but even in the larger towns it can take a long time to collect your money (in small towns, it's impossible). The US dollar and Singapore dollar are recommended for traveller's cheques. Credit cards are usable if you stay in the big hotels. International airline offices, a few big city restaurants and duty free shops will also accept them, but they are useless elsewhere.

HEALTH

Yellow fever vaccinations is required if you arrive within six days of leaving or passing through an infected area. It is also advisable to be vaccinated against cholera, typhoid and paratyphoid. If you intend staying in the more isolated parts of the Riau archipelago for some time, particularly outside of the big towns, gamma globulin injections are recommended; they won't stop hepatitis, but many physicians believe that the risk of infection is greatly reduced.

A supply of malaria suppressant tablets is also highly recommended if you are going to stay in rural areas for an extended time. Make sure the suppressants are effective against all the strains of malaria. It was discovered that a malaria strain was resistant to the usual kind of malarial prophylactic (chloroquine). Consult your physician.

All water – including well water, municipal water and water used for making ice – MUST be purified before consumption. Boiling water for 10 minutes is an effective method. Iodine (Globoline) and chlorine (Halazone) may also be used to make water potable. All fruit should be carefully peeled before eaten and no raw vegetables should be eaten.

Last but not least, protect yourself against the equatorial sun. Tanning oils and creams are expensive in Indonesia, so bring your own or stock up in Singapore.

WHAT TO WEAR

Light, informal, summer-wear – preferably in natural fibers – is best for the heat of the Riau islands. However, as Batam and Bintan are predominantly Muslim and conservative, you should follow a few basic rules. Women should not wear dresses, skirts or shorts that are too short and should always wear a bra. While in towns and cities, government offices or passing through immigration, stick to conservative dresses or long pants. In mosques, legs should be covered to below the knee and it's a good idea to carry a scarf as some places of worship require that arms and the head are also covered. Topless and nude sunbathing is frowned upon. Men can wear T-shirts and open toed sandals.

CUSTOMS

Visitors are allowed to bring in 200 cigarettes, 50 cigars or 100gms of tobacco; a liter of wine or spirits; and a reasonable amount of perfumes and gifts with a value of up to US$250 per adult or US$1,000 per family. Check Singapore's customs regulations (page 265) before stocking up on duty-free goods for the return tip.

GETTING ACQUAINTED

TIME ZONES

Batam and Bintan are seven hours ahead of Greenwich Mean Time, and one hour behind Singapore time. For example 8am in Singapore is 7am in Indonesia.

CLIMATE

The Riau islands have a typically tropical climate, hot and humid throughout the year with cool breezes near the coastal areas. The average annual temperature at sea level is about 78°F (26°C). The monsoon months are between November and March when you can expect heavy rain.

BUSINESS HOURS

Government offices are open from 8am to 3pm, Monday to Thursday; 8am to 11.30am on Friday and 8am to 2pm on Saturday.

General office hours for commercial enterprises are 9am to 5pm with a 1pm to 2pm lunch hour. However, many employees leave early on Friday.

Shops are open from about 9am to at least 6pm. Larger shops and department stores open a bit later but stay open until 9pm.

LANGUAGE

Although over 350 languages and dialects are spoken in Indonesia, the national tongue, Bahasa Indonesia, will take you from the northernmost tip of Sumatra through Java and across the string of islands to Irian Jaya. In fact, Bahasa derives from a form of Malay originally spoken in the Riau islands.

Although formal Bahasa is a complex language demanding serious study, the construction of basic Indonesian sentences is relatively easy. A compact and cheap book called *How to Master the Indonesian Language* by Almatseier is widely available in Indonesia and should prove invaluable in helping you say what you want to say. Indonesian is written in the Roman alphabet and, unlike some Asian languages, is not tonal.

ELECTRICITY

The voltage is 220 volts, 50 cycles.

GETTING AROUND

BY ROAD ·

Batam has acquired a sophisticated road network over the last five years as the Indonesian government tries to develop the island into a mini version of Singapore. Excellent two-lane highways connect all the major towns and ports. Bintan and the other islands have more primitive road systems, although the highways on Bintan should improve markedly in years to come.

Batam island has a large fleet of Japanese-made taxis which can be hailed from the ferry terminals and major hotels. Quality varies from cab to cab. Some are air conditioned and quiet, while others offer open windows and loud radios. If a meter is present, ask the driver to use it. Otherwise you will have to negotiate. As a rough guide, a journey between Kabil (east coast) and Sekupang (west coast) should not cost more than Rp15,000 (US$7.50).

Bintan's taxis look like rejects from a used car lot, a motley collection of vehicles that includes many Holdens and Chevys from the 1960s. Air conditioning is a scarce comfort, meters even rarer. Be prepared to negotiate. A return trip to Trikora Beach – including an hour or two wait for a dip – should cost around Rp40,000 (US$19). You can usually find a ready supply of taxis at the main pier and around the clock tower on Jalan Merdeka.

Shared taxis to Trikora Beach depart from the bus depot next to Bank Duta each morning between 7am and 11am. The ride costs about Rp4,500 (about US$2). There are buses every hour to Tanjung Uban at the western tip of Bintan, between 7am and 4pm. The fare is about Rp2,000 (US$1).

Around Tanjung Pinang you can travel by bemo for about Rp300 or pillion on a motorbike taxi (*ojek*) for about Rp 500. Alternatively, you can rent your own motorbike for about Rp30,000 (US$14) a day – including a helmet and a tank of petrol – from near the main ferry pier. No driving license necessary, but they require a photostat of your passport.

BY BOAT

The only way to get between Batam and Bintan is by speed boat ferry. The westbound service runs from Pier One (Pelantar Satu) in Tanjung Pinang, arriving at Kabil on the east coast of Batam about

45 minutes later. Boats leave every hour (on the hour) from 8am to 4pm. The eastbound service leaves from the end of the wooden jetty at Kabil, also a 45-minute trip. Boats leave every hour (on the half hour) from 9.30am to 5.30pm. The one-way journey costs Rp 10,000 (US$5). Bring our own food and water because nothing is served on the boat.

Boats to places near Tanjung Pinang can be caught from various points along the waterfront. Boats to Penyengat depart from the small wooden pier to the south of the main ferry terminal. The cost is negotiable, but should be roughly Rp500 per person. Boats to Senggarang and Kampung Bugis leave from Pier Two (Pelantar Dua) near the central market. The cost is similar to Penyengat boats.

There are also ferries to the other points in Riau province including Tanjung Balai (on Karimun island), Pekanbaru, Selat Panjang, Tanjung Batu (Kundur), Pancur (Lingga) and Dabo (Singkep). Prices are very reasonable. For example, the journey to Dabo costs Rp25,000 one way and Rp40,000 return. For more information contact PT Netra Service Jaya in Tanjung Pinang (Tel: 21384).

WHERE TO STAY

BATAM

Batam Jaya Hotel, Jln Raja Ali Haji, P.O. Box 35, Batam Island 29432. Tel: (778) 458708/458622, Fax: (778) 458057. 300 rooms, Indonesian and Chinese restaurant, bar, convention room, ballroom.
Batam View Beach Resort, Jln Hang Lekir, Nongsa. Tel: (778) 453746/322281, (Singapore: (65) 2354366), Fax: (778) 453747. 218 rooms, Seafood, Chinese and Thai restaurants, 24-hour coffee house, bar, karaoke, health centre, pool, sea sport facilities, squash and tennis courts, meeting rooms.
Hill Top Hotel, Jln Ir. Sutami No 8, Sekupang. Tel: (778) 322482/391, Fax: (778) 322211. 65 rooms, coffee house, pool, lobby and karaoke lounges, meeting rooms.
Nagoya Plaza Hotel, Jln Imam Bonjol, Lubuk Baja. Tel: (778) 459888/457880, Fax: (778) 456690. 138 rooms, coffee house, bar with live entertainment, karaoke lounge, business centre, convention room.
New Holiday Hotel, Jln Imam Bonjol, Nagoya. Tel: (778) 459308-311, Fax: (778) 459306. 260 rooms. 24-hour coffee house, seafood and Japanese restaurants. Disco, karaoke and lobby lounges. pool, fitness centre, conference facilities, ballroom shops.

Puri Garden Hotel, Jln Teuku Umar No 1, P.O. Box 1053, Nagoya. Tel: (778) 458888, Fax: (778) 456333. 144 rooms, Balinese coffee house serving Oriental cuisine, bar, karaoke lounge, meeting room, business centre.
Sei Nongsa, P.O. Box 47-BAM Pantal Bahagia, Nongsa. Tel: in Singapore (65) 3352383/2255235. Air-conditioned cottages each with attached bathroom, TV, IDD, mini bar. Coffee shop, open-air seafood restaurant, lounge and bar. White sand beach, pool.
Turi Beach Resort, P.O. Box 55/BAM, Batu Ampar. Tel: (778) 310078/83 (in Singapore: (65) 2735055), Fax: (778) 310042. 152 beach front cottages, Oriental and Chinese restaurant, grill room, bars, lounge and karaoke room, health centre, pool, sea sport facilities, tennis court, conference facilities.

BINTAN

Asean Hotel , Jln Gudang Minyak, Tanjung Pinang. Tel: (771) 22161, Fax: (771) 22162.
Bintan Beach Resort, 1 Jln Pantai Impian, Tanjung Pinang. Tel: (771) 23661/23803/23732 (in Singapore: (65) 2874621), Fax: (771) 23995. 103 rooms, Chinese restaurant, bar, karaoke, pool, tennis court, games room.
Garden Hotel, Jln Gatot Subroto 282, km 5. Tel: (771) 22344/22071. 33 bungalows on a landscaped hillside.
Hotel Kartika, Jln M T Haryono Km 3.5, Tanjung Pinang. Tel: (771) 22446/23389 (in Singapore: (65) 722 9271), Fax: (771) 22518. 38 rooms, restaurant, sauna, gym, pool, tennis court.
Pinang Island Cottages, 133, Complex Rimba Jaya, Tanjung Pinang. Tel: (771) 21307/22384, Fax: (771) 22099. 17 cottages.
Riau Holiday Indah, Jln Pelantar II No 53, Tanjung Pinang. Tel: (771) 22573/22644 (in Singapore (65) 2251693). 50 rooms built on stilts over the Riau River. Indonesian restaurant, meeting rooms.
Sampurna Jaya Hotel, Jln Yusuf Kahar No 15, Tanjung Pinang. Tel: (771) 21555/21264/21269 (in Singapore (65) 5324711). 77 rooms, Indonesian and Chinese restaurant.
Trikora Country Club, 37km Jln Teluk Bakau, Tanjung Pinang. Tel: (in Singapore) (65) 2219655. 8 rooms, Indonesian and Chinese restaurant, pool.
Wisma Riau Hotel, Jln Yusuf Kahar No 8, Tanjung Pinang. Tel: (771) 21023/21133, Fax: (771) 24082. 40 large, older style rooms with private bathrooms, some with air-conditioning. Indonesian restaurant.

KARIMUN

Wisma Gloria, Pantai Taman Wisata, Tanjung Balai, Karimun Island. Tel: (777) 21082/21088. Restaurant, coffee house, bar, karaoke, salon, mini shop.

FOOD DIGEST

SHOPPING

Dining in the Riau islands can be a delightful experience. Locals seek out obscure roadside stalls (*warung*) for a special *soto* or *sate*. But overseas visitors should be careful if they want to avoid 'Batam belly'. It's possible to eat a good meal in a clean restaurant for US$2 and truly excellent Indonesian or Chinese food can be had for US$5 a head. A meal at the best restaurants will rarely cost more than US$10 per person, all inclusive.

Seafood of any sort is excellent, so be sure not to leave Batam or Bintan without sampling grilled carp (*ikan mas bakar*), fried prawns (*udang pancet*), barbecued squid (*cumicumi bakar*), conch with a spicy sauce (*gong-gong*) or fish curry and pepper crab. In Batam, the best place to eat seafood are the big beachfront restaurants at Batu Besar, or further inland at the King Prawn Restaurant. In Bintan, the Night Market (*pasar malam*) on Jalan Pos offers a mouth-watering array of seafood plus other local favorites. For a more relaxed setting, try the popular Teluk Keriting at 15 Jalan Usman Harun, where you dine *al fresco* at the end of the pier.

You should also try and get a group together for *Nasi Padang* which is a veritable feast comprising of about a dozen dishes of various meats and vegetables eaten with steamed white rice.

Other delicacies not to be missed are raw vegetable salad with shrimp paste and chilli sauce (*lalap/sambal cobek*), raw vegetables with a peanut sauce (*gado-gado*), grilled chicken (*ayam bakar*), spicy chicken soup (*soto ayam*) and (*gudeg*) which consists of young jackfruit boiled in coconut cream and spices, served with buffalo hide boiled in chili sauce, chicken pieces, egg and gravy. Other 'musts' are spicy chicken broth with noodles or rice (*soto madura*) and the ever popular chicken, beef or mutton barbecued on meat skewers (*sate*).

The large Chinese influence in Indonesia results in an abundance of Chinese food and there is also a growing selection of Japanese restaurants (mainly at hotels) catering to the Japanese golfers who flock to Batam. And if you can't get through your holiday without some American fast food, Batam has a Kentucky Fried Chicken (Jalan Raden Patah) and Dunkin' Donuts (Indah Permai Centre).

As Batam is a duty-free port, alcohol, cosmetics and cigarettes are considerably cheaper than Singapore and elsewhere in Indonesia.

Duty-free shops cluster around the ferry terminals at Sekupang and Batu Ampar, as well as Hang Nadim Airport on Batam. Most larger hotels have their own duty-free stores but there are also independents outlets in some of the large towns. **CV Prima Jaya** at Komplek Nagoya Business Centre has a large selection of imported beers, wines and spirits.

Not a lot of indigenous handicrafts are produced in the Riau region, but there are shops that stock other popular Indonesian arts and crafts. For instance **Tiara Indah Trade Centre** on Batam boasts items from all 27 provinces – paintings, wood carvings, rattan, silverwork, furniture etc. Tiara Indah also hosts artisan displays and cultural dances, so its worth dropping by to see what's on. **Bali Arts** on Jalan Raja Ali Haji in Nagoya also sells Indonesian arts and crafts. Meanwhile, the duty-free shops at Sekupang ferry terminal sell batik, wooden masks, sculptures and other items.

General household goods, electronic items, books, clothes and travel accessories can be purchased at modern strip malls and shopping plaza in Nagoya: **Indah Permai Centre** on Jalan Raden Patah as well as **Lucky Plaza** and **City Plaza**. The malls also contain fast-food outlets for quick snacks.

In Bintan, there is a small duty-free shop at the main ferry terminal. Otherwise shopping is confined to the market area along Jalan Merdeka and Jalan Pasar Ikan where you can buy traditional Indonesian items such as batik, prawn crackers, bird's nests, peanuts and dried fish.

USEFUL ADDRESSES

TOURIST INFORMATION

Batam Tourist Promotion Board
Jalan R.E. Martadinata, Sekupang, Pulau Batam
Indonesia. Tel: 322852 or 322857, Fax: 322898

Indonesia Tourist Promotion Board
#15-07 Ocean Building, 10 Collyer Quay, Singapore 0104. Tel: 5342837, Fax: 5334287

TRAVEL & SHIPPING AGENTS

Singapore:
Auto Batam Ferry/Kalpin Tours
1 Maritime Square, #02-40 World Trade Centre, Singapore 0409. Tel: 2714866
Dino Shipping/Channel Holidays
1 Maritime Square, #02-39 World Trade Centre, Singapore 0409. Tel: 2702228, Fax: 2701113
Indo Falcon Shipping & Travel
1 Maritime Square, #08-01 World Trade Centre, Singapore 0409. Tel: 2706778 or 2783167, Fax: 2782923
Sinba Cruise & Holidays
1 Maritime Square, #02-56 World Trade Centre, Singapore 0409. Tel: 2782788 or 2707779
Sincar Travel & Tours
3 Maritime Square, #15-00 Cable Car Towers, Singapore 0409. Tel: 2708855, Fax: 2740525

Batam:
PT Bintan Baruna Sakti
Terminal Ferry, Sekupang, Pulau Batam, Indonesia.
Tel: 322599 or 322639, Fax: 321799
PT Hanita Wisatama Tours & Travel
Ferry Terminal, Sekupang, Pulau Batam, Indonesia.
Tel: 321429 or 322107, Fax: 321358

Bintan:
PT Bintan Baruna Sakti
Jalan Samudera No. 1, Tanjung Pinang, Pulau Bintan, Indonesia. Tel: 21657
PT Netra Services Jaya
Jalan Pos No. 2, Tanjung Pinang, Pulau Bintan, Indonesia. Tel: 21384

OTHER INSIGHT GUIDES

Other *Insight Guides* which highlight destinations in this region are:

This book will bring you to the obvious and not so obvious corners of the surprising island state.

Insight Guide: Southeast Asia is the definitive guidebook that unravels the complexities of regional travel in Southeast Asia.

Much more than a field guide, this book answers the call of all wildlife lovers.

More than 280 superb photographs and an entertaining text capture the heart and soul of Malaysia.

More than 13,600 islands comprise the most extraordinary collection of places and peoples on earth.

ART/PHOTO CREDITS

Photography by

Pages 55, 66/67, 197, 249	S.T. Amerasinghe
33, 56, 57, 68, 72/73, 88/89, 94/95, 96, 106/107, 122, 132/133, 134/135, 146, 178, 189, 200, 204/205; 207, 220, 228, 234, 252, 258, 214	Apa Photo Agency
80, 254, 255	Marcus Brooke
232, 235	Alfred Chan
168	Compost, Alain
28/29	Courtesy of Col-L.T. Firbank, OBE
38, 46	Courtesy of National Library
32, 34/35, 36, 37, 39	Courtesy of National Museum
149	Ray Cranbourne
225	Lance Dowring
59, 76, 79, 104/105, 125, 131, 138, 187, 210	Jean-Leo Dugast
8, 22, 44/45, 52, 53, 62/63, 64/65, 71, 77, 78, 84, 85, 91, 97, 98/99, 102, 148, 188, 191, 193, 209	Alain Evrard/APA Photo Agency
130	Jill Gocher
152/153, 194/195, 202/203	Manfred Gottschalk
140, 147, 151, 251	Hans Höfer
Cover, 6, 25, 60, 86/87, 92, 93, 100, 101 103, 123, 126, 127, 156/157, 182/183, 190, 192, 198, 199, 201, 211,213, 227, 230/231, 236, 238, 239, 240, 257	Ingo Jezierski
16/17, 50, 116/117, 118/119, 150, 237	Rainer Kraek/APA Photo Agency
120, 224	J. Kugler
10, 14/15, 26/27, 40/41, 82/83, 114/115, 128, 129, 158, 164, 176, 215, 219, 229	Philip Little/APA Photo Agency
49	Ian Lloyd
141, 181, 186	Joe Lynch
139, 142, 143, 144, 145	Reg Monison
244	Kal Muller
43	National Archives S'pore
61	R.C.A. Nichols
216/217	Robin Nichols
90, 212	Michael Ozaki
124, 177	G.P. Reichelt
51	Blair Seitz
233	Frank Salmoiraghi
174/175, 179, 221	Ivan Soh
208	Paul Von Stroheim
47, 48, 54	Straits Times Archives
154/155, 160, 161, 162, 163, 166L/R, 167, 169, 170, 171, 172, 173	Strange, Morten
226	Adina Tovy/APA Photo Agency
12, 18/19, 180	Denise Tackett/APA Photo Agency
136/137	Larry Tackett
253	Tsuji, Atsuo
250	Yap Peng Kiah
20/21, 58, 74/75, 81, 108, 222, 223, 241, 242/243, 247, 256, 259, 260, 261	Joseph R. Yogerst
121	Rendo Yap
Maps	Berndtson & Berndtson
Illustrations	Klaus Geisler
Visual Consulting	V. Barl

INDEX

U & V

W – Z

A
B
C
D
E
G
H
I
J
a
b
d
e
f
g
h
i
j
k
l